DATE DUE

AP 7 '99			
FE 7 '00			
JE 7 '05			
JY 11 '05			
AG 4 '05			

DEMCO 38-296

TWENTIETH-CENTURY
SPANISH AMERICAN FICTION

Texas Pan American Series

Twentieth-Century Spanish American Fiction

Naomi Lindstrom

UNIVERSITY OF TEXAS PRESS
AUSTIN

Research for this study was supported by a grant from the
Andrew W. Mellon Foundation, administered through the
Institute of Latin American Studies of the University of
Texas at Austin, and by summer research funds provided by
the College of Liberal Arts.

Requests for permission to reproduce material from this work
should be sent to Permissions, University of Texas Press,
Box 7819, Austin, TX 78713-7819.

♾ The paper used in this publication meets the minimum
requirements of American National Standard for Information
Sciences—Permanence of Paper for Printed Library
Materials, ANSI Z39.48-1984.

Library of Congress Cataloging-in-Publication Data
Lindstrom, Naomi, 1950–
    Twentieth-century Spanish American fiction / Naomi
Lindstrom.—1st ed.
        p.   cm.—(Texas Pan American series)
    Includes bibliographical references and index.
    ISBN 0-292-78119-9.—ISBN 0-292-74682-2 (pbk.)
    1. Spanish American fiction—20th century—History and
criticism.
I. Title. II. Series.
PQ7082.N7L53   1994
863—dc20   93-42557

To Michael, Rick, and Mara

Contents

Introduction   *1*

ONE   Twentieth-Century Modernist Prose,
1900–1920   *13*

TWO   Realism and Naturalism, 1900–1930   *34*

THREE   Avant-Garde, Imaginative, and Fantastic
Modes, 1920–1950   *62*

FOUR   Realism and Beyond, 1930–1960   *110*

FIVE   The Boom and Its Antecedents, 1950–1970   *140*

SIX   The Postboom: New Voices and Belated
Discoveries, 1968–1990   *197*

Conclusion   *222*

Notes   *227*

Selected Bibliography   *237*

Index   *241*

TWENTIETH-CENTURY
SPANISH AMERICAN FICTION

Introduction

In this presentation of twentieth-century Spanish American narrative, the intention has been to allow for a fair amount of summary overview of trends and patterns of development, but also for some substantial critical commentary on individual works that are outstandingly original, important, or representative of a tendency. This plan precludes discussion, or even mention, of every work that could be considered significant in the development of this area of literature. Many readers may find their personal favorites missing or briefly mentioned. Yet a process of selection was necessary. Any attempt at all-inclusive coverage would swiftly have eliminated the space reserved to take a closer look at particular texts. Hard choices were necessary concerning the selection of works covered and the amount of attention each text would receive.

The main point of this book is to orient readers, especially English-language readers, to the principal tendencies, texts, and writers of twentieth-century Spanish American narrative and to convey why they are held to be so major and significant. In many cases, this purpose entails giving the most detailed scrutiny to those works of Spanish American narrative that have been the object of the most public attention and critical examination—the texts that would most readily come to mind if one were asked to name distinguished examples of this fiction. But the general fame enjoyed by these works and writers could not serve as the sole guide to their inclusion and prominence in this overview. In some cases, the acclaim accorded to single works, especially those that were commercial successes in translation, has tended to distort the larger picture of twentieth-century Spanish American prose fiction as a continuum. The present overview seeks to represent all decades more or less equally, including the earlier years of the century.

A special difficulty was raised by the fact that one period in Spanish American prose fiction has received more critical study and publicity, particularly outside Spanish America, than any other. This is the era known as the "boom," stretching from approximately the beginning of the 1960s into the early 1970s. It was during this time that such monumental and original works as *Hopscotch* (1963) by Julio Cortázar of Argentina and *One Hundred Years of Solitude* (1967) by the Colombian Gabriel García Márquez dazzled critics and readers internationally. A new public began reading Spanish American narrative for the first time in a spirit of discovery. During the same period, the international reading public also encountered certain predecessors of the boom, the first practitioners of the "new narrative" (1940s onward) such as Alejo Carpentier of Cuba, the Guatemalan Miguel Angel Asturias, and Juan Rulfo of Mexico. This innovative fiction appeared on the world scene as stunning individual texts isolated from their literary context, the development of Spanish American narrative over the successive decades. It must have often seemed to these new readers that Spanish America had hardly possessed a literature until recent years. The region's writing appeared nearly coterminous with the much-translated, widely sold narrative works of the 1960s, together with their precursors of the 1940s and 1950s. Beyond any doubt, the boom merits an extensive chapter, not simply because of its success in riveting world attention on Spanish American writing, but because of the outstanding works of Spanish American fiction published during these years. While it is true that during the boom a few massively publicized writers tended to monopolize international attention, they had earned their renown by writing with exceptional originality.

It is in treating the next period—the provisionally named postboom that begins in the late 1960s, before the boom is even over—that a dilemma arises. On the one hand, the boom writers, who had succeeded as no one before in bringing Spanish American literature to the world's attention, continued to publish fiction that was significant and widely read, if less groundbreaking than their work of the boom years. At the same time, it is important not to allow these writers, who enjoyed the good fortune of publishing their most important fiction during a period of widespread excitement over Spanish American writing and editorial prosperity, to occupy more than their share of the stage. For this reason, the chapter on the postboom concentrates principally on those writers who came to general attention later (even if they had begun publishing earlier) and who represented diverse alternatives to the type of fiction that most typically enjoyed success during the 1960s. One of the main points of this survey is that Spanish American literature has been characterized by significant developments and new texts worthy of study during the entire twentieth century, not only during those years when Spanish American writers were able to capture the international limelight. The great novels of the boom writers and their predecessors deserve to be singled out, but they should also be placed in the context of a literature that is constantly changing and producing new movements and variants, only some of which reach an international readership in translation.

Other, younger writers, who were newly emerging into international fame during the 1970s, 1980s, and 1990s, deserve greater attention in the coverage of this period because they are the ones who represent the "postboom." They are the ones who present alternatives to the mode established by the major boom figures. A strength of the postboom is, indeed, that the work of more different writers is now able to claim attention, including the fiction of authors who had long been productive but who were obscured or upstaged by the celebrated figures dominating the Spanish American literary scene. For instance, during the boom period, no Spanish American woman writer was able to achieve international renown. The postboom saw two women—Isabel Allende of Chile and Luisa Valenzuela of Argentina—earn large worldwide readerships and commercial success. Many new and rediscovered women writers attracted less vast audiences. Works by members of native peoples and African Hispanic populations appeared and became the topic of critical study. The continuing careers of the boom writers, who in a sense had already had their turn, are treated more briefly to make room for the writers who were signaling new directions in Spanish American narrative.

In the case of writers with long, productive careers, greatest attention goes to those works with which the authors made their greatest impact. The baroque short stories that Jorge Luis Borges produced between about 1936 and 1954 are the ones on which his world fame rests and the ones that influenced other writers so strongly. The brief fiction Borges wrote after his long absence from the short story genre—tales published after 1966—never aroused the same excitement and received much less critical study. The late stories are simpler and plainer on the surface, with strong, easily summarized plotlines. The late stories may well prove, as some critics have asserted, no less complex than the celebrated narratives of *Ficciones* and *The Aleph*. Still, the fact is that the stories of Borges's most flourishing years are the ones that have made a difference to both Spanish

American and world literature. When readers refer to "the Borges story" as a type, they mean the baroque texts of the author's high period, not his late revival of the tale-teller's art.

It will be immediately obvious that this study treats more novels than short stories. The reason for this preponderance is that more novels than short stories have established their authors' importance and created a stir among the reading public. Certain authors built their reputations on their expertise in the short fiction genre. The most memorable cases are those of Borges, who deliberately refrained from writing a novel, and the Uruguayan Horacio Quiroga, who excelled only in the short story. There are even specialists in the exceedingly short story, or *microcuento;* Augusto Monterroso, a Guatemalan residing in Mexico, is especially singled out here for his cultivation of the art of compression. Still, the authors whose fame rests on their short fiction are in the minority. To return to an earlier-cited example, García Márquez will always be known as the author of *One Hundred Years of Solitude* and not primarily for his short fiction. A well-written and original novel has a greater chance of staking a claim for itself and its author than an equally able short story. This circumstance has colored the present study. Yet there has been an effort throughout to recognize outstanding examples of briefer fiction, including those by authors generally referred to as "novelists," such as the Chilean José Donoso.

In nearly every case, the texts selected for discussion belong to the category of prose fiction; they are imaginative and creative literature rather than exposition. The first work treated, though, is an exception to the rule. This is the book-length *Ariel* by the Uruguayan José Enrique Rodó. Though generally classed among essays, *Ariel* is unique for its type. It relies at least as heavily on the techniques of imaginative literature as on those of expository writing. Allegorical figures, particularly the spirit who gives *Ariel* its title, carry its message. Rodó constructed *Ariel* as a narrative that unfolds as one reads. Besides the fact that it is poised between the essay and creative narrative, *Ariel* is exceptional in other ways that also justify its inclusion. Not only is it one of the prose works that best exemplify turn-of-the-century *modernismo,* *Ariel* is the modernist text that most deeply influenced Spanish American thought and intellectual life. Finally, its publication date of 1900 makes it an excellent baseline from which to observe the evolution of twentieth-century Spanish American prose through and beyond *modernismo.*

While *Ariel* merits extensive consideration, other essays are more briefly mentioned. In the case of *The Labyrinth of Solitude* (1950) by Octavio Paz of Mexico, there is no ignoring the effect this study produced on the way Mexican intellectuals thought and wrote. However, *Labyrinth* will be discussed for the changes it brought about on the intellectual scene, not for its own textual qualities. While it refers abundantly to literature and is more creatively written than most essays, no careful reader would mistake it for a narrative.

The final, postboom chapter includes several works that are not, strictly speaking, creative literature. These belong to the category of documentary literature that gained such prominence and excited such controversy from the late 1960s onward. This is the class of writings that includes the famous *I, Rigoberta Menchú: An Indian Woman in Guatemala* (1983). In texts of this type, the rhetorical moves of fictional narrative serve to communicate a story that the protagonist, who is generally the narrator, experienced in the real world. The ambiguous relation of documentary literature to imaginative writing is much of what has sparked the lively interest of literary critics in this difficult-to-define category of texts. It would make no sense to exclude such hybrid works, which force critics to think harder about the way they define literature, from an examination of significant developments in literary narrative.

It is common to find translators lamenting that their work receives scant or no recognition in reviews and criticism. They are right to complain, since the words an international public reads are the translator's, even if the work is still of its author. Talented translators have been essential to the creation of a worldwide audience for Spanish American literature. This study makes a special effort to note the contribution of such pioneers as the persevering Harriet de Onís, who produced early English versions of Spanish American prose fiction, and of such stellar translators as Gregory Rabassa, Margaret Sayers Peden, Suzanne Jill Levine, and Helen R. Lane, who helped win this body of writing its massive audience in the English-speaking world. Younger translators attuned to the new voices from Spanish America, such as Andrew Hurley with his special empathy for Cuban exile writers, are named in the postboom chapter. (When no translator receives credit for a quotation and a Spanish-language edition is cited, the English version is mine.)

Most of the works this study singles out enjoy a high critical reputation, but some are less-cited works chosen as exemplifying a type of text or tendency. An example is *Rosa at Ten O'Clock* (1955) by the Argentine Marco Denevi. Though it won the Guillermo Kraft Novel Prize and critical admiration for its ingenuity, this elegant murder novel has not established itself as a staple item of required reading. Yet, better than any similar work with more visible literary pretensions, it typifies the expertly plotted crime and detective novels that became a specialty of Spanish American literature.

In the final, postboom chapter, the requirement that works enjoy an established reputation has been relaxed. Contemporary readers and critics have a notoriously poor record of judging which new works will find a permanent place on standard reading lists. There is no claim here that the postboom writers and works discussed are the ones that will be famous thirty or fifty years from now. Three of the writers who appear in this last chapter currently hold thriving international reputations: Manuel Puig and Luisa Valenzuela of Argentina and Isabel Allende of Chile. Others are either of more regional renown, as are the *onda* (hip) writers of 1960s–1970s Mexico, or possess rising reputations that may become solidified, like the Cuban American Heberto Padilla. The selection of writers and texts functions to present as varied a sample as possible of the lines of innovation now being explored in Spanish American fiction. It is not intended to sort out which of the recent writers is most significant in a literary history still unfolding.

This study is designed to be useful above all to English-language readers, some of whom will be dependent on translations for access to Spanish American writing. For this reason, when a choice presented itself between two equally worthy and appropriate works, the space usually went to the text available in an English-language edition. In-text references are provided to guide readers toward English translations, especially to outstanding English versions of Spanish American fiction. At the same time, there is the hope that this book will help point out works, especially those from the neglected early decades of the century, overdue for English translation or reissue. For instance, the 1925 short story collection *Cuentos de la oficina* (Office stories) by the Argentine Roberto Mariani is not available in English, but it should be, and that is one reason for its extended discussion here. This practice is in line with the goal of introducing English-language readers to those texts and tendencies in Spanish American narrative that tend to remain obscure to the international reading public.

With regret, Chicano literature has been left for study elsewhere. The writing of members of Latino groups in the continental United States—U.S.-born Cubans and mainland Puerto Ricans as well as Mexican Americans—is only in some senses an extension of Spanish American writing. Chicano literature is, with increasing frequency, composed in English, a circumstance that sets this body of writing at a remove from Spanish American letters. Whatever its language, this important literature is am-

biguous in identity and can be viewed either as regional writing of the
U.S. Southwest or as a Latin-culture literature. Though they cannot re-
ceive discussion here, it should be noted that certain Chicano writers con-
tribute to Spanish-language narrative as well as to U.S. regional fiction.
These include Tomás Rivera, with his 1971 . . . *y no se lo tragó la tierra*
(*This Migrant Earth*), Rolando Hinojosa, author of the Klail City Death
Trip Series, and Miguel Méndez-M. For a study dedicated to Mexican
American fiction, readers are referred to Ramón Saldívar's 1990 *Chicano
Narrative: The Dialectics of Difference* (1990).

The decision, motivated by the need to keep this overview compact,
has been to remain within the bounds of Spanish American narrative by
presenting only works by authors who were born or made their names in
Spanish American countries. This applies to all groups; for example, Cuban authors who went to the United States in exile after establishing
themselves receive discussion, but not those who began their careers as
Cuban American writers.

Though space was limited, it has proven necessary to include in many
cases quotations from critics. The goal here is not just to see what fiction
Spanish American authors wrote, but how that narrative has been regarded and the significance commentators have attributed to it.

A clarification is necessary regarding the use of
the terms *modernism* and *postmodernism* in this study. In the Spanish-
speaking literary world, *modernism* refers to a movement that originated in
Spanish America in the nineteenth century, becoming fully evident during the 1880s and later spreading to Spain. It drew considerably on European sources, particularly the Parnassian and Symbolist currents in
French poetry. Spanish American writers recombined and reworked these
tendencies to produce an original mode of expression unlike any seen in
European writing. The modernist esthetic predominated in Spanish
American letters into the 1910s, when it began to cede ground to the
tendencies known as *postmodernism*.

The movement known in Hispanic literature as *modernismo* does not
greatly resemble the European and U.S. phenomenon designated by the
same term, associated with such typically twentieth-century innovators as
James Joyce, Ezra Pound, and T. S. Eliot. The style of Spanish American
modernists is apt to strike unaccustomed English-language readers as
mannered and laden with embellishment. Its decorative, frankly artificial
splendor sets it apart from the streamlined expression, stripped of orna-

ment, that was valued and developed by twentieth-century European and U.S. modernists.

In the study of Hispanic literatures *postmodernism* designates a movement that, in reaction to modernism, sought to reduce the degree of evident artifice in literary language. The postmodernist writers strove for an effect of simplicity and directness. They gave greater prominence to the representation of human experience than the formal novelty that dominated many modernist texts. The postmodernists' focus on the here and now, and especially on phenomena unique to Latin America, offered an alternative to the modernists' preoccupation with settings remote in time and place. In Hispanic literary studies *postmodernist* is a term applied to poetry; its application to narrative prose is fairly uncommon.

The term and concept *modernism*, as understood in European and English-language literature, does have a counterpart in Spanish American writing. During the 1920s, avant-garde movements arose in a number of Spanish American literary capitals. Avant-garde writing manifests the search for a streamlined, fragmented expression, representative of the new century, that characterized European and U.S. modernism.

This survey will utilize the terminology that provides the standard frame of reference in the discussion of Spanish-language literature. *Modernism* designates the turn-of-the-century movement. *Avant-garde* refers to the experimental writing, first notable in the 1920s, that prides itself on its distinctively twentieth-century form, denuded of adornment and, as befits the era of modern technology, its accelerated pace. The next term used to denote a surge of technical innovation is *boom*, referring to the ingenious, complex type of narrative that was at its height during the 1960s.

In the chapter devoted to the postboom, the term *postmodernism*, as it is used in the discussion of late twentieth-century culture, will appear briefly. Many postboom narratives exhibit features of international postmodernism. Any thorough examination of postmodernist features in current Spanish American fiction would require a book-length inquiry. Here the relation between postboom fiction and postmodernism will be pointed out rather than analyzed in any detail.

Beyond the selection of the works to be mentioned and discussed, another necessary decision concerned the organization of the material. The most obvious plan, a strictly chronological ordering, had a major drawback in treating the first half of the twentieth century. It placed next to one another works that were too dissimilar and represented the unfolding of very unlike lines of innovation. Since the book is intended to present Spanish American narrative as a whole, a division by regions or countries was undesirable, although in some cases several works from one country are discussed in a series.

Instead of grouping works into chapters by chronology or geography, the plan of this book has been to divide early twentieth-century Spanish American narrative into two principal tendencies. One of these stresses a highly visible element of artistry and makes esthetic issues plainly a part of the text; fantasy and myth frequently come into play. This current is present, at the beginning of the 1900s, in the prose writing of *modernismo*. The same eagerness to draw attention to the artfulness of literature shows up in narratives of the twenties, thirties, and forties strongly colored by fantasy, myth, and magic. At the same time, though, these prose works that so plainly manifest a concern with artistic stylization and with imaginative freedom often convey as well a commentary on society. Indeed, the experimentation with form is in many cases the vehicle for questioning the arrangements of society as it exists.

In a type of complementary or even interdependent opposition to this tendency is the line of realist writing that insistently gives first place to the depiction of social realities. This fiction may well reveal itself, on closer examination, to be as artfully planned and executed as any in the earlier-described category; nonetheless, it generates an effect of artlessness and disguises its own designed and constructed character. This is the fictional mode that early twentieth-century writers most typically employed to deal overtly with such issues as indigenous peoples, the urban working force, and women's status and role.

The distinction between the two currents is, beyond any doubt, itself something of an artifice and a fiction. In this survey the separation of the two tendencies is utilized, but always with an awareness of its fragility and arbitrariness. The purpose is to show how this bifurcation was a firmly established part of Spanish American literature as the century opened but was less and less maintained in succeeding decades, finally becoming the viewpoint of a small minority of literary intellectuals. It is now unusual to hear polemical defenses either of art for art's sake or of pure social realism. The polarity's somewhat unnatural character is confirmed by the fact that it needed to be sustained by manifestos, debates, and polemics between literary intellectuals. Yet this opposition is not only useful but highly characteristic of the way contemporary writers and readers viewed Spanish American narrative and its options. (In this overview changes in prevailing beliefs about literature receive special attention.) The opposition, even if it cannot always be verified by reading actual texts from both tendencies, has a firm existence as part of literary culture. During the first half of the twentieth century, debates raged and factions banded together, pitting estheticist writing against social literature. Although modernist literature is a valuable source of insights into the era's social attitudes, modernist writers were cast, and often cast themselves, as esthetes. In the often exaggerated discourse of cultural polemics, the modernists were inevitably placed on the side of art and against realism and social writing. They frequently found themselves defending, if not exactly art for art's sake, at least an intense focus on the artistry involved in the making of the literary text. They were viewed as inherently in competition with the realists who flourished during the same years. Though modernist writers are associated with detachment from society, there was an identifiably modernist outlook on society, with followers of this tendency sharing a disdain for mechanization and the definition of progress as technical and material development. The first chapter of this book, "Twentieth-Century Modernist Prose, 1900–1920," and the second, "Realism and Naturalism, 1900–1930," reflect, in their bifurcation of literature, two literary categories clearly recognized by contemporary authors and readers.

With the advent of the twenties and the formation of avant-garde groups in Spanish American cities, the opposition between the two tendencies was played up for dramatic, attention-claiming effect. A well-publicized case is that of the 1920s Buenos Aires literary scene. Argentina's younger writers vigorously and showily polarized themselves into rival avant-gardes, and in manifestos and interviews placed social literature in stark opposition to the cultivation of artistry. The third chapter, "Avant-Garde, Imaginative, and Fantastic Modes, 1920–1950," is designed to follow the typical categories of Spanish American narrative into two general modes, but at the same time to draw attention to the overgeneralization involved in separating this body of work from realist writing. The works discussed in the third chapter do, indeed, exhibit avant-garde, imaginative, and fantastic properties, but these qualities are at times only barely predominant over other features that allow them to generate a social critique.

While the split between estheticist literary innovation and realism as social critique held during the first three decades of the century, by the 1930s it was revealing its arbitrary character. Writers and critics were less eager to support such a dichotomy. Myth, fantasy, and magic began to claim an undisguised place in literary works that delivered a commentary on society. Contemporary readers and critics of Chile's María Luisa Bombal regarded her as an imaginative and fantastic writer. Yet later readings of her texts, the most important of which appeared in the 1930s, have brought out her bitter criticism of the confining lives of upper-middle-class Chilean women. She now stands as a proto-feminist writer as well as one able to depict convincingly oneiric states and ultranatural occurrences.

In the 1940s the old distinction was plainly becoming useless to describe new developments in Spanish American prose fiction. Now Miguel Angel Asturias of Guatemala and Alejo Carpentier inaugurated the mode that would retrospectively be categorized as *magical realism*. Asturias, with the 1944 publication of his *Men of Maize*, made it clear how great a change was occurring in the literary treatment of Indian issues, which only shortly before had been generally regarded as a subject suitable for social-realist writing. In *Men of Maize* Asturias draws on the *Popul-Vuh*, the sacred book of Maya civilization, and on modern Central American Indian tale-telling to generate a magical, legendary ambience for his novel. At the same time, the work speaks in favor of Central American Indians and encourages respect for their rich cultural inheritance. In Carpentier's case, Caribbean social history is his prime topic, and his fiction subjects his historical material to a critical reading with special emphasis on the class and racial hierarchy. But his narratives, particularly those of the 1940s, also create a world in which matters function according to mythical and magical patterns at odds with strictly rational concepts of time, space, and causation.

The organization of the chapters of this book reflects the move, during the mid-century decades, away from a polarization of Spanish American narrative into realist and esthetic or imaginative tendencies. Chapter 4, "Realism and Beyond, 1930–1960," shows the rapid abandonment of the concept, always a somewhat forced one, that realism could stand distinctly apart from imagination and fantasy. Spanish American writers who in earlier decades might have cast themselves in the role of realists, based on their desire to criticize the prevailing social order, now felt less inhibited about drawing on the set of resources identified with fantastic writing.

By the 1960s there was an old-fashioned quality to the idea that the fictional representation of and commentary upon social conditions was opposed to a highly imaginative and esthetically elaborated textual treatment. Occasionally a literary intellectual would attempt to revive the polemical distinction. The critic Oscar Collazos sustained a long-running dispute with Julio Cortázar; Collazos accused Cortázar of neglecting society's concerns in favor of experimentation with narrative form. Yet even as the polemic was at its height, observers noticed that it seemed less appropriate for the 1960s than for an earlier part of the century, when competing "isms" vied for prominence.

In consequence, the last two chapters, "The Boom and Its Antecedents, 1950–1970" and "The Postboom: New Voices and Belated Discoveries, 1968–1990" are not separated by the type of texts discussed, but only by chronology. The abandonment in the final chapters of the earlier dichotomy corresponds to an acceptance, now general in the Spanish American literary world, of the proposition that formally innovative fiction, even narratives with a strong mythic and fantastic strain, can serve as a medium of social criticism. However, changes in what may be considered socially committed fiction do not imply any relaxation of the assumption, a sturdy one in Spanish American intellectual life, that writers carry a responsibility for helping to set society's agenda.

If there is one principal effect this study should achieve, it is to show readers the progressive unfolding of Spanish American narrative over the course of the entire twentieth century up to the present. This includes the early years, more difficult to recover and appreciate, whose main works and tendencies are often largely unknown to an international readership. It also covers recent decades, when it is difficult to know which of multiple lines of innovation will prove of lasting significance. Beyond the discussion of particular writers, texts, and trends, the survey aims to portray a literature characterized both by salient continuities that unite diverse periods and constant new permutations.

One

TWENTIETH-CENTURY MODERNIST PROSE, 1900–1920

As the twentieth century began, Spanish American prose was still receiving the renovating impetus of the modernist movement that had originated in Spanish America during the 1880s. While often thought of as a movement of poets, modernism had brought about profound changes in the character of Spanish-language literary prose. Nearly all modernists experimented in this form, including many who would later be remembered only as poets. In particular, José Martí (1853–1895), equally celebrated as an advocate of Cuban independence from Spain and as a literary innovator, had devoted considerable thought and practice to giving new, vital rhythmic qualities to prose. Martí's short stories, one novel, essays, and journalism are all distinguished by notable, eloquent rhythms. Rubén Darío (Nicaragua, 1867–1916), the single most important figure in modernism, had achieved impressively unusual effects in prose during the movement's early years. His sensuous, rhythmic pieces in the 1888 *Azul . . .* (Azure . . .), often consisting almost exclusively of description, made the point that prose was an artistic, as much as a communicative, medium.

The 1890s found modernism in a state of transition owing, in part, to the deaths of all but one of its main practitioners.[1] The survivor, Darío, had assumed responsibility for restoring the depopulated modernist literary movement and making a modernist program out of his belief in the artistic use of language to achieve a far-reaching harmony. During this period not only were the chief actors in modernism changing, but the movement was becoming more geographically centered. Modernist activity had at first simply occurred wherever the writers were, chiefly in countries north of the equator. But after Darío moved to Buenos Aires in

1893, he grew increasingly involved in organizing a modernist literary scene. The Argentine capital, with its cafés, literate reading public, and well-developed publishing industry, served as a center of operations. Many members of this reconstituted modernism were from Argentina, like Leopoldo Lugones (1874–1938) and Enrique Larreta (1873–1961); or from neighboring Uruguay, like José Enrique Rodó (1871–1917), the poet Julio Herrera y Reissig (1875–1910), Horacio Quiroga (1878–1937), who would go beyond modernism in his famed short stories, and Carlos Reyles (1868–1938). Others lived in Buenos Aires, like the Bolivian Ricardo Jaimes Freyre (1868–1933), or at least published there. After Darío left for Europe in 1898, Buenos Aires was less pivotal, but modernism still relied on geographically specific literary scenes.

While Darío never again made as great an impact with his creative prose as he did in *Azul . . .*, his critical essays in the 1896 *Los raros* (The strange ones) were widely looked to as a guide to advanced tastes in literature. He at moments announced projects for extended works of fiction; in 1897 he tantalized his public by publishing installments of a novel, *El hombre de oro* (The man of gold), only to abandon it in mid-plot. Darío never completed this or any other novel. The Colombian José Asunción Silva (1865–1896) had written a widely read novel, the 1896 *De sobremesa* (After dinner; published in 1925). Martí had published in installments, under a female pseudonym, the 1885 novel *Amistad funesta* (Woeful friendship). He expressed some frustration and embarrassment over this lightweight work, though he later made plans for its publication as a book, under his real name and with the new title *Lucía Jerez*.[2] All in all, briefer forms had more successfully lent themselves to modernist prose expression. Darío never abandoned fiction and descriptive vignettes in prose, but he was really able to make a profound impact only with his rapidly evolving poetry. There was clearly an opening for an imaginative writer to make a breakthrough with a monumental, memorable work of modernist prose.

At this juncture a work appeared that, as well as taking modernist prose in a new direction, electrified the Spanish American intellectual world with the program of ideas it set forth. The 1900 book-length *Ariel* (also *Ariel* in Margaret Sayers Peden's English version), by the Uruguayan Rodó, is by all accounts the outstanding application of modernist literary principles to the essay. It is a showcase for the highly polished "artistic prose" (to use the contemporary phrase) favored by the movement. Sentences and paragraphs are crafted into balanced, well-measured cadences, and words are painstakingly selected for an effect of meditative refinement. The essay's central propositions are often posed obliquely, through thoughtfully constructed metaphors and allusions ranging from classical antiquity to the turn-of-the-century intellectual world. The essay is set within a narrative frame in which a wise teacher inspires his exceptional students with a farewell lecture, making emblematic use of a statue charged with meaning.

The language and construction of *Ariel* made readers feel part of an educated few capable of appreciating such stylistic delicacies and learned references. Whoever reads the teacher's lecture is addressed in the second person as one of the highly valued students to whom this mentor assigns a moral mission. These features well suit the essay's message, an urging to Latin American youth to cultivate spiritual nobility, elevation of thought, a wide-ranging knowledge, and sensitivity to beauty and harmony. Aníbal González observes that *intellectual*, used as a noun, never appears in Rodó's famous essay. The term was just then rapidly gaining a place in public discussion; as González shows in his study of the modernist novel, modernist writers frequently discussed the role of the intellectual in Latin American life.[3] It is impossible to know why Rodó avoided the term; perhaps he considered it too new and voguish for his prose, which strives for a classical, timeless effect. Yet its absence draws attention to the fact that his celebrated essay is not exactly about intellectual individuals and elites, but rather a broader concept. *Ariel* concerns itself with a form of personal growth that involves more than intellectual development.

Rodó addressed the anxiety many Latin Americans were experiencing over the sudden preeminence of the United States. While recognizing the vigor of U.S. society, Rodó cautioned Latin Americans not to mimic its utilitarian emphasis. To give a fresh prestige to a devalued heritage, *Ariel* traces a "Mediterranean" cultural legacy from the ancient Greeks to Spain to current-day Latin Americans. Such an outlook brings with it the disinterested love of beauty and wide-ranging mental activity pursued for its own sake. To impress these ideas on the students in *Ariel*, the teacher contrasts Ariel (present in the form of the statue), with his noble detachment from worldly interests, with Caliban, representative of base strivings. This contrasting pair, adapted from Shakespeare to serve Rodó's rhetorical goals, exercised a hold on the imagination of many Latin American readers, and the figures of Ariel and Caliban continue to be cited and discussed. Many readers eagerly identified Ariel with Latin America and

Caliban with the United States. While this interpretation no doubt provided comfort, it omits the complexities of Rodó's formulation. *Ariel* does not offer the possibility of rejecting the U.S. example. Instead, Latin Americans must continually evaluate U.S.-style progress, deciding which of its features will, if adopted, lead to greater well-being and which to mindless striving for material gain. Several similarly difficult tasks of discernment are urged upon Latin Americans. Rodó is particularly concerned with the balance between democracy and the maintenance of an elite whose spiritual distinction will entitle it to make decisions for others.

Ariel is very much a work of its cultural moment, illustrating both the strengths and the shortcomings of the contemporary artistic and intellectual scene. Its elaborately wrought prose and framing story make it a showpiece of the literary craftsmanship then much admired, although these characteristics have rendered the essay somewhat dated and mannered to subsequent generations. Though Rodó published many other important essays, especially the 1909 *Motivos de Proteo* (*The Motives of Proteus*), he made them less self-consciously literary than *Ariel*.

No sooner had *Ariel* won its success than it drew fire for elitism, and its aristocratic outlook has troubled readers increasingly over the years. The essay is full of reminders that the Latin American youth addressed by the teacher are upper-class boys, receiving private instruction in a beautifully appointed room. As the group leaves after the uplifting lecture, intruding on its elevated state of mind is "the harsh contact of the crowd."[4] In considering Latin America's cultural situation, *Ariel* offers a new appreciation of what Rodó calls the Mediterranean legacy and its continuation in Latin America, but is silent about indigenous and African-source cultures. The Cuban critic Roberto Fernández Retamar, in his 1973 *Calibán*, suggests that Latin Americans should see themselves in not Ariel but the slave. The latter is perceived as savage and grossly material, rather like the unskilled labor and unprocessed minerals and foodstuffs Latin America exports, while technologically advanced nations view themselves as living on their expertise, ingenuity, and entrepreneurial imagination.[5]

Whether the reaction was to embrace *Ariel*'s teachings, as did so many that an *arielista* movement developed, or to react against them, Spanish American intellectual culture received a long-lasting impact from the work. Despite objections to *Ariel*'s treatment of its central questions, there was no dispute that Rodó had accurately targeted issues requiring critical analysis. He had recognized that Latin American culture required examination, not in historical and geographical isolation, but in its evolving relation with the cultures of other world regions (later analysts would add, and their economies). Rodó pinpointed an inequity that would continue to provoke discussion: regions or nations at an economic advantage easily appear to have cultures worthy of emulation, while economically weaker areas struggle to establish, even to themselves, the value of their culture.

It should be noted that often the very features that cause modernism to be categorized as detached or escapist can also be cited as evidence of a questioning outlook on society. A text in the modernist mode is as capable as any other of generating a comment on culture and society. From the movement's inception, modernists were prepared to express social criticism through their writings, especially castigating the utilitarian, mercantile outlook they saw developing as Spanish America grew closer to the highly industrialized nations of Western Europe as well as the United States. Standing apart from this concern with efficiency, they favored a disinterested rejoicing over objects pleasing to the senses. The celebration of costly beauty offers a retort to widespread contemporary urgings that Latin Americans invest for economic expansion.

The related attribute of elitism is too quickly assigned to modernism. Beginning with Martí, a populist in cultural matters, throughout the movement's history there were, together with aristocratic postures, moments when modernists paid admiring tribute to grassroots expression. As a movement whose continued life depended on variation and novelty, modernism could not completely exclude any thematic material. For all its aloof image, modernist writing has included social protest and borrowings from folk culture.

Darío and others kept modernist prose in the public eye with short stories and sketches. Many of these appeared in newspapers and magazines of quite popular appeal as modernists often looked to creative prose as a source of income. Their work in this vein was not always critically valued. For example, in 1904 Darío published a collection of his prose vignettes, *Tierras solares* (Ancestral lands). This volume was accorded little of the significance attributed to the same author's contemporaneous books of poetry; recent years have brought a belated recognition of Darío as a writer of artistic prose and an effort to recover examples of his work left uncollected in back issues of magazines and newspapers.

Modernism remained widely perceived as dedicated to art for art's sake. This notion receives support from many pronouncements made by members of the movement, especially Darío. But while all modernists were intent on giving literary language a surprising expressivity, beauty, and musicality, in other respects their characteristics are less easily specified; there is unending critical debate over the most accurate way to describe the movement.

            While modernism was seeking to maintain its vitality and Spanish American intellectuals were struggling to come to terms with recent changes in the region's identity and place in the world, Spanish American republics, particularly the more economically developed ones, were swiftly becoming involved in economic relations with industrialized Western Europe and the United States. These connections, bringing increased cultural influences along with an unaccustomed prosperity, moved the former Spanish colonies farther from their traditional Hispanic culture, long a source of identity. With Spain's fortunes at a low ebb after the Spanish American War, many Latin Americans devalued their Hispanic legacy and looked to the more industrialized countries, especially the booming United States, as models of a vigorous modernity. The close connection between the rise of modernism and the greater engagement of Latin America with the economies of powerful countries has been the topic of illuminating studies in recent years, with the work of Angel Rama particularly contributing to this line of research.[6] While Rama and others struck with his approach are frequently critical of modernist poets, their assertions establish modernism as a phenomenon of more profound impact than was previously assumed; rather than limit modernism to an esthetic universe detached from the forces transforming Latin America, this type of research makes the literary movement part of the historical dynamic.

Even before Rama began to study modernism as a dimension of social history, there had been lengthy debate over the movement's relation, or lack of it, to Latin American realities. Modernists were closely attentive to tendencies in French- and English-language literatures and referred with pride to European influences on their writing. Understandably, they have been accused of disdain for their Spanish American heritage. Here, too, the issues are complex. While modernists drew upon other literatures, these borrowings were thoroughly, and inevitably, transformed. Such European trends as French symbolism and parnassianism necessarily assumed unexpected forms, unlike anything existing in European letters, as they became part of Hispanic American writing. Jean Franco summarizes the sea change that literary tendencies undergo in entering

literatures of the Spanish-speaking New World: "From Independence onwards, the assimilation of Latin America into a 'universal culture' has been
as powerful a stimulus as the assertion of the originality of the American
experience. Yet as far as literature is concerned what can be assimilated is
little enough; for some strange oddness marks even the work of those
writers who labor most strenuously to enter into the paradise of universal
culture."[7]

In a sense, Spanish American modernism as a whole can be seen as a
response to the contemporary situation of the region; though increasingly
involved with the modernity of French- and English-language countries,
the population of Spanish America was ineluctably different and experienced the modern in a distinctive way. The argument just summarized,
eloquently stated by Octavio Paz in his 1964 essay "The Siren and the
Seashell" and expanded upon in his influential 1974 book *Los hijos del limo*
(*Children of the Mire*), has won wide acceptance, and the current critical
tendency is to see Spanish American modernism as very much a part of
the regional culture in which it originated. As Paz put it, "Darío and his
friends . . . were not anti-Latin American; they wanted a Latin America
that would be contemporaneous with Paris and London."[8]

Modernists considered the available repertory of lexical options in literary Spanish to have become depleted. They claimed that the vocabulary
had grown impoverished, beginning with the neoclassical reaction against
the baroque period, through puristic efforts to obtain a more sober, homogeneous, and strictly Spanish language. Looking beyond the expected
possibilities, they enriched the texture of their writing with memorable,
evocative, and at times eccentric word choices. They enjoyed a notable
liberty to adapt words from other languages and were often accused of
Frenchifying or otherwise corrupting Spanish; in addition, some of their
bolder lexical innovations involved the coining of new words. In their
view, well-chosen adjectives had a particular power to give beauty and
elegance to a text. The naming of objects, and particularly objects possessed of a degree of splendor and refinement, was a task to which modernists devoted great care. They used exactly correct, and often rare,
nouns for precious stones and gemstones, costly fabrics and furs, objets
d'art, ornate receptacles, tableware, furniture, fine metals, building materials, and cultivated plants and animals. The effect is so strictly determined by the exact words chosen, with their specific sound properties,
that much modernist writing is extremely difficult to translate with any
degree of success.

Under an imperative to innovate, modernism required continual new variations to keep from turning into a set of fixed conventions. Modernists believed that the rhythms and harmonies of esthetically crafted language, though neglected by their romantic predecessors, held limitless expressive potential. They developed variegated patterns capable of suggesting to the reader's mind moods, attitudes, and musical and other sensory stimuli, this last a point of special concern. Darío, whose esthetic outlook had an occult and mystical tinge to it, asserted that the sonorous harmony of a text could attune readers to the unity of the cosmos.

Of the writers who helped Darío launch the second wave of modernism, the most influential and original was Lugones. Although Lugones formed part of the modernist literary scene, he was in many ways an isolated creator whose literary innovation was motivated by his own strongly held, if shifting and idiosyncratic, beliefs. Lugones grew skilled at exercising influence as a distinguished man of letters. Together with his literary principles, he promoted educational and cultural policies and political ideas. After starting out as a utopian anarchist, then passing through a socialist phase, he grew conservative and developed an odd philomilitarism, abhorrent to his fellow writers. At the time of his suicide, he was cultivating a quasi-mystical variety of fascism. Lugones's ideological mutations are most evident in his speeches and essays; they at times manifest themselves in his verse, which moved toward nationalistic themes. Yet his prose fiction gives little sign of the author's political outlook.

Lugones was equally a poet and a prose writer. Pedro Luis Barcia, an experienced editor of Lugones's texts, estimates that he published some one hundred and fifty items of prose fiction, making him the most productive writer of stories in the modernist mode.[9] Lugones's poetry requires some effort of adjustment for later readers to appreciate. So does his eccentrically beautiful regional novel of 1905, *La guerra gaucha* (The gaucho war). Composed in an artificial style, with an abundance of showily strange metaphors and a vast, bizarrely eclectic lexicon, *La guerra gaucha* takes to an extreme the baroque aspects of modernism. But Lugones's short stories retain their beauty and ability to horrify. In short fiction Lugones favored the cold story, or cruel story, popularized in Europe by such writers as Guy de Maupassant. (In current-day terms, his tales would be called fantastic.) This subgenre features either eyewitness or "as told to" accounts of disturbing events that contradict the usual operating principles of the world, such as entities that move between the animate and the inanimate world and encounters between beings from different dimensions of reality. Among the implicit rules for this subgenre is the avoidance of compassion or sentimentality, although the narrator should express such emotions as revulsion and terror. In Lugones's work the spine-chilling tale is well served by modernist prose, developed to evoke a variety of sensations.

The often reprinted stories of *Las fuerzas extrañas* (Strange forces), first collected in 1906, have proven equally successful as thrilling reading matter and as complex, subtle texts prized by literary analysts. These fictions present themselves as documents of various types. Individual stories pose as a reporter's notes, a chapter from an ancient history book, a suicide's deposition, and a saint's life. Lugones was an expert mimic who could produce a convincing simulacrum of a text from Middle Eastern antiquity or medieval Europe. Several tales from *Las fuerzas extrañas* center on experimenters who, working on the far edges of science or spiritualism, have tampered with the norms of nature, unleashing unknown powers. Though in one text the researcher gives an account of his own misguided work, a more frequent narrative arrangement has a relatively normal observer tell with horror of his encounter with science gone wild. In other stories the natural equilibrium is disturbed by decadence and excess, bringing punishment upon humankind. Two of the tales feature pious men as protagonists. One, a monk, succumbs to diabolical temptation; the other, a crusader, is brought down by a cruel infidel, in both cases triggering events beyond the natural order. One character suffers a bizarre fate for the seemingly insignificant infraction of killing a toad; however, the offense is compounded by his family's snobbish disdain for folkloric warnings concerning this creature's vengeance.

Las fuerzas extrañas illustrates several important features of modernism. Members of this movement, as part of their search for the hidden harmonies of the cosmos, were given to attending séances, consulting mediums and ouija boards, and studying theosophy and other esoteric systems. Such themes as the transmigration of souls and mystically perfect numbers and vibrations appear frequently in modernist writing. Such concerns have a prominent place in Lugones's stories; characters often discuss spiritualistic theories at length before the main action begins.

Much admired among modernists was the ability to suggest physical sensations through descriptive prose. Lugones's eyewitness narrators are adept at evoking such disturbing phenomena as a wall evenly coated with human brains ("La fuerza Omega" [The Omega force]) and an icy slime that forms on the participants when a séance goes out of control ("El origen del Diluvio" [The origin of the deluge]). In the tales of *Las fuerzas extrañas* and in other Lugones stories, tactile sensations often give the narrators the first clue that matters are direly amiss. Human beings may be disturbingly cold, while objects that should be inanimate may be warm to the touch. "Kábala práctica" (Practical Kabbalah), a story Lugones left uncollected (later reprinted by Barcia), is constructed to lead to the narrator's lengthy, horrified description of holding in his arms a woman with no skeleton: "But that contact left a horrible impression on me that will haunt me as long as I live. Instead of the svelte body whose elegance I had often admired, I felt a heavy, squishy mass, like a mushy pillow, fall into my arms, and when I squeezed her arms to hold her up, my fingers sank into them without feeling any resistance." [10]

Characteristically modernist, too, is the inclusion of exotic details. In "La lluvia de fuego" (The rain of fire), a free adaptation of the Sodom and Gomorrah narrative, the jaded narrator offhandedly describes a city where women and men, elaborately adorned and perfumed, uninhibitedly stroll the streets to sell their favors or advertise rare sexual entertainments. The ancient Middle East appears recreated in several Lugones tales, with an abundance of orientalist flourishes. Modernists were studious writers who ransacked the cultural past in search of reusable and adaptable themes and forms and unusual items of information. In their outlook, the contemplation of bygone civilizations provided relief from the here and now, with its banal emphasis on commercial and technical development. *Las fuerzas extrañas* is full of skillfully integrated borrowings from literature, folk narrative, and diverse mythical traditions. Lugones brings from his readings such motifs as the living statue, the severed yet vengeful body part, the partly human hybrid, the magic mirror, and the fatal utterance.

Later Lugones undertook to learn Arabic and became an adept of the arcane side of Oriental studies. His 1924 collection *Cuentos fatales* (Fatal tales), in which Lugones the amateur Egyptologist and his Arabic tutor figure as characters, reflects his absorption in the occult doctrines and sects of the Arab world. He particularly relished the thought of ancient belief systems, such as the original cults of desert tribes, surviving underneath a surface of Islamic orthodoxy.

The fantastic short stories of Lugones are instances of modernist prose that could appeal even to readers with little interest in literary language and construction, but simply a desire for tightly constructed, hair-raising "tales of effect." Other early twentieth-century writers of modernist prose gave first priority to satisfying esthetic criteria and allowing their readers to experience sensations elicited by the subtle suggestion of the literary text. The Venezuelan Manuel Díaz Rodríguez (1868–1927), especially in his early writing, and the Mexicans Amado Nervo (1870–1919) and Luis Gonzaga Urbina (1868–1934) exemplify writers who followed this latter path. Díaz Rodríguez enjoyed, at the turn of the century, a fame that has all but dissipated over the years. He made his name with his 1899 *Cuentos de colores* (Stories of colors). Each piece bears the name of a particular color, which then dominates the abundant descriptive passages and the mood and tone of the text. Díaz Rodríguez continued to specialize in painstakingly and precisely wrought prose pieces. His journalistic travel pieces, to which he gave the aptly modernist name of *sensaciones de viaje* (travel sensations), won their readership by reconstructing, in elegant language, the exact sense impressions the author had experienced upon visiting new scenes. Even when his newspaper columns were thematically unremarkable, Díaz Rodríguez rendered them in a language bordering on poetry. It was a point of pride among modernists to be able to generate a memorable and artistically satisfying text with a minimum of subject matter.

This author's early novels, the 1901 *Idolos rotos* (Broken idols) and the 1902 *Sangre patricia* (Patrician blood), are showpieces of the richly worked style and of the symbolic descriptive passages that were much cultivated at the height of modernism. The 1902 work, much noted at the time for its beauty and its pervasive sense of futility, is a novel-length illustration of the modernist concept that very little plot is required to sustain a narrative text. Shortly after the novel begins, the hero's young wife-by-proxy, sailing to Europe to join him, suddenly dies and is buried at sea. The widower, one of many neurasthenic, listless protagonists of contemporary fiction, finds himself unable to obtain a fresh start on life. His trip through the Mediterranean provides the occasion for elaborate descriptions of landscape and water—the latter a growing obsession of the hero's—but fails to revive him. After slowly concluding that he has no other worthwhile course of action, he begins a sea voyage toward South America, then casts himself into the ocean at the spot where his wife's body was placed. In its leisurely progress from one death to another, *Sangre patricia* offers intricately rendered interiors and lengthy philosophical exchanges between the main character and his friends. The novel's pessimistic outlook and its aristocratic hero unable to adapt to real-world situations are characteristic of much writing from the turn of the century. What sets it apart is the variegated and complex way its prose has been worked—and perhaps, for current-day tastes, overworked.

Sangre patricia exemplifies a tendency strong in the early twentieth century: the commingling of realistic and naturalistic writing with such modernistic elements as a reliance on symbol and metaphor. Hernán Vidal, for instance, characterizes *Sangre patricia* as "naturalist-symbolist" and argues that symbolic representation enhances the novel's lifelike qualities by making the main character's subjective states of mind vividly present to the reader.[11] John S. Brushwood points to *Sangre patricia* as a novel in which the modernist strain predominates, but realistic and naturalistic elements also lend a coloration.[12] If the latter are emphasized, the novel becomes the depiction of a representative of a decayed aristocracy unable to deal with, and unsuccessful at transcending, the coarse and commercial tenor of contemporary life. Such a thematic emphasis is especially present in a lengthy account of the protagonist's family history and in the figures of his shipboard companions, who, preoccupied with entrepreneurial ambitions, are insensitive to his suicidal condition.

Sangre patricia offers an unusually clear illustration of how modernist prose, most typically composed in brief, self-contained fragments, can serve to move along the characterization of a novel. For instance, when a friend of the protagonist's reencounters him after his supposedly restorative trip, the narrator sums up the alarming impression:

> . . . *Tulio seemed to contain, as in a very subtle jewel-case, a single, tenuous strand of soul. All of his being had been condensed into the strength of his voice and the light in his eyes, changing, restless, and alive. His eyes burned at times as if they wanted to consume everything in one of their flames; and his fragility was so out of proportion to the strength of his voice that the latter, just by sounding, threatened to break him into tiny pieces, like a brittle crystal container, from which his life would fly out and dissipate into the atmosphere like a drop of essence.*[13]

Of another member of this same circle, the narrator remarks that his friends learned

> *to see in Martí, beneath the smooth water of an immutable serenity, the gold of his spirit; through his words and actions they learned to see as if through very pure panes of glass. Sincerity surrounded him like a diapha-*

> *nous stream. It flowed from his lips, his eyes, all of*
> *him, in particular from his habitual posture, during*
> *conversations, when, bending forward, he leaned with*
> *his hands on his knees.*[14]

Mexico City flourished as a modernist center. It was there that the *Revista Moderna* (1898–1911) was published. The celebrated *Revista Azul* had been published there from 1894 to 1896. Mexico City would assume particularly great importance in the late years of the movement (roughly 1910–1920), when the search for fresh inventions took both poets and prose writers well past the bounds of modernism.

The Mexicans Nervo and Urbina both brought the esthete's prose to a fairly wide audience of newspaper and magazine readers. The more important of the two, Nervo, exerted a charismatic hold on a sector of the literary public. Though Nervo's fame today rests on his poetry, he first gained wide notice with his 1895 novel *El bachiller* (The graduate). Creating a scandal with its hero's act of self-castration, this work also aroused admiration for the wealth of noteworthy artistic touches in its prose. After publishing his third novel in 1899, Nervo appears to have abandoned the genre. But he continued to work in prose, writing sketches of contemporaries, travel notes, pained reflections on global conflict, vignettes, and stories.

While Nervo's short stories often involve mysterious happenings, they are certainly not standard ghost tales relying on rigorous plotting and well-timed climactic scenes. The emphasis is on the painstaking recreation of sensations, often rare or pathological ones, experienced by characters. The portrayal of emotional response is important, too, for Nervo is a student of feelings as well as a modernist. For example, when he deals with characters who traverse the space between life and death, their situation is grounded in their states of mind. The dead-in-life are apt to be driven between worlds by a longing for love. This effort to create a human context for mysterious events stands in contrast to the ghastly and blood-curdling effects that are the highlights of Lugones's cruel stories.

The author, who enjoyed a reputation as an eclectic, modern mystic, was well read in parapsychology and associated topics. At the same time, he knew many facts that, while culled from mainstream science, concerned little-known, startling phenomena. He was a self-taught student of contemporary scientific research into consciousness, pathological neurology, and cognition. This curious erudition went into his short stories.

Many of his texts generate esthetic effects from the presentation of other-worldly forms of consciousness and bizarre neurological disorders affecting perception. Like a number of modernists, he found literary uses for such esoteric concepts as the projection of the soul via an astral body and communication across time, or between worlds, by means of vibrations.

Nervo's metaphysical and scientific concerns frequently converged in the same text. An example is the very brief story "La serpiente que muerde la cola" (The serpent that bites its tail, 1912). The text narrates a verbal exchange between a doctor and a patient afflicted with extreme and persistent déjà vu. After the patient has detailed his experience of reliving every instant, the doctor offers him two explanations of his situation. The first of these is neurological:

> . . . *your sensory apparatus instantly and mechanically*
> *registers the external phenomena that the neurons trans-*
> *mit to it. What you see or hear is placed into your*
> *brain with extraordinary speed, thanks to your special*
> *sensitivity. So: after this registering (a fraction of a*
> *second later) you find out you're seeing an object or*
> *hearing a sentence, already seen and heard unbe-*
> *knownst to your consciousness. Then, naturally your*
> *memory remembers the impression previous (even by a*
> *fraction of a second) to the other one, and this memory*
> *gives you the sensation of doubleness you're telling me*
> *about.*[15]

Concluding this scientific-sounding account of déjà vu, the doctor presents a metaphysical explication of the problem, meditating aloud on the possibilities of a perfectly cyclical temporal structure to the universe. The text ends with a quick descent to the mundane, as the doctor offers his patient some common-sense health advice. The closing twist illustrates a device typical of many Nervo stories: homespun, down-to-earth touches give a human dimension to a character who, after experiencing extraordinary forms of consciousness, might otherwise seem too unlike the common run of humankind.

Far removed from Nervo's intimate and sympathetic effort to explore his characters' subtlest consciousness, down to their very neurons, is the broad sweep of the earlier *La gloria de don Ramiro*

(The glory of Don Ramiro). This intricate novel is the work of the Argentine Enrique Larreta, who spent six years laboriously reworking it before publishing it in 1908. *Don Ramiro* represents an original departure for modernism, applying the movement's principles and stylistic tendencies to the historical novel. The resulting text made a considerable impact upon its appearance and continues to be reprinted. It is the work most frequently pointed out as exemplifying modernism in the novel. The influential critic Amado Alonso chose *Don Ramiro* as his case in point for a 1942 monographic study largely on modernist textual practices, *Ensayo sobre la novela histórica. El modernismo en "La gloria de don Ramiro"* (Essay on the historical novel: Modernism in "The glory of Don Ramiro"). The novel also has served as a lightning rod for the indignation aroused by modernism.

Although the protagonist ends his days in 1605 in the New World, most of *Don Ramiro* is set in late sixteenth-century Avila. Larreta's fascinated recreation of a distant place and time was, for some readers, proof of the escapist character of modernism. Undeniably, the text reveals a museum curator's delight in reconstructing the architecture and interiors of Avila. However, the novel's portrait of Spanish culture, particularly its Catholic side, shows a critical outlook. Spanish life appears stifled and constricted by the Inquisition-era church, inflexible regal governance, anxiety over "purity of blood," and pressure to maintain one's honor and good name. Don Ramiro, coming from this context, is drawn into the Moorish community of Avila, not realizing for some time that his father is a Moor. Though he struggles to resist contamination by the new environment, he gradually absorbs its values and recovers a sensuality that mainstream Spain has self-defeatingly sacrificed in its efforts to purge itself of Islamic culture. Those portions of the novel set in the Moorish environment, where Don Ramiro becomes entranced by an ill-fated Arab beauty, exemplify a modernist ideal: evoking the experience of the senses, and an environment of pleasurable sensuality, through literary means. At the same time, they stand as a reproach to Christian Spanish culture for its cultivation of repression and fear of pleasure. As in many contemporary works, the protagonist is afflicted with an inability to accomplish results in the real world, and his actions are often futile and misguided. Don Ramiro has grandiose notions of what he will achieve, but his attainments are persistently meager; the titular reference to glory grows increasingly ironic.

The plot of *Don Ramiro* has its share of events, some of them verging on the melodramatic, and in this sense does not exemplify the modernists' experimentation with actionless prose. Yet the novel provides many instances of a modernist specialty, the still life painted in words, like this portrait of Avila:

> *Outside, in the city, the grim restfulness of the Castilian siesta.*
> *The noon light burns rabidly onto the stony walls, heating up iron, burning the moss off the rooftops. The streets are solitary and mute; but, on an occasional afternoon, the harsh voice of a Moor, a vegetable vendor, profanes the monastic silence, making more than one sleepy gentleman fume in the darkness of his bedchamber.*
> *Roosters crow, hoarse and drowsy.*[16]

By the 1910s it was becoming obvious that modernism was exhausting its inherent possibilities. Modernist style and construction alone could not sustain interest in a work; different subject matter and varieties of literary language had to be added, resulting in works of heterogeneous character. It becomes more difficult to find prose vignettes, short stories, or novels that can be classified under modernism without stretching the term considerably. Even such an author as Lugones, who at the time was perceived as a die-hard practitioner of modernism, in retrospect appears to have been undergoing changes in esthetic orientation, so that his later work is modernist only in an extended sense. Newer prose writers who came on the scene in the 1910s, as well as many authors long identified as modernists, now moved away from the tendency or at least variegated it greatly.

The 1910 novel *Los gauchos judíos* (*The Jewish Gauchos of the Pampas*) by Alberto Gerchunoff (1883–1950) shows how an author formed in the dominant mode of modernism could significantly vary this current by bringing in distinctive thematic material. Gerchunoff had come to Argentina as a small child and grown up in one of the agricultural colonies established by Jewish immigrants. His famous novel is cast, for the most part, as reminiscences of Jewish-Argentine life in a farming settlement. It exhibits a notable strain of Eastern European Jewish thought, particularly in its lyrical expressions of hope for a Zion remade through regenerating labor on the land.

The Jewish Gauchos, which had appeared as sketches in the newspaper *La Nación*, was published as a book in 1910 to coincide with the centennial of Argentina's independence. It is a highly ideological text. For instance, the novel expresses a servile gratitude toward Argentina for its willingness to admit Jews, omitting the real-world circumstance that the national government was actively recruiting Jewish immigrants. The novel's distortion of the relations between the immigrants and the Argentine state has provoked disgust among readers in subsequent decades. Yet the much reprinted *The Jewish Gauchos* continues to be by far the best-known text by a Spanish American Jewish author. The success of this anomalous text would seem to owe much to its use of the lyrical prose of modernism to smooth over elements that, when viewed in less poetic terms, would be painfully contradictory.

During the waning years of modernism, Spanish American prose writers began to utilize elements of this tendency, including its fantastic side, as they moved toward a more realistic type of representation. This synthesis of realism and fantasy would later become a celebrated distinguishing feature of Spanish American fiction designated as *magical realism*. In its early manifestations it is best represented in the prose fiction of the Chilean Pedro Prado (1886–1952). The poetic prose of modernism, regionalistic realism (Chilean *criollismo*), and fantastic literature come together in two lyrical, symbolically charged novels by this author. These are *La reina de Rapa Nui* (The queen of Rapa Nui, 1914) and the 1920 *Alsino*, named after its protagonist. While the author's reputation rests chiefly on the latter work, both are innovative texts and may jointly be considered as exemplifying magical realism long before the popularization of this term.

Prado's writing took on its special character when he began combining poetic prose, a good deal of information about Chile's geography and peoples, and highly inventive narrative events and description. The 1914 text offers more of the lyrical and imaginative than the realist element in this original admixture. A fictional prologue presents the main text as a manuscript that the author has discovered, edited, and published. Left by a mysterious friend of the author's, it is an account of a voyage to Rapa Nui, or Easter Island, Chile's colony, where the narrator gains privileged knowledge of one of the remaining isolated, indigenous peoples of South America.

The main text is not only an autobiographical story of exotic adventures but also an ambiguous meditation on the relations between more urbane cultures and the more insular ones that the former discover, explore, and colonize. The narrator states that he was drawn to Rapa Nui because it gave him a rare opportunity to feel part of colonial power: "When I studied geography, my favorite subject, I was filled with pride by the paragraph that says: 'Chile possesses in Oceania Easter Island, the only colony of which South America can boast.' The only colony was ours! I found it natural for us to be compared with the English." [17]

Once the story brings the narrator to the island, he has a continual struggle maintaining his ideal of an exotic native idyll. The landscape is as unspoiled and breathtaking as he had hoped, providing the material for a number of poetic-prose descriptions synthesizing geographically accurate and fantastically inventive elements. The islanders at first appear winsome and childlike, and there is even a beautiful queen with whom he becomes passionately involved. However, when the protagonist spends enough time to learn something of the island dwellers' cultural and social history, what he discovers calls into question his original assumption that the local people are irreflexively at home in a continuous, relatively static culture of their own. Instead, the inhabitants have long had a disrupted, uneasy relation with their cultural past, and a fresh set of troubles has arisen from their contacts with cosmopolitan, modern cultures. They have no clearer information than other Chileans about the great stone heads on Easter Island and have denied, perhaps untruthfully, any relation to the megalith carvers. An artisan crudely proclaims his ignorance of the meaning of the ancient writing system he reproduces on exportable handicrafts. Suicide, self-destructive risk-taking, and carelessness toward others are disturbingly prevalent. The local people's explanations of their concepts of morality sound like defensive rationalizations for a general breakdown of ethics, with deceit and guile accepted as virtually the norm.

The ending of *La reina de Rapa Nui* is a puzzling one. Although the narrator has frequently expressed bafflement and disorientation when describing his glimpses into the islanders' intricate and disordered social organization, once his tale comes to his departure from Rapa Nui, his outlook suddenly becomes much simpler. He thinks back upon the island in a romantically nostalgic mode, rhapsodizing over the untroubled life its "innocent and naked" [18] inhabitants lead: "Happy the life of your children, who live far from the fever and the ambition of new men," he says in the closing paragraph, addressing the island as he sails away. [19] John R. Kelly finds the ending words a mistake in the construction of the novel: "Prado destroys the impact of his message." [20] Still, since the narrator's conclusions are so saliently out of alignment with his experiences, his last remarks might be read as an ironic comment on the robust persistence, even in the face of contrary evidence, of the belief that tribal societies are un-selfconscious and free from the stress of cultural change.

Alsino aroused a good deal of contemporary admiration and is one of the few modernist novels to enjoy continuing popularity. The influential Chilean critic Arturo Torres-Rioseco particularly recommended it to readers, calling it "a beautiful work, one of the most beautiful conceived on our continent,"[21] although he also cautioned against assigning too monumental a significance to such a slight text. The literary language of *Alsino* may seem somewhat effusively lyrical for current-day tastes, particularly in the passages that represent the protagonist's own words and thoughts. Yet the novel continues to be well regarded for its ability to bring down-to-earth, realistic detail convincingly into direct contact with fantastic occurrences. Any summary of *Alsino* should include mention of the text's many specifically Chilean allusions, particularly evident in the regional geographical, botanical, and zoological details Alsino surveys in his wanderings.

The protagonist is a Chilean peasant child, the son of two alcoholics, who is at first distinguished only by his attempts to fly. After being injured in a launch from a treetop, Alsino's back grows a hump that then sprouts wings. The power of flight does not transform Alsino into an ethereal being. He is still a rambunctious peasant boy who for a time enjoys such boisterous pleasures as buzzing a terrified herd of horses. But his anomaly sets him apart from his fellow beings and excites their animosity. Alsino is repeatedly the target of gratuitous ill treatment because of his difference. His peculiar existence as the only known winged specimen of an earthbound species gradually forces him to develop certain unhappy insights about human nature. As well as hostile reactions, Alsino arouses a certain awe; he is twice taken for an angel. As he grows apart from other human beings, he develops an intimate rapport with the natural world. His experiences take him farther and farther from the human norm, and his exceptionality, when joined with his knowledge of folk medicine, gives him an unasked-for celebrity as a magic man with healing powers.

At first, Alsino's flights bring him release and excitement. His early enrapturement is represented by long segments of poetic prose evoking the delights of aerial movement. Alsino himself grows lyrical in his expression, and, addressing himself to nature, rhapsodizes in mid-flight:

> *"Oh, moon of the solitary heights!" he exclaimed deliriously. "Forgive my startling you, forgive my having*

*come, not knowing how, to this deserted region where
you, perhaps, trustingly, will display your charms at
closest range. Forgive me! But what could I do? One
day, attached to my legs, I saw them move and take me
to fulfill a secret destiny. Back then, on fire with curiosity, happy with feeling free, free with all possible
freedom, I still didn't go so far as to feel at the same
time this terror of seeing myself bound to something
that now pulls me beyond the limits of action set for
my life.*

*"Just as I once felt my legs, now I feel my wings as
if they are and aren't mine. My blood runs toward
them, and they, in turn, take me completely away.
When we feel ourselves being pulled along the marvel-
ously hidden channel of our destiny, everything is confused expectation, and we can't even know whether
anything truly is ours."*[22]

Despite such surges of euphoria, matters deterio-
rate when Alsino is captured and his wings clipped. Transferred to the
estate of a landowner who is plotting to exhibit him as a freak, he falls in
love with his captor's daughter. Their love is frustrated not only by Alsino's exceptional condition but also by class divisions. The section of the
novel that narrates this doomed love provides the best support for one
interpretation of the novel. Julio Arriagada A. and Hugo Goldsack, two
articulate exponents of the social reading of *Alsino*, argue that the novel is
an allegory of class antagonism.[23] In this vision of the work, Alsino's drive
toward flight is a metaphor for the Chilean peasant's struggle to rise above
conditions of misery; his eventual defeat emblemizes the impossibility of
this aspiration given the existing social hierarchy. The notion of warring
class interests and the exploitation of the poorest, most vulnerable Chileans is certainly inherent in the events of the plot. Yet class struggle never
surfaces as such in the novel. The landowner's daughter dies and Alsino
escapes before the novel can play out the conflict that appears to have been
building up between the winged peasant and his would-be exploiter.

In further contrast to the playful, high-spirited segments evoking Alsino's early experience of flight are the final chapters. The protagonist is
impelled by grief to wander until he comes to stay with a small farmer's
family. The local healing woman is envious of Alsino's reputation for
curing ailments and contrives to have him blinded. The sightless Alsino

grows more anomalous yet and attracts droves of sufferers hoping for a cure, although they receive more embittered wisdom than medicine from him. Alsino regains the use of his wings, but without sight, his first new flight ends in a catastrophic fall. Even though the forces of nature come to his aid, Alsino fails to recover from his infected wounds and passes his last days wandering about in a virtual delirium. Unable to distinguish between waking and dream, he flies straight upward into the night, then plummets earthward with such speed that he is reduced to a wisp of ashes.

The ending leaves it unclear what significance to assign to Alsino's deterioration and death. Clearly, human beings are ethically at fault for their ill treatment of a fellow member of the species, but it is ambiguous how much their cruelty and indifference arises from social factors and how much their treatment of Alsino is rooted in the human character. There is also a metaphorical tale of fatally grand aspirations: the parallel with the Icarus myth is readily apparent, especially in Alsino's fiery death. Because the novel so often calls attention to its Chilean setting, the ending has been interpreted as having meaning for Chile. Arriagada A. and Goldsack, for instance, orient themselves by the novel's current of social criticism and read the finale as a negative vision of the future open to the nation's poor.[24] Aníbal González, though, believes that the last sections of *Alsino* show the work's kinship to other modernist novels that narrate case histories of intellectuals. When he becomes a blind prophet, "It is then that Alsino begins to speak and act like an intellectual."[25] From then on his story can be understood the way González interprets other modernist novels, as illustrating the painful trade-off between meditative detachment and engagement with needy, noisy humankind.

As modernism recedes, the other strong current in turn-of-the-century prose, the realistic one, comes more fully into play. In addition, writers become increasingly eager to avoid the heavily worked, self-consciously artistic language of modernism and seek a style that is less cluttered and ornamental. Still, many features that were part of modernism continue to appear in creative prose, particularly the showcasing of elaborate descriptive passages and the favoring of symbolic over literal representation. Brushwood has observed that, just as many predominantly modernist novels show many characteristics of realism and naturalism, modernist traces occur in novels in which realism and naturalism are the prevailing tendencies.[26] The presence of modernism, particularly in elaborate descriptive passages and a preference for symbolic representation, continues to make itself felt to the present day.

Two

REALISM AND NATURALISM, 1900–1930

While Spanish American modernists were developing spectacular innovations in literary form, a less showy tendency was also making itself felt. This was literary realism: in the most general terms, the construction of texts so as to give the impression of representing, with as little distortion as possible, the realities of human life. In most cases, social realities were the primary focus, although some realists concerned themselves particularly with psychological issues or manifestations of culture. In Spanish American literature regional and ethnic folk cultures were often an attractive subject matter for literary realists.

Modernist prose had most characteristically taken the form of lyrical sketches, with the writing consisting of tenuously connected wisps of descriptive material. Even when modernists undertook lengthier works, their tendency was to downplay plot and action in favor of subtle, evocative set pieces. Realism brought a vigorous resurgence of the short story and novel, with clearly delineated characters engaged in easily summarized sequences of events.

Realism is inherently hard to define, and in the case of early twentieth-century Spanish American writing the difficulty is made more acute by the co-occurrence of naturalism. Naturalism may be a variant of realism or a subcategory of it. While naturalist beliefs may be stated, in actual works of literature the division between naturalism and realism is difficult to specify. At the turn of the century, Spanish American literary intellectuals and readers were keenly aware of naturalism, which was still quite recent. It should be remembered that naturalism, unlike the relatively spontaneous realism, had been deliberately formulated as a movement

(Emile Zola's 1880 *Le Roman experimental* is often cited as its programmatic statement), and its existence was marked by discussion and debate, beginning in France and spreading to other countries.

In Spain and Spanish America there were expressions of concern lest the deterministic outlook of naturalism undermine Christian belief and its emphasis on sordid matters deprive literature of its beauty and decorum. But for all the discussion of naturalism, very few Spanish American works consistently exemplify this current as it occurred in France. In a characteristic pattern, a movement that had seemed relatively homogeneous and clear-cut when first seen in its European forms grew increasingly eclectic and diffuse as Spanish American writers integrated it into their literature.

When naturalism first arrived in Spanish America in the 1880s, a few indisputably naturalistic texts appeared, the fiction of Eugenio Cambaceres (Argentina, 1843–1888) being probably the most definite example. But by the time the twentieth century began, the impact of the movement had become more generalized as it spread through Spanish American fiction. A number of works of basically realist tendency show only certain touches of naturalism. The narrator may take a detached, clinical view of the characters' sufferings at times, yet at other moments inject an undisguised note of empathy and pathetic appeal. The text may attribute characters' behavior to factors of heredity and environment, yet leave open the possibility that an effort of will, or the lack of it, was what really set their course in life. It is common to find a single work of Spanish American fiction accommodating realism and naturalism together with significant features of modernism. In addition, romanticism, with its violent contrasts, scenes of high emotion, and pathetically appealing characters, enjoyed a new flowering in Spanish American writing as one component of naturalistic works.

Some modernist prose writers who had always exhibited a certain current of naturalism in their fiction, sensing that modernism had nearly run its course, rebalanced the mixture so that realism and naturalism predominated in their new work. For example, the Venezuelan Manuel Díaz Rodríguez, discussed in Chapter One as a modernist novelist, adapted features of naturalism. By the 1920s, Díaz Rodríguez had edged over into a realistic mode, with rural Venezuelan life as his raw material; from his early specialization in refined settings and protagonists, he had moved toward rough and coarse ones. Yet he continued to work into his fiction elements, such as descriptive passages loaded with sensory details, that were clearly derived from Spanish American modernism. The same partial accommodation of naturalism typified other writers who had come onto the scene as modernists, such as the Venezuelan Rufino Blanco Fombona (1874–1944). So while naturalism was not a movement originating in Spanish America, as modernism had been, it took on a substantially different character in the course of becoming part of New World writing.

Javier de Viana (Uruguay, 1868–1926) produced some of the clearest cases of naturalism in twentieth-century Spanish American literature. Viana's best texts are short stories taking an unsentimental look at Uruguayan and Argentine gauchos; the 1901 *Gurí* stands out as especially successful among this author's many collections. The stories show this rural, mestizo population just as its longtime way of life is breaking down under such measures as the conversion of open range to fenced property and more efficient cattle-raising, resulting in less employment for ranch hands. The plots of these narrations often involve brutal revenge, with the hardened characters seeming to accept violent injustice as usual. Narrators of these events, observers who are conscious of the gap between themselves and the country people, are quick to compare the coarsened protagonists to animals, in the naturalistic tradition of "human beings as beasts." The clinical outlook of naturalism is evident in a number of observations about such matters as characters' ailments and drinking habits. Viana's stories reflect a belief, then much in vogue, that a racially mixed population will, by the laws of heredity, tend to degenerate physically and morally.

The rural people of the Southern Cone are more positively valued in the stories and loosely strung-together novels of Roberto J. Payró (Argentina, 1867–1928), who practiced a satirical regional realism. Payró was an anarchist; many of his texts support an attitude of confidence in the ability of unsophisticated people, free of the corrupting ambition to become leaders, to pursue their own business and maintain a rough-and-tumble justice. When their social system, with its inherent self-balancing mechanisms, suffers the interference of local politicians or government agents bent on applying formal regulations, the results are ridiculous. While the official ideal of efficiency and rigor in government—usually accompanied by corruption—receives the most stinging mockery, the wiliness and venality of the country folk also come in for satirical treatment.

Payró adapted elements of the picaresque novel, including sly characters and the satirical illustration of society's shortcomings. The raucous humor and acute observation of the rural scene gave his work a considerable popularity with the Argentine public. His stories in *Pago Chico* (1908), named for its fictional setting, an agreeably unruly small town, and his novels *El casamiento de Laucha* (Laucha's marriage, 1906) and *Las divertidas aventuras del nieto de Juan Moreira* (The entertaining adventures of Juan Moreira's grandson, 1910) are more critically valued today than they were by commentators at the time. In retrospect, it is evident how much Payró's works stand out, among contemporary writings, for the unusual respect they show toward less-educated provincial characters and their speech. While Viana's narratives reduce peasants to an inarticulate sullenness, Payró creates a successful literary equivalent for their sharp-witted, ironic talk, while at the same time keeping his characters' speech intelligible to readers unacquainted with the local dialect. His work uses a great deal of dialogue between, or stories told by, rural characters.

El casamiento de Laucha appears as the transcript of a lengthy autobiographical monologue by its protagonist, who is a great raconteur as well as a great rogue in his little region, to a gathering of intimates whom he can trust to appreciate his tale of outwitting a well-off widow. *Las divertidas aventuras* is also narrated by its own picaresque hero. However, this rogue is a more worldly, ambitious individual who leaves behind local scheming and mischief to become part of the larger political scene. Consistent with the distrust of leaders that typifies Payró's writing, the power-mongering narrator of *Las divertidas aventuras* is characterized so as to arouse much more distaste than the engaging rascal Laucha. Whether the characters are appealing scamps or corrupt wielders of influence, Payró's mimicry of local speech is admiring. He imitates not just dialectal features but also the wry, inventive, malicious subtleties of country talk. Rural, lower-class characters seem alert, expressive, linguistically innovative, and skilled in the art of narrative rather than ignorant and substandard.

The adaptation of the picaresque mode to Spanish American regional realism enjoyed a lengthy popularity. Among its successful practitioners was the Colombian Tomás Carrasquilla (1858–1940). Carrasquilla's fiction shows his concern with oral tradition, particularly popular storytelling and jokes. Though he did not make as detailed an effort as Payró to find suitable literary equivalents for the talk of rural populations, Carrasquilla illustrated an appreciation, slowly growing among populist intellectuals, for the capacity of verbal expression found among those with less formal education. This tendency would become increasingly pronounced in the latter part of the century as more writers sought to move away from the dominant central narrator of conventional realism, who speaks in an elite register of the issues confronting nonelite groups.

      Santa, the phenomenally popular 1903 novel by Federico Gamboa (Mexico, 1864–1939), brought to an unprecedentedly large public the manifestations of a somewhat softened naturalism. In his novels of this period, Gamboa repeatedly favors erotic subject matter, but typically the eroticism comes in a form that blights the characters' lives. In *Santa* the tormented figure is a greatly suffering prostitute. Successive editions totaling 65,000 copies were printed during the author's lifetime, and publishers continue to launch successful reprints, often mass marketed. This success is even more notable considering that *Santa* had to distinguish itself among many contemporary novels featuring prostitutes as heroines. The 1901 *Juana Lucero, o los vicios de Chile* (Juana Lucero, or the vices of Chile) by the popular Chilean author Augusto d'Halmar (real name Augusto Geomine Thomson, 1882–1950) is only one of the many competing works on the same theme and in a more or less naturalistic mode that enjoyed a limited vogue before dropping into an obscurity that *Santa* has never experienced.

  The narrative of *Santa* follows a young woman from her arrival at a Mexico City bordello, through her heyday as a celebrated demimondaine, and on to her decline and death. What would otherwise be the descriptive account of a rising and then falling career has two deviations that give it a more empathetically involving tone. Near the beginning of the novel, a flashback explains that Santa came to a brothel after being seduced, abandoned, and expelled from her rural home; giving this background serves to create sympathy for her as the victim of an intolerant society. As Santa's story nears its end, she manages to escape prostitution through the love of the bordello's blind piano player; she dies alcoholic and cancerous, but inwardly redeemed. The heroine's transformation through love is one of the best examples of the way in which a sentimental romanticism found its place as part of the highly eclectic Spanish American adaptation of naturalism.

  Although the novel often dwells upon the causes of Santa's career in prostitution, its message is not that Santa was forced, in any strictly deterministic fashion, to the downward path. She has the opportunity to improve her status to that of kept woman, and one of her long-term lovers is a good-hearted bullfighter who behaves quite honorably toward her. Nonetheless, she disrupts their stable relation to return to prostitution.

The narrator reports that, while living with the bullfighter, Santa confessed that "she missed her old life!" There follows a summary of Santa's thoughts on the matter. The narrator refrains from assessing the heroine's beliefs, leaving it ambiguous whether she had an alternative: "That attempt at an honest life bored her, probably because she was lost beyond all hope, because she had gone bad to the core; she didn't deny that was likely the case."[1]

The force, and the injustice, of social circumstances is made vividly present in certain episodes. In one of the strongest scenes, Santa's brothers, who had driven her from home, track her down to a chic bar where she has been holding court. It has been " . . . an exceptional night, when Santa was considered queen of the entire corrupt city,"[2] but the brothers burst in, abruptly take her aside, and inform her point-blank of her mother's death. They then revile her for turning to prostitution (although they had left her without resources for survival), forbid her all further contact with her family, and stalk out.

In a coda to this scene, whose impact depends partly upon the unfairness of the heroine's treatment, Santa visits a church to say a prayer for her mother. The sacristan ejects her, in disregard of the Christian ideal of charity. The narrator ends the sequence of unhappy events with a meditation designed to elicit sympathy for Santa: " . . . she was an orphan and she was a whore; she was laboring under the weight of a hopeless double orphanhood."[3] Yet there are many indications that an effort of will is still effective against inequitable fate and that Santa can reasonably be faulted for not struggling harder. These suggestions helped make the novel generally acceptable, despite inevitable expressions of outrage over its subject matter, in a Catholic culture where there was much anxiety lest literature undermine faith in free will.

The novel's popularity has certainly aroused curiosity and speculation. Its mass appeal taints it with the suspicion of being simplistic subliterature. Yet *Santa* is a work of fairly complex design, with many memorably constructed and elaborated scenes. The descriptions of characters and scenes stand out for their well-chosen details. Some of these descriptive passages dwell upon the sumptuous, fashionable highlife that Santa enjoys in her prime; here the novel manifests a strain of modernism in its evocation of material splendor and elegance. But equal skill is evident in the rendering of sordid or revolting matters; for instance, the piano player's sightless eyes come in for disturbingly minute description.

From the time the novel first won its anomalously large audience, there has been suspicion that many readers turn to *Santa* for titillation. There may be some validity to the conjecture, although many passages of the novel exhibit a clinical tone toward sexual matters. Narrator and characters often discuss Santa's body; the narrator repeatedly draws attention to the admirable firmness of the young Santa's flesh. Describing a character's reactions to the heroine, this narrator emphasizes such perceptions as "the delightful line of Santa's hip," "that soft fleshiness," "her fleshy shoulders."[4]

Margo Glantz has given intelligent thought to the representation of Santa's body, concentrating her analysis on the text's method of describing the heroine's appearance. She concludes that the novel often piques interest by offering up, as a butcher would offer up prime cuts, descriptions of Santa's body in piecemeal, peek-a-boo flashes and by chastely but tantalizingly veiled references to sexuality. Of the heroine's name, Glantz asks: "What greater pleasure exists than to sin with flesh seasoned with the epithet of *saintly?*"[5] She also remarks upon the coy strategy whereby the narrator makes it known that Santa is using a term such as *prostitute* or *whore*, but the actual word does not appear. Glantz's analysis is well formulated, but it still does not account for the success of film versions of *Santa*, in which Gamboa's oblique and reticent mode of referring to sexual matters is largely lost, while the plot and characters, and above all the figure of Santa, carry the day.

Chile had a long-running tradition of realist writing. Since the last quarter of the previous century, a number of Chilean writers had concentrated on rural regions, a literary tendency known as *criollismo*. With a literary culture that valued realistic representation, such tendencies as naturalism and "proletarian" social-protest writing prospered in Chile. The short story writer Baldomero Lillo made a memorably strong impact with his disturbing glimpses of the lives of Chilean miners. Of his collections of stories, the 1904 *Sub terra* is the one that most centers on this thematic material. Shocking to the contemporary public, these texts still retain their ability to horrify readers with vividly detailed accounts of the adverse effects of mining. To win readers' empathy for the miners and rouse indignation against the owners and operators, Lillo's texts seek to exert a strong pathetic appeal. In "Inválidos" (Invalids), a group of miners gathers excitedly to watch as an old horse is pulled up out of the mine and put out to pasture. Any idea of celebrating the animal's retirement vanishes when the horse emerges and is seen in daylight for the first time in years. The narrator details the horse's deterioration, contrasting its present state with the condition in which it descended into the mines:

> *The hide that was once soft, shiny, and black as jet had*
> *lost its sheen, scored with countless scars. Great cracks*
> *and suppurating wounds showed where the hauling*
> *harness had gone, and the hind leg joints displayed old*
> *spavins that deformed the lithe legs of earlier days.*
> *With a dragging belly, long neck, and bony flanks, it*
> *had nothing left of its former sprightly, svelte self, and*
> *its tail hair was nearly gone, torn out by the whip*
> *whose bloody mark could be seen, still fresh, on the*
> *sunken back.*[6]

Not only is the horse painfully disabled, but it has grown unaccustomed to normal light and proves unable to survive on the surface. The focus then moves back from the dying horse to the miners, who are last seen moving off with no hope of escaping their lives underground.

Lillo's contemporary readers were shocked at the real-world circumstances to which his stories alluded; many had been hitherto unaware of working conditions in the mines and their deleterious effects. His new and alarming raw subject matter tended to upstage the literary treatment he gave it, to the point that the texts were at times taken almost as a journalistic exposé. It is true that part of Lillo's achievement was to identify and utilize previously untreated, startling raw material, with a sure knowledge of his subject. For example, Jean Franco notes that "Lillo's stories are the first in Spanish American literature to picture man as a victim of industrialisation."[7]

With time and successive critical readings, though, Lillo's descriptive passages have won recognition for the complexity and skill of their rendering, and his writing has come in for detailed stylistic analyses. For instance, "La compuerta número 12" (Gate number 12), a famously upsetting story in which a family's poverty forces a father to set his terrified eight-year-old son to work in the mines, stimulated indignation over child labor. This same text can support a close examination of literary style such as the one Carmelo Virgillo offers in his study of its symbolic imagery.[8] Lillo had been struck with the approach of the French naturalists and studied Zola's writing; his own work displays a certain naturalism in its insistent attention to sordid details. Yet again naturalism is softened and humanized in Spanish American writing. The outlook in Lillo's work is not one of detached, clinical determinism. The narrator expresses in quite personal terms his distress at characters' misery and his indignation over the exploitation whose results he surveys; a pathos and undisguised emotionalism of romantic intensity is evident in many passages.

Manuel Gálvez (Argentina, 1882–1962) is among the writers most often mentioned as practicing a Spanish American variant of naturalism. As is frequently the case in Spanish-language literature, the naturalistic mode is adapted to avoid a direct challenge to the Christian concept of free will, and the narrator tends to manifest more human empathy with his characters than do the clinical observers who narrate Zola's novels. The first of Gálvez's texts to make a major impact was *La maestra normal* (The schoolteacher). This 1914 novel gave surprisingly personal offense to many readers. Its setting is the provincial town of La Rioja, depicted as such a monotonous, stifling, stagnant social environment that groups formed to defend their hometown's image. The heroine is a barely competent, insecure schoolteacher who drifts into being seduced by a jaded big-city man.

Lugones seized upon this plotline to denounce the novel as an attack on the public school system by a writer favoring Catholic education. Teachers, feeling collectively maligned, demanded that Gálvez resign as a school inspector. Such responses seem petty, but they reveal the accuracy with which the novel had targeted the nation's sorest anxieties. There was wide unease over the failure of the provinces, underfunded and neglected vis-à-vis Buenos Aires, to measure up to the dynamic, progressive ideal Argentina had set for itself during the economic boom of the late nineteenth century.

Gálvez published a swift succession of realist novels, winning so much attention that he rivaled Lugones as the nation's leading literary figure. His 1916 *El mal metafísico* (Metaphysical anguish), a long, meditative work with an intellectual protagonist ill adapted to life, has probably been most valued by critics. But Gálvez earned his best sales—though not so striking as those of *Santa*—with the fictional life story of a prostitute. This work is his 1917 *Nacha Regules*, named after an errant heroine who, like Santa, achieves redemption through love.

Gálvez had written a dissertation on aspects of prostitution, and his 1917 novel appears to promise a usefully remedial exposé of social ills. Yet critics are reluctant to see *Nacha Regules* as a text conducive to or promoting social reform. Doubts about the novel's efficacy in this regard have come not only from analysts hostile to Gálvez, as is Noé Jitrik, but even from such a critic as Myron I. Lichtblau, who has made a careful and sympathetic effort to appreciate this novelist's approach. Recognizing *Nacha Regules* as "a novel of social protest," Lichtblau points out that it "fails to offer solutions to problems or even constructive comments."[9]

Jitrik notes that, although Nacha's rescuer and eventual husband editorializes aloud, blaming society for prostitution, the novel centers attention on individual causes of and remedies for the phenomenon. Once the male protagonist moves from words to concrete behavior, he pursues "the project of saving Nacha in particular and not all prostitutes."[10] Nacha's rehabilitation is ascribed to her finally mustering the will to mend her ways, with the encouragement of a man whose concern for her becomes predominantly personal.

During the author's heyday, the mid-1910s to the early 1930s, the publication of a new Gálvez novel was a widely anticipated event. Yet in the second half of the century, his fiction began to seem old-fashioned and stodgy; reissues of his novels are relatively infrequent. One reason is the author's heavy reliance on a central narrator who not only knows everything about the characters, but also is quick to indicate how their personalities and behavior ought to be viewed. The characters' speech does not occupy much space, nor does it appear to carry much significance. Lichtblau, who finds many aspects of Gálvez's technique well developed, concedes that dialogue "is not a distinctive feature of Gálvez' fiction. As a means of revealing character and personality, it plays but a small role; the novelist relies almost exclusively on his own narrative."[11] David William Foster observes that Gálvez's narrator is typically so much more articulate than the protagonists as to make these characters, who are often low in the social hierarchy, appear deficient and incompetent in dealing with their difficulties.[12] More negative still are the comments of Jitrik, who sees in Gálvez's overpowering narrators a strategy to discourage readers from making their own independent assessment of the figures and events of the story.[13]

Of the many similarities between *Santa* and *Nacha Regules*, one is particularly telling. Gamboa and Gálvez were perceived as somewhat daring progressives at the time they published their respective best-selling novels centered on prostitute heroines. Both authors shortly afterward exhibited, in their writing and in their public statements, an increasingly conservative, Catholic outlook. Their best-selling novels, with time, no longer strike readers as expressing liberal thought or a drive for thoroughgoing social change.

As noted, a number of the themes of Spanish American realist and naturalist fiction were basically those favored by European writers of similar tendency, such as prostitution, slum life, and the careers of criminals. So it was an invigorating new development when literary realism encountered a mother lode of previously untouched, distinctively Spanish American material in the 1910 Mexican Revolution, both its initial decade of active violence and the convulsions that national politics suffered throughout the 1920s. Literary intellectuals turned their attention to this event, producing the novel of the Mexican Revolution.

The most outstanding work in this category, and a novel that continues to attract both general readers and critics, is *Los de abajo* (*The Under Dogs*). It is the one undeniable success of Mariano Azuela (1873–1952), who composed several short novels using the subject matter of the Revolution and related events. It was first serialized in 1915 in a newspaper in El Paso, where the author had taken refuge after the retreat of Pancho Villa's campaign. He had been supervising medical services for a pro-Villa general and had written a considerable portion of the novel while in the field. *The Under Dogs* was twice issued in book form (1916, 1920) before a 1925 edition captured the attention of a wide readership.

With its episodic structure composed of quick scenes, this short novel reduplicates the succession of experiences registered by participants caught up in the sometimes random swirls of a great, disorganized conflict. The feature of *The Under Dogs* that has most drawn commentary is its ability to suggest a world in the grip of uncontrollable movement, change, and activity—the novel's image of Mexico during the Revolution. The effect arises both from the narrative construction, designed to look helter-skelter, and from the events described. Though sympathetic to the revolutionaries, the work shows them brawling, taking out their pistols on the least provocation, bringing prostitutes along on their campaigns, and looting and vandalizing the houses of the rich. Many passages in the novel narrate action in a spare style with short sentences and relatively few descriptive adjectives; at the same time, *The Under Dogs* includes some stretches of descriptive prose that are unmistakably in the modernist vein.

While it manages to give the appearance of following no plan in its flow of scenes, *The Under Dogs* has an organizing pattern in the field career of one soldier who sums up in his person the Revolution. Demetrio Macías is an illiterate peasant of Indian ancestry, tough, pragmatic, spontaneous, and accepting of violence and brutality as the norm. He is so little given to thinking ahead that he disdains the idea of gathering advance information about the site of an upcoming battle. After a period of leading a local, wildcat band of rebels, Demetrio joins the larger national Revolution, affiliating with a general allied with Villa. Yet he has no political thought that he can articulate and no overall concept of the Revolution and its significance; he only has clearly in mind a desire to strike back after mistreatment from the local landowner and the *federales*.

During the course of the novel, the quick-witted Demetrio leads several successful battles and comes to be, or at least to be called, "Colonel" and then "General." Though a glib, opportunistic intellectual attaches himself to Demetrio and tries to supply him with ideology and grandiose left-wing rhetoric, this pragmatic leader continues to make revolution through action, not words or ideas. He never learns to make even a simple victory speech and is so remote from the political aspect of the Revolution that he can barely name an important opposition leader.

Demetrio's military career is represented cyclically; at the end of the novel, he is defeated and killed at the very spot where he had obtained his first notable success in battle. John S. Brushwood observes that Demetrio comes full circle as well in his personal approach to making revolution.[14] For example, during his rise as a commander, he loses the concern with his men as individuals that had earlier typified his style. In the last battle, he watches his soldiers fall and thinks of them in human terms, by name. *The Under Dogs* manifests a populist and, to some degree, anarchistic outlook on the Revolution. The protagonist comes to the Revolution from a grassroots, popular uprising and does best when he remains close to his men. The text includes many notes of warning against leaders who lose touch with the people and their fundamental needs.

The novel's closing words can be construed to have more than one meaning. Demetrio, whose troops are being mowed down all around him, presumably is himself killed. But instead of telling readers that the protagonist has died, the narrator makes this assertion: "Demetrio Macías, with his eyes fixed forever, keeps aiming the barrel of his rifle. . . ."[15] Brushwood observes that these words can equally well point to the end of Demetrio's life or the continuing action and movement of the Revolution.

Novels of the Revolution continued to appear long after the actual conflict had subsided, assuming new forms in response to changing esthetics and a changing vision of the basic significance of the phenomenon. *The Under Dogs,* with its manifest distrust of the abstract and elite aspects of the struggle, stands in contrast to the work of Martín Luis Guzmán (1887–1976), whose works reflect a top-down view of the Revolution. While Azuela evokes the roily armed conflict of the 1910s, Guzmán, even when writing of the early years, reflects the outlook of the 1920s, in which the revolutionary struggle became an issue of political leadership. Guzmán was drawn to the new elites that emerged from the upheaval, and makes the Revolution a study in leadership—specifically, in the forms of leadership brought into being by the conditions prevailing after ten years of violent struggle in Mexico and the displacement of the long-standing elite.

In 1928 Guzmán published *El águila y la serpiente* (*The Eagle and the Serpent*), a nonfiction work that nonetheless is frequently cited in studies of the novel of the Revolution. It consists of essays on major revolutionary figures. Guzmán could rely on his personal contact with these men as well as his research into and analysis of their personae and careers. Yet his essays are not, strictly speaking, political reportage. The prose exhibits distinctively literary qualities and, in some of the portraits, imaginative interpretation of the personality and actions of subjects. With his undisguised focus on the leading figures in the Revolution and his desire to see them devise and implement an overall plan for the nation, Guzmán proves disturbing to readers who conceive of the Mexican Revolution as first and foremost a movement of the people.

The Eagle and the Serpent is realistic in working hard to convince readers that its portraits of revolutionary figures are faithfully lifelike. This persuasion relies in part on the accumulation of telling descriptive details, a standby of realist fiction. The effect of a real or true account also comes from a feature made possible by the nonfiction format: Guzmán, appearing to write as his real-world self, gives his portraits the form of an insider's memoirs, centering on his own first-hand involvement with and close-up observation of the leaders.

His 1929 novel *La sombra del caudillo* (The shadow of the *caudillo* [political boss]) is a barely disguised portrait of Plutarco Elías Calles, his allies and hangers-on, and those who run afoul of him. After leaving the presidency, Calles had retained his hold on power through both ingenious and crude strategies, which Guzmán reconstructs with intimate knowledge in his novel. As does the earlier work, *La sombra del caudillo* creates the impression of describing the real partly by appearing to divulge to anyone who reads the novel details previously known only to insiders. Technically the work is fiction; the words are presented as those of the novel's narrator, not of Guzmán himself. Yet *La sombra del caudillo* has been widely taken as a knowing account of a corrupt régime, based on Guzmán's privileged information.

In denouncing the abuse of power and mismanagement of the Revolution, *La sombra del caudillo* stops short of questioning the direction the revolutionary movement had taken. Guzmán appears to accept as natural the Revolution's shift of emphasis from social change to the achievement and exercise of political power. In this regard, his writing accurately reflects, albeit in a somewhat irreflexive manner, the outlook that prevailed during the 1920s. This feature of the work, in addition to irritating intellectuals who prefer a farther-reaching and more probing critique of the Revolution, exemplifies an often-observed weakness of realism. While realist representation is efficacious in describing the concrete manifestations of a problem, it is not necessarily the best instrument for probing the underlying structural disorder and may even obscure the deeper issues. This point will later be emphasized by socially critical writers seeking alternatives to realism; they must work against a generalized belief that realism is the most suitable vehicle for the literary expression of concerns about society.

Amid the many Spanish American realist writers who, during the period 1900–1930, brought attention to bear primarily on social conditions, the Chilean Eduardo Barrios (1884–1963) is most distinctive for his skill in the representation of psychological problems, although it should be noted that late in his career his realism would move toward more social themes. He developed, as his most striking literary specialty, an ability to mimic the expression of characters whose minds are reeling under the assault of turbulent feelings. The 1915 *El niño que enloqueció de amor* (The boy who went mad from love) and the 1922 *El hermano asno* (Brother donkey) are both presented in the first-person, present-tense, self-divulging form of personal diaries. The presumption that nobody will read their words and the hope that finding words for the experience of a crisis will help resolve it motivate the protagonists to reveal their turmoil.

The earlier work, really a long short story, is one of the clearest examples of psychological fiction in Spanish American letters. The author of the fictional diary is a ten-year-old boy who falls catastrophically in love with an adult woman. This anomalous event precipitates the mental deterioration that is reflected in his writing. The actual plot is so simple that it can be summarized, without loss of nuance, in the six words of the title; yet the novel gains complexity through its representation of the linguistic signs of mental disorder. At the outset the text reads like the writing of an extraordinarily precocious, but otherwise normal, young person. As obsessive love affects the child more and more profoundly, *El niño que enloqueció de amor* imitates with alarming verisimilitude the increasingly demented child's loss of the ability to give a logical coherence to his discourse.

A common reaction to this work is the realization that the events narrated are implausible by real-world standards but that, as presented through the boy's words, they acquire a gripping, artfully created truth. Arturo Torres-Rioseco sums up this insight: "In *El niño que enloqueció de amor,* the immediate value lies in the wave of heartfelt identification that is established between the reader and the child character," even though "for a psychologist perhaps there is no scientific truth to this little work." [16]

El hermano asno takes as its title Francis of Assisi's allusion to the human body with its animal drives. The phrase, implying anxiety over and unease with bodily existence, accurately gives the tone of the work. It appears as the diary of a man who has spent six years in a Franciscan monastery, yet postpones entering the order, still struggling with his unshakable attachments to worldly existence. As in the earlier novel, the protagonist is thrown into a crisis by an unexpected love, in this case with a young woman whose sister had earlier rejected him.

As well as introspectively describing his own inner state, the narrator chronicles another troubling case occurring in the same monastery. A friar becomes venerated as a saint, yet also destroys himself, in pursuit of the Franciscan ideals. The diarist, and the reader with him, make progressively more worrisome discoveries about the fanatic's mortification of his flesh and conversations with a long-dead monk, who some friars suspect of being an agent of the devil. The two stories come together at the end in a satisfyingly gothic climax and dénouement.

In those regions with a substantial Indian population, Spanish American authors had near at hand distinctive New World material and a potentially fascinating subject for their fiction. Yet they were slow to turn their attention, as writers, to contemporary indigenous peoples. Throughout the early twentieth century, more and more Spanish American intellectuals had gained an increasingly knowledgeable awareness of the difficulties facing Indian peoples. The result was a good deal of stimulating public discussion and some well-argued essays. José Carlos Mariátegui (Peru, 1894–1930) offered a groundbreakingly insightful analysis in his 1928 collection of essays, *Siete ensayos de interpretación de la realidad peruana* (*Seven Interpretive Essays on Peruvian Reality*, 1971). However, it would be some time before Spanish American creative writers could produce an equally intelligent and unsentimental treatment of indigenous issues.

In imaginative writing there had been a long-standing convention, particularly evident in literary celebrations of independence from Spain, of floridly glorifying the great Indian civilizations that flourished before the European conquest. As the twentieth century began, though, only one work of fiction had made a widespread impact through the realistic treatment of current-day Indians. This was the 1889 novel *Aves sin nido* (Birds without a nest) by the Peruvian Clorinda Matto de Turner (1854–1909). It made a melodramatic, denunciatory appeal comparable to that of *Uncle Tom's Cabin*.

By the 1930s there would be an entire movement of *indigenista* writers in the Andean countries, with their approximately 80 percent Indian population. During the first decades of the century, though, Spanish American authors were still working out an approach to the theme of native peoples. Ventura García Calderón (1886–1959), a Peruvian who resided for some time in France, for a time enjoyed a vogue with his action-filled Indian stories, many of which were collected in his 1924 *La venganza del cóndor* (The revenge of the condor). His fiction gives the image of a violent, dangerous Indian given to strange rites and superstitions; it is often cited as exemplifying what more serious Indian-theme writers sought to avoid.

Enrique López Albújar (Peru, 1872–1966) had an unusually good knowledge of Andean Indians based on his work as a judge in a heavily indigenous region. Unlike most contemporary intellectuals who took up a concern with Indians, López Albújar was not intent on protesting the treatment accorded this group. In his stories he strives for a literary re-creation of the typical behavioral traits and outlook of Andean Indians. The texts collected in his 1920 *Cuentos andinos* (Andean tales) and 1937 *Nuevos cuentos andinos* (New Andean tales) frequently have as their point of departure a moment of crisis, in many instances a court case, that brings out the tendencies of thought and behavior of the Indian characters.

Alcides Arguedas (Bolivia, 1879–1946) made an important advance in this subject matter with his novel *Raza de bronce* (Race of bronze), a 1919 reworking of his less successful *Wata-Wara* (1904). This work, which shook many contemporary readers, shows the route that would be taken when the trend toward realist, Indian-theme fiction became a full-fledged movement. Arguedas was a historian and sociologist specializing in indigenous issues. His 1909 book-length essay *Pueblo enfermo* (A diseased people) had succeeded in convincing many Bolivians that the "Indian problem" was also, or primordially, a problem of the white elites. The same concept—that unconscionably exploitative and abusive whites maintain the Indians in misery—is also central to *Raza de bronce*.

Raza de bronce is above all a novelistic exposé of the mistreatment of Andean Indians by well-off white landowners and the *mestizos* to whom they delegate power over their estates. The episodes of the novel show the whites not only taking economic advantage of the Indians under their purview, but engaging in disturbingly gratuitous acts of cruelty to them. These events, and the narrator's comments, convey the idea that the enjoyment of unchecked power over everything and everyone on one's estate leads to a generalized insensitivity to others' well-being. In several scenes the young landowner who is the novel's villain is seen directing his cruelty against the animals living on his property. All members of this class feel free to berate and strike the Indians on their family's holdings, while the men believe they should enjoy sexual access to the indigenous women. Secondary to its denunciatory function, the novel serves to provide a novelized ethnography of Andean Indian life. The indigenous characters appear performing ceremonies and customs typical of the region of Lake Titicaca, while the narrator, with unabashed didactic intent, explains the traditions involved.

Motivating the entire exposition is the idea that it is high time for the Andean-area elite to emerge from its disregard for and ignorance of Indian life and issues. With open indignation, the narrator characterizes the attitude of this social class, referring specifically to the young landowner and his friends:

> *They were the owners, and their estates remained, in their young hands, just as they had received them from the lazy hands of their idle fathers; but, it's true, they believed themselves to be, in relation to Indians, infinitely superior beings, different in their very essence; and that was a naive, atavistic conviction. They never took the trouble to meditate on whether the Indian could break away from his enslaved condition, acquire*

an education, skills, emerge. They had seen him from
his mother's lap, miserable, humble, making himself
unobtrusive, small, and they believed that that was his
natural state, that he couldn't and shouldn't be emanci-
pated without throwing the order of things into chaos,
and he should die like that. The opposite of that seemed
to them absurd, inexplicable; for if the Indian became
skilled and educated, who would plow the fields, make
them produce, and, most of all, be the houseboys? [17]

The element of social protest and the informative
aspect of the work both depend upon the story of a young Indian couple.
The main plotline of *Raza de bronce* follows this pair through courtship and
marriage, described with close attention to ethnic folkways. At every step,
the couple's life together is complicated by mistreatment from members
of the white elite and the *mestizo* estate supervisor. During their courtship,
the man is sent away to harvest under unjustifiably hazardous conditions,
which the text chronicles with hair-raising vividness. Back home, the
woman is required to submit to exploitative sexual relations. Despite these
difficulties, the two marry, but the woman is killed by the landowner's
heir when he and his houseguests attempt to rape her. This last abuse
exhausts the patience of the Indians, who have hitherto swallowed all
types of humiliations without protest, and the novel ends with an unsuccessful uprising.

Raza de bronce exhibits a number of features that later indigenous-theme
writers would strive hard to avoid. Perhaps prime among these is the
dominating presence of a narrator whose view is that of a reform-minded
white social scientist who has made a study of Indian affairs. In Jean Franco's assessment, even those passages that purport to transmit the Indians'
thoughts seem permeated by the same outlook.[18] Later writers began to
feel uncomfortable with this textual arrangement, in which the Indian is
depicted from without by an observer who, however well versed in his
subject, is not part of the culture. Authors of a subsequent wave of Indian
novels would accordingly strive to give a greater sense of the indigenous
characters' own perception and understanding of their situation.

Also typical of the early generation of Indian-theme novels is the frequency with which the Indians appear defeatedly submitting to exploitative and sadistic treatment. Until the final episodes of *Raza de bronce*, the
indigenous characters respond to abusive treatment with outward resig-
nation, waiting until their oppressors are out of earshot to express their

resentment. Ariel Dorfman sums up the change that would later occur in Spanish American fiction on Indian themes: "As opposed to the naturalist novelists, who showed *oppression*, contemporary writers emphasized rebellion in its many forms, seeking especially to portray the collective psyche that motivates and makes possible that violence."[19]

The regional realism that had enjoyed such success in Chile in the late nineteenth and early twentieth centuries continued to prosper into a twentieth century now well underway. It is true that more vividly imaginative modes, including fantastic fiction, held an increased attraction for contemporary writers and readers. For example, Augusto d'Halmar, previously noted as a practitioner of turn-of-the-century naturalism, came to abandon naturalism and, more broadly, to shift his writing away from realistic representation. In his later writing, d'Halmar won an enthusiastic following among the Chilean reading public by developing a more ethereal, playful type of writing with features of the fantastic. The most celebrated contemporary Chilean writer, María Luisa Bombal (discussed in the next chapter) moved far from realism, although it should be noted that she made her career outside Chile.

Yet despite the increased competition from the literary alternatives to realism, the Chilean reading public still exhibited an appreciation for realist writing, and the *criollista* tendency retained its vitality. A new generation of writers began to publish work that owed much to the tradition already established by *criollista* writers, but demonstrated a conscientious effort of adaptation to the changes that had taken place both in Chilean social realities and in the concept of what constituted literary realism. Among these younger writers, Manuel Rojas (1896–1973), who was born in Argentina but made his lengthy literary career in Chile, and the Chilean Marta Brunet (1901–1967) were particularly cited as giving a fresh impetus to *criollismo*.

Rojas would eventually gain considerable fame as a writer of realistic novels, scoring an international success with his 1951 novel *Hijo de ladrón* (English version *Born Guilty*). He was able to make good literary use of his first-hand knowledge of Chile's diverse regions and many of the forms of livelihood practiced by its citizens, from skilled laborers down to hobos and thieves. When he first came onto the literary scene in the 1920s, it was with such short stories as those collected in *Hombres del sur* (Men of the south, 1926) and in *El delincuente* (The delinquent, 1929). These stories were admired for the plain quality of their style; using a good deal of unembellished description and little commentary on the part of the narrator, they successfully sustained an effect of direct and straightforward communication. The subject matter with which Rojas worked drew readers interested in an insider's account of life among such groups as dockworkers, vagrants, day laborers, and radicalized workers and students. Turning to lengthier narratives, Rojas eventually became the foremost representative of Chilean realism.

Marta Brunet, who won respect as an editor as well as a writer, was a discovery of the celebrated Chilean critic and arbiter of tastes known as Alone (real name Hernán Díaz Arrieta). She tended to favor a more artful and subtle presentation than the famously rugged manner of Rojas; her narrative prose frequently exhibits a stylized, poetic quality. Although Brunet is considered part of the literary current of *criollismo*, her fiction is more urban in setting and generally concentrates on less impoverished characters than was traditionally the case in this regional realism. She particularly stands out for her focus on women characters and on a middle class in financial straits and anxiously struggling to maintain its claim to gentility; the complex issues of social status are often more clearly present than those of economic survival.

Pedro Prado, with a substantial literary career already behind him, also helped give a fresh start to *criollismo*. *Un juez rural* (1924; *Country Judge*, 1968) was a surprise to readers of his modernist verse and first two novels, and convinced many that this Chilean author had discarded fantasy and lyricism in favor of a straightforward realism. It is true that the plot, in which a high-strung engineer serves a stint as a judge in a lower-class Santiago suburb, is less exuberantly imaginative than the story lines of the earlier works. Still, this text also has its departures from verisimilitude. One uneasy night the protagonist is reported by the narrator to gallop a horse through the night and leap into an abyss, only to appear in the next chapter going about his usual daytime activities.

Of the many contemporary writers who sought to transform their hitherto modernist writing by infusing realist elements, by far the most successful was Horacio Quiroga (1878–1937). During his early career, the Uruguayan-born Quiroga did little that would make him stand out among the many young people attached to the Buenos Aires–Montevideo modernist scene. After he accidentally killed a close friend during preparations for a duel, Quiroga acquired a macabre local celebrity. Lugones heard that the protagonist of this gothic real-life story was living in Buenos Aires, took a special interest in the depressed young writer, and invited him on an expedition to photograph old Jesuit missions in Misiones province. Lugones was at that time wearying of the cosmopolitan attitude typical of much modernism and seeking renewed contact with the roots of New World culture.

The wild, near-tropical landscape exercised a hold on Quiroga. Within a short time he had become a Misiones landowner and transformed himself from a dandy into a rough and ready countryman adept in agriculture, carpentry, and rustic handicrafts. Quiroga's reinvention of himself would not have become so famous if not for the new mode of writing that accompanied it.

The fiction he published beginning in the late 1910s quickly won over readers looking for riveting turns of plot and hair-raising scenes. It was also of concern to literary intellectuals pondering the direction Spanish American writing might best take after modernism and ways in which this literature might become more clearly marked as Spanish American. The passage of time has not diminished the effectiveness of Quiroga's postmodernist fiction, which continues to grip readers and provide inexhaustible points of departure for critical analysis.

Quiroga carried out his most notable work in the short story. His achievement in this genre is equaled, in all of Spanish American literature, only by that of Jorge Luis Borges. His texts are widely regarded as models of the taut, economical construction that is especially admired in short fiction. Literary analysts have repeatedly taken Quiroga's best stories apart in an effort to discover the exact textual mechanisms that generate their riveting effect, while aspiring short-story writers are still apt to pattern their early efforts on Quiroga's work.

Quiroga combined a modernist emphasis on striking and memorable sensory perceptions with the spine-chilling tale, as had Lugones, but his original contribution was to bring into this mixture a distinctive type of existential realism. This last element was produced by pitting isolated human characters against the forces of nature, or, more broadly, an inhospitable universe. The comfortless scenario of human existence was often, though not invariably, emblemized by a literary version of the Misiones countryside; even if the setting is not near-jungle, the stories exhibit an unmistakably Spanish American frame of reference. The characters may have their vulnerability exacerbated by the threat of tropical fevers, parasites, poisonous snakes, and the hazards of rough farm work. Even if the protagonists are not out in the wild, they are subject to attack from unsuspected adversaries, such as the monstrous bloodsucking parasite of "El almohadón de plumas" (The Feather Pillow).

In the midst of this hostile environment characters are left radically alone by the severance of normal human bonds. Some have lost part of their families through death; others have cut off relations with their fellow beings; others have been abandoned or shunted to one side. Although clearly at a hopeless disadvantage, the protagonists strive mightily to persist in their existence as long as possible, and the reader is empathetically drawn to their struggle. As the effort to maintain life is conducted against such formidable opposing forces, premature and violent deaths are prominent throughout Quiroga's fiction and constitute one of its best-known features.

The text that most clearly exemplifies what readers think of as a Quiroga story is the author's much-anthologized "El hombre muerto" ("The Dead Man"). The story begins just as a farmer receives a fatal injury, follows his thoughts as he lies dying, and ends a moment after his death. The nameless hero has invested a great deal of work into transforming a stretch of wild land into well-kept farmland, and in his dying moments still takes pride in this order-making accomplishment. Yet it is this very endeavor that brings about his death; after a morning's work keeping his groves in perfect condition, he slips and falls on his own machete.

"The Dead Man" follows, in its textual construction, a number of internal rules whose purpose is to give the reader a sense of the dying man's situation. Until the protagonist is actually dead in the closing lines, all descriptions are given from his point of view. He is so weakened by his abdominal wound that he cannot lift his head, restricting his field of vision in a way the text carefully duplicates. Descriptions of other sensory information are similarly limited to what the hero is able to register from his spot on the ground. This includes not only data obtained through the usual sensorium but also an out-of-body experience at the moment of death. The third-person narrator alternates between giving an only slightly mediated transcription of the thoughts that pass through the dying man's mind and stepping back to summarize and comment upon the protagonist's mental processes. Immediately after incurring his wound, the man rationally makes mental calculations that lead him to the conclusion that he will soon die. But as his general condition and consciousness deteriorate, he struggles against the obvious truth that had already registered clearly in his mind, and his last moments are spent trying to argue himself out of a belief in his impending death.

The story continues slightly beyond its protagonist's death. In its final lines, the narrator switches from representing the awareness of the human hero to reporting on the perceptions and thoughts of the protagonist's mare, who has been observing the scene. One of Quiroga's unusual specialties was the use of narrative procedures to show what life must look like through the eyes of farm animals. In this case, the mare focuses upon a single issue raised by the scene of death: whether her master, with his eagerness to maintain order and discipline, continues to hold the authority he had earlier established over her while he is now lying motionless on the ground.

Margaret Sayers Peden has ably translated the closing passages of this celebrated story:

> *What a nightmare! But, of course, it's just one of many days, ordinary as any other! Excessive light, yellowish shadows, oven-still heat that raises sweat on the motionless horse next to the forbidden banana grove.*
>
> *. . . Very, very tired, but that's all. How many times, at midday like this, on his way to the house, has he crossed this clearing that was a thicket when he came, and virgin brush before that? He was always tired, slowly returning home with his machete dangling from his left hand.*
>
> *But still he can move away in his mind if he wants, abandon his body for an instant and look at the ordinary everyday landscape from the flood ditch he himself built—the stiff grama grass in the field of volcanic rock, the banana grove and its red sand, the wire fence fading out of sight in the distance as it slopes downward toward the road. And further still, the cleared land, the work of his own hands. And at the foot of a bark-stripped post, thrown on his right side, his legs drawn up, exactly like any other day, he can see himself, a sunny little heap on the grama grass—resting, because he is very tired.*
>
> *But the horse, striped with sweat, cautiously motionless at a corner of the fence, also sees the man on the ground and doesn't dare enter the banana grove, as she would like to. With the voices nearby now—"Pahpah!"—for a long, long while, the mare turns her mo-*

*tionless ears toward the heap on the ground and finally,
quieted, decides to pass between the post and the fallen
man—who has rested now.*[20]

Among the intellectual and artistic tendencies
that came with the postmodernist moment was a new concern with women's writing and women's issues. Four of the writers most known for moving Spanish American poetry beyond modernism were women. Such stress was laid on their gender that postmodernist poetry became, in the public's perception, closely associated with women's expression. The most celebrated of the poets involved was the Chilean Gabriela Mistral (real name Lucila Godoy de Alcayaga, 1889–1957), the first Spanish American winner of the Nobel Prize for Literature. Though not enjoying Mistral's international fame, three other women poets achieved considerable renown: the Argentine Alfonsina Storni (1892–1938) and the Uruguayans Juana de Ibarbourou (1892–1979) and Delmira Agustini (1886–1914). Of the four, only Storni could accurately be described as a feminist; she was a liberal journalist who often wrote on women's status. But all of them exhibited a special concern with the literary presentation of experience specific to women.

In prose, the woman writer who gained the widest notice was the Venezuelan Teresa de la Parra (real name Ana Teresa Parra Sanojo, 1889–1936). De la Parra was a well-read, socially prominent young woman whose winning personal presence, wit, elegance, and above all her powers of verbal expression had placed her in demand as a speaker at public events and writer of occasional pieces. As was typical for a woman of her time and social class, she had had to pursue on her own the extensive literary background that she later put to good use in her celebrated novels. From the outset of her career, the public was very insistent in attributing special qualities of femininity to De la Parra and her writing. At the same time, the author often appeared to invite such an attribution by employing a type of writing that her public would tag as feminine. She exhibited a preference for intimate and domestic subject matter, a mannered style of somewhat whimsical, teasing humor, and, broadly, a chatty, gossipy mode. Her first publications, the journalistic pieces she began publishing in 1915, were certainly in this vein. A critic dubbed her "Miss Frivolity," and her choice of a pseudonym, Fru-Fru, is a good clue that her own judgment of her early work was not so different.[21] The issues raised by a discourse that readers readily perceive as feminine are important in her first full-length novel, *Ifigenia (Diario de una señorita que escribió porque se fastidiaba)* (*Iphigenia [The diary of a young lady who wrote because she was bored]*). (Between her early journalism and her famous novel, De la Parra had pseudonymously published two short narratives with Oriental themes and settings.) *Iphigenia* makes a more purposeful use of a hyperfeminine discourse, full of gossipy asides and capricious remarks, this time to make a critical examination of women, their role, and their ability to speak of important issues.

While staying in Europe, the author had witnessed the growth of feminism in European intellectual circles and had considered how feminism might apply to the Spanish American context, particularly among women who had little if any exposure to contemporary currents of progressive thought. She was worried particularly about women who, through travel or hearsay, had glimpsed the possibilities for unprecedented independence, but were frustrated when they tried to inject some of this freedom into their own situations.

These concerns appear in her *Iphigenia*, whose five hundred pages were begun in 1922 and finished in somewhat under a year. *Iphigenia* was serialized in both Spanish- and French-language magazines and first published as a book in 1924. According to Louis Antoine Lemaître, when the first chapter completed was published in *La Lectura Semanal*, the Caracas magazine sold out its print run of 6,000 on the day of publication.[22] Encouraged by the novel's first-person form (the first pages are a long letter to an intimate friend, followed by a diary), the public tended to view *Iphigenia* as the direct, confessional outpourings of its author, unmediated by either artistry or critical irony. Readers of the novel without hesitation identified the author with her excitable, high-strung heroine, María Eugenia, an incompletely educated young woman who often floundered in her efforts to articulate a critical outlook on society and personal relations. The linkage between the two did not make much sense, since De la Parra was a public literary intellectual known for her ability to find the right words for any occasion. De la Parra was well aware of this perception of her novel and complained that her readership was insensitive to the strong satirical component in her work.[23]

The heroine of *Iphigenia* is an upper-class young woman, though she has been despoiled of her personal fortune and must be paired off with a wealthy match. She lives in the personal and private sphere and has only the most tenuous, second-hand notions of the feminism developing in the world at large. Nonetheless, she is so intelligent, independent-minded, and eager to attain happiness that she develops her own version of feminism based on her experiences and observations. María Eugenia can utilize these insights to analyze, sometimes rather ingenuously and sometimes with some sophistication, the situations in which she finds herself. María Eugenia's ability to set her new insights down in effective words fluctuates widely throughout the novel. In some passages she melodramatizes her own plight and falls into a self-indulgent lyricism; in others, she is a sharp observer of individual and collective behavior, as able to mock herself as to satirize those around her. From time to time she bursts into a stiffly didactic speech on society and morals; the reader must sympathize with her ardor even while cringing at the awkwardness of her expression.

For all María Eugenia's intelligence, it is a difficult task for her to generate a critical feminist analysis out of the scanty materials she has at hand. One of the fascinating aspects of the novel is that the reader frequently observes María Eugenia faltering and blundering in her efforts to think and act with a new freedom. In her mind, liberation is often confused with simply getting her own way. At various times in the course of the novel, the heroine appears to associate personal liberation with the wearing of low-necked gowns, dancing "American dances" in public, associating with worldly friends, and coming and going at less restricted hours and unchaperoned. María Eugenia persists in her reading despite the disapproval it raises in her household; yet she reads only for pleasure, and it never occurs to her to undertake a program of study.

By the end of the novel, María Eugenia faces only a choice between marriage to a successful, family-approved, but plodding candidate and life as the mistress of a more imaginative and engaging, but married, man. Until nearly the end of the novel, María Eugenia swings back and forth between the respectable and the exciting alternative. The author is willing to resort to melodramatic twists and turns of plot to engage the reader in the heroine's inner conflict.

While De la Parra was the object of a widespread public fascination during the time she was writing and serializing *Iphigenia*, she became the target of negative criticism after the book was published. While the complaints were many and varied—some local readers felt that Caracas was not described in its proper beauty—the dominant objection was that the novel was immoral and might harm young women readers. A number of readers were offended that the heroine considered her respectable marriage a defeat in life, and criticized her as a light-minded creature obsessed with showing off her beauty and seeking pleasure. De la Parra vigorously defended her book; among other arguments, she stated that the book's detractors were men, while women readers recognized the accuracy of *Iphigenia*'s vision of society.

Teresa de la Parra has been coming in for a rediscovery in recent years, principally for *Iphigenia* but also for her 1929 *Las memorias de Mamá Blanca*. Translated into English as *Mama Blanca's Souvenirs* (1959), the later novel offers a more lyrical and celebratory treatment of the culture of traditional upper-class women. Here a household full of women, with their feminine occupations and their intimate conversations, is nostalgically recalled by a narrator now well into adulthood.

Perhaps because of its genteel setting, upper-class heroine, and the subtly ironic way it presents ideas, *Iphigenia* was not fully perceived as a work of social criticism until after the resurgence of feminism in the 1960s and 1970s, which affected the reading of many existing literary texts. The novel is now especially valued for its early recognition that Latin American women living in conservative environments, while no less in need of change than their counterparts in fast-moving European and U.S. cities, would necessarily approach the issues of women's role and status from a different background and perspective, and face a different set of obstacles.

In their search for a model of social-protest writing that would go beyond naturalism, a number of Spanish American authors turned to Russian literature and, particularly, Soviet writing of the late 1910s and early 1920s. Movements inspired by this example arose in several Spanish American cities, although the writers involved often found it difficult to acquire translations of Russian texts and a good familiarity with cultural developments in the Soviet Union.

The Buenos Aires group known as Boedo was a particularly clear example of this tendency. Attracting principally writers born around the turn of the century, this loosely constituted movement flourished in the 1920s. The left-wing and largely unknown practitioners of proletarian literature had little to do with the mainstream, best-selling realism of Manuel Gálvez. The fellow writers to whom they were closest, and with whom they conducted a much publicized feud, were the equally youthful members of the estheticist avant-garde.

Of the novels and short stories produced during the 1920s by the writers most identified with Boedo, such as Roberto Mariani (1892–1946), Elías Castelnuovo (Uruguay, 1893–1982), and Alvaro Yunque (real name Arístides Gandolfi Herrero, 1889–1982), none won a wide readership. The more intellectual public took some note of the group, which, with its declarations and public statements, maintained the image of a radical artistic movement determined to remake literature. Yet during the 1920s the Boedo writers were generally somewhat romantic anarchists, and their fiction was not particularly innovative in literary language and textual construction.

The principal new accomplishment of the Boedo writers' fiction was the elaboration of scenes of labor and of interaction in the workplace. Castelnuovo brought to his work an extensive knowledge of the publishing and printing industries. The title story of his 1923 *Tinieblas* (Darkness), his most noted piece, has as its outstanding feature a detailed representation of the working conditions of typesetters, for whom lead poisoning was a normal occupational disease. In most respects, the text continues the naturalism that was already long established in Spanish American writing.

Mariani, who was an aggressive spokesman for proletarian literature, developed two specialties in his fiction: psychological studies of mutually tormenting couples and stories set among clerks and bookkeepers. His white-collar subject matter, which had never been so thoroughly explored in Spanish American writing, earned him the widest recognition. The tales of clerical workers collected in the 1925 *Cuentos de la oficina* (Office stories) have aroused admiration, above all, for their ability to evoke the wearing tedium of paperwork and the petty jockeying for position that occurs even in the lowest rungs of a hierarchy.

After the late 1920s, realistic fiction underwent a number of changes that reflected growing urbanization, the influence of the social sciences, and new currents in Latin American social thought. Spanish American writers produced a greater number of texts capable of interesting an international public. These developments will come in for discussion in Chapter 4.

Three

AVANT-GARDE, IMAGINATIVE, AND FANTASTIC MODES, 1920 – 1950

While Spanish American modernism held sway, writers seeking an alternative to realistic representation found it natural to turn to this movement. As the modernist era waned, many authors still favored a stylized way of offering up images of the world, one in which the element of imaginative artistry enjoyed a prominent place. Many younger writers were antirealist in this sense, but disdained modernism as an outdated, establishment mode. In particular, the modernists' tendency to ornament and embellish and their expanded range of lexical choices had provoked a desire for a sparer expression, with the creator under less of an imperative to attain elegance, balance, and fluidity, now considered rather suspect qualities. A number of Spanish American authors were seized by the avant-garde impulse that had been coursing through European literatures during the decade of the 1910s.

At first, they directed their attention toward European precedents, learning what they could about such movements as Italian futurism and the expressionism that had flourished in German-language literatures; they eagerly described their discoveries and attempted to launch projects at home along the same lines. In a few fairly isolated cases Spanish American writers, most notably the Chilean poet Vicente Huidobro (1893– 1948), began to grope toward an avant-garde esthetic as early as the mid- to late 1910s. However, these early manifestations of avant-gardism often prove, on close examination, to be tentative and precarious. For example, despite Huidobro's desire to be a precursor figure (he is widely suspected of misstating the dates of composition of his most innovative writing), he did not produce his most recognizably avant-garde work until the 1920s.

In most cases, Spanish American avant-gardism arises approximately at the beginning of the 1920s.

As avant-garde ideas achieved a more secure hold on Spanish American literary scenes, the initial preoccupation with studying and imitating European movements began to fade. The avant-garde groups that formed in Spanish American literary capitals often came to assume their own distinctive outlooks and characteristic practices. Though still dependent to varying degrees on the models provided by European movements, the avant-gardes of Spanish America, in the best of cases, began to take into account the special cultural and historical circumstances and needs of their own regions and nations. Perhaps even more significantly, the innovative concepts and literary practices developed in avant-garde circles spread to the general literary culture and became the property of any writer able to benefit from them and further their evolution.

The deliberately cultivated avant-gardism of the early 1920s—when advocates of competing literary programs issued manifestos, published factional journals, and eagerly proclaimed their youthful newness—ceded to a widespread, eclectic spirit of invention. Writers enjoyed a greater liberty to adapt and recombine features of the various "isms" once perceived as rivalrous and mutually exclusive. While writers affiliated with avant-garde groups of 1921–1927 defined themselves primarily as poets, the authors who continued the movement's innovative drive into the late 1920s and subsequent years were as likely to carry out their creative work in prose as in verse.

At this point it is worth noting again the inexact correspondence between European and U.S. literary-historical terminology and that standardly used in the study of Hispanic letters. The *modernismo* that prevailed in Spanish America from the 1880s to the 1910s is only tenuously related, through a common emphasis on innovation, to *modernism* as English-language readers understand the term. But Spanish American *avant-gardism* is closely allied to *modernism* in the European and U.S. sense, the phenomenon whose landmark figures include Joyce, Pound, Eliot, Dos Passos, and Faulkner. Spanish American avant-garde writers were *modern* in their sharp awareness of belonging to the fast-paced twentieth century. Like European and English-language modernist writers, they sought an accelerated, streamlined expression, stripped of embellishment and ornamentation, suitable to the rapidly changing times; discontinuous, fragmented texts became common, as did experimental treatments of time, space, and person.

Fantastic narrative had already established itself, during the modernist years, as a significant current in Spanish American prose. The fantastic mode appealed to writers of fiction looking for opportunities to transcend realistic description and narration. In addition, fantastic fiction, with its ability to absorb and thrill readers, held out the potential for attracting a fairly general public.

As had been the case with *modernista* prose, much avant-garde prose came into being primarily to serve the purposes of artistic experimentation. With the esthetic element standing out above all others, isolated as if in a laboratory from any reader satisfaction that a substantial narrative might provide, this prose could arouse keen excitement among readers with a strong commitment to a given movement's program of goals. Still, readers less concerned with testing out the limits of the movement in question typically found such highly experimental prose difficult to appreciate. Even more than the artistic prose sketches of modernism, which at least possessed a sumptuous appeal to the senses, the sketchy, bare, antirhetorical prose of dedicated avant-gardists found only a small audience. But when many of the avant-garde's techniques were applied to the creation of fiction with a strong, often fantastic plot, full of thrillingly unexpected turns, a broader readership warmed to the results. This was particularly the case in literary environments where, among the reading public, a taste for nonmimetic, boldly imaginative fiction was already well established, such as the cosmopolitan literary capitals of Buenos Aires and Mexico City.

The single individual who most clearly illustrates both the early 1920s drive to establish avant-garde beachheads in Spanish America and the subsequent spread of the avant-garde impulse into nonrealistic narrative prose is Jorge Luis Borges (Argentina, 1899–1986). Borges, when he later attained world renown for his short fiction, was much given to denigrating avant-gardism and publicly expressing embarrassment over his involvement in it. Yet it is difficult not to see a continuum from his early experimentation to the stories he wrote in his prime, carrying forward the avant-garde drive toward innovative construction, avoidance of the straightforwardly verisimilar, and other important features.

Borges spent the years of his adolescence in Europe, principally in Switzerland (1914–1919) and Spain (1919–1921). The first stay coincided with the rise of literary expressionism in German-language writing. As a schoolboy in Geneva, Borges was hardly in a situation to participate in this movement. Yet he became swept up in the excitement it generated, learning to read German just as expressionist works became available. He was won over by the expressionists' fragmented way of structuring a text, favoring of the irrational, and creation of a figurative language that was only partially accessible even to the most adept readers. Borges liked to recall that Gustav Meyrinck's 1916 novel *Der Golem*, which brought expressionist techniques to a popular audience by utilizing them to tell an exotic tale of mysterious events, was the first book he managed to read in German. He also became a reader, translator, and imitator (in his own Spanish-language verse) of German expressionist poetry, famous for its discontinuous syntax and emotive, or, in the contemporary term, "shrieking" manner.

Ultraísmo was the form avant-gardism took in Spain. Supposedly beyond (*ultra*) all isms, this movement was distinguished by its extreme reliance on innovative metaphors, with little connective matter and an avoidance of descriptive adjectives (these last were closely associated with modernism). *Ultraístas* prided themselves on their Spartan ability to appreciate a bare literature, bracingly stripped of decorative, sensuously appealing, and emotionally engaging features. The purest examples of *ultraísmo* are poems consisting exclusively of one such unusual figure after another, not arranged in any apparent progression and at times virtually opaque in meaning. As was often the case with Spanish American writers discovering the European avant-gardes, Borges was too young and too little known to play a major role in Spanish *ultraísmo*, but he published in the movement's outlets and was part of the café sessions of Rafael Cansinos-Asséns, the group's most visible leader.

In 1921 Borges came back to Buenos Aires, where he set about organizing an avant-garde similar to the ones he had known in Europe. Even before Borges's return, often cited as the beginning date for Argentine avant-gardism, Buenos Aires had seen scattered manifestations of interest in avant-garde movements. Scrimaglio, who has examined these earliest stirrings, concludes that the first Argentine enthusiasts of avant-gardism had no substantial understanding of the phenomenon, which they were quick to conflate with the nineteenth-century symbolism admired by their modernist forebears.[1] Nonetheless, these faltering efforts testify to a widely generalized eagerness, strongest among young writers, for a thoroughly different tendency, one that would stand apart from modernism as sharply as modernism had distinguished itself from romanticism.

This avant-garde ideal resulted in a small, not very tightly coherent group of younger creative people who were primarily poets and painters, with little concern for narrative prose. However, experimental prose was cultivated in prose poems as well as the self-consciously artful, abstract criticism of the visual arts much practiced in the movement, cultural essays, the elaborate jokes frequently printed in avant-garde magazines, and statements of esthetic principles. It should be kept in mind that, in the contemporary literary environment, it was common to use the term *poema* to refer equally to texts in verse format and to prose poems. To cite a famous example, *Veinte poemas para ser leídos en el tranvía* (Twenty poems to be read on the streetcar) by Oliverio Girondo (1891–1967) has a substantial component of poetic prose. Examination of avant-garde periodicals shows that prose of these various types frequently occupied as prominent a place as verse writings.

The nucleus of the group—its most vocal segment—was committed to the ideal of an experimental, highly metaphorical, and quintessentially twentieth-century expression. But many of those who published in avant-garde periodicals and participated in group festivities were not dedicated to its program. They were simply creative people eager to move beyond modernism and are most accurately described as postmodernist. In addition, certain writers who were highly innovative, but followed a program of their own rather than the avant-garde pattern, became associated with the movement. Two such original prose writers, Ricardo Güiraldes (1886–1927) and Macedonio Fernández (1874–1952)—claimed by the avant-gardists as "tribal elders"—will come in for discussion in this chapter.

Despite their differing projects, the avant-garde of Borges and his colleagues maintained close ties with the other major youthful movement on the Argentine scene, the social or proletarian literature discussed in the previous chapter. It should be recalled that avant-gardism included movements that were not primarily concerned with the beauty or novelty of artistic expression, but rather its efficacy in promoting social change. Both the estheticist and the social factions of the Buenos Aires literary youth scene were known for their banquets, café-going, and insistent public derision of modernism, establishment literary figures, and, particularly, Leopoldo Lugones. Both groups issued manifestos, launched literary reviews, and started publishing projects. Of the many youthfully spirited and short-lived reviews of the era, by far the most important was the tabloid *Martín Fierro* (1924–1927; Evar Méndez, editor), espousing esthetic change as the top priority. The fourth issue (1924) helped consolidate a true movement by publishing the much-reprinted "Manifiesto de MARTIN FIERRO."[2] This and other rousingly programmatic statements were the work of Oliverio Girondo, who became the movement's co-leader with

Borges. Girondo, over the course of his career, remained within the avant-garde program and achieved the greatest success of any group member in utilizing such concepts as the basis for poetry, prose poems, and lyrical essays on art; he is the only Argentine avant-gardist to achieve major status without moving substantially away from the group's principles. *Martín Fierro* was such a rallying point for youthful innovators that Argentine avant-gardism is frequently referred to as *martínfierrismo*, and when the newspaper ceased publication, the group lost much of its cohesion, although its ideas continued to exercise an influence and its dispersed members furthered their individual lines of innovation.

Girondo's *Veinte poemas*, originally published in Europe before he joined the *martínfierrista* group, nonetheless provides some of the best-realized examples of Argentine avant-garde prose, as in this text:

STREET NOTES

> *On the terrace of a café is a gray family. Some cross-eyed breasts go by seeking a smile atop the tables. The noise of cars fades the leaves of the trees. On a fifth floor, someone crucifies himself, throwing a window wide open.*

> *I think about where to keep the kiosks, the street-lamps, the passers-by, that come into me through my pupils. I feel so full I'm afraid I'll burst . . . I'd need to leave some ballast on the sidewalk . . .*

> *When it comes to the corner, my shadow separates from me, and suddenly throws itself in among the wheels of a streetcar.*[3]

The course that avant-gardism ran in Buenos Aires exemplifies, in several respects, the way this tendency became increasingly eclectic as it reached Spanish America, with various isms fusing together into a heterogeneous *vanguardismo*. In early 1920s Buenos Aires there was a fascination, which reached well beyond avant-garde circles, with Italian futurism and the aggressive, imperious manifestos launched by F. T. Marinetti as futurist spokesman. *Futurismo* was often used as a global term for the entire avant-garde tendency. Many educated Argentines kept a close watch on the latest intellectual and artistic developments in France, and it is common to see allusions to cubism and to the early surrealists in contemporary Argentine cultural journalism. Borges awakened some interest in German-language expressionism.

Still, Spanish *ultraísmo*, and innovative Spanish writing generally (especially that of Ramón Gómez de la Serna, who visited and finally moved to Buenos Aires), probably supplied the most available avant-garde model, and so became the most important antecedent for Argentine experimental writers. Beyond the obvious circumstance of a common language, the sparely metaphorical, deliberately abrupt, and ungainly *ultraísmo* appeared to offer a bracing remedy for what was perceived as modernism's mindlessly perpetuated display of beautifully flowing harmony.

Of Spanish American movements that were avant garde in the strict sense, Argentine *ultraísmo* was the one that most thoroughly engaged the attention of the nation's readers as well as its writers. Several important authors and editors began as *ultraístas*, or at least enjoyed an association with the *ultraísta* group in its social and literary activities. Established Argentine writers became involved as allies, critics, or targets of satire of the movement. A number of texts produced under the stimulus of Argentine avant-gardism have found a place in the nation's literature, appearing in anthologies or reprinted in their entirety.

Second in importance to the Argentine movement is Mexican avant-gardism, which, while its impact was not as widely generalized to the overall literary scene, also stands out as an innovative phenomenon, and one that produced a fair amount of experimental prose as well as its more often mentioned verse. The first and most unalloyed manifestation of avant-gardism in Mexico was *estridentismo* (1922–1927), which had as its leader and virtual inventor Manuel Maples Arce (1898–1981). Bringing together writers and visual artists—in addition, there was *estridentista* music—it was an extreme movement that stood apart from the established literary life of 1920s Mexico. Seen in retrospect, *estridentismo* is a fascinating episode in Mexican literary history, and as such has attracted scholarly study. Yet no *estridentista* became a major contributor to the nation's literature, and no texts originating in and during this movement have earned a place as standard reading. Nonetheless, the movement had an impact over the long run; many of its innovative features later appeared incorporated into more widely accepted Mexican writing. Certainly the *estridentistas'* project proved of more lasting importance than that of their contemporary rivals who painstakingly reproduced colonial settings for their traditionalist historical novels.

Of the group's principal members, Arqueles Vela (1899–1972), who specialized in the *relato*, or short, loosely narrative text, is the one who stands out as having produced *estridentista* prose of some literary interest. The short fiction cultivated in *estridentista* circles minimized sequentiality, giving an effect of, to some degree, aleatory construction. Plot was a minor consideration. The principal focus of attention was isolated, bizarre turns of phrase clearly intended to disconcert and shock readers.

Younger Mexican writers, like those all over Spanish America, had become eager to construct alternatives to modernism and to apply to their own work concepts analogous to those of the European avant-gardes. Consequently, *estridentista* writing exhibits many of the same features as the texts of Argentine *ultraísmo*. There was the same attempt to move away from the fluid cadences of modernism, with writers favoring instead an abruptly shifting, telegraphic, even helter-skelter effect. Features that might be considered ornamentation or embellishment, and particularly the descriptive adjectives cultivated by modernist writers, were kept to a minimum. *Estridentistas* gave importance to dynamic images suggesting force and movement, in contrast to the often languid, static portraiture-in-words of modernists. Frequent allusions to mechanical devices, technology, and science, familiar landmarks of the Italian futurist writing attentively studied by Mexican avant-gardists, gave *estridentismo* a characteristic subject matter as well.

These references at times took on social meanings, although the anarchistic *estridentismo* never clearly defined itself as a political avant-garde. It should be recalled that the Mexican Revolution was still being worked out at the political level, and creative intellectuals often felt compelled to respond to the country's social upheaval. *Estridentistas*, particularly in the last years of the tendency, expressed solidarity with the industrial proletariat, portraying workers amid the complex modern machinery that engaged the movement's imagination.

Estridentista writers maintained, as a group, a social and cultural life apart, and as different as possible, from what they considered the stultifying routine of the establishment. Their deliberate eccentricity combined with their inherently anomalous situation—neither part of revolutionary social literature nor admissible in more refined literary circles—to isolate them from Mexican literary culture as a whole.[4] Conducting significant literary business in unlikely milieux seems to have typified the *estridentistas*, and important position papers were issued from provincial cities.

The *estridentistas'* chief gathering place, an unfashionable Mexico City restaurant, provides the title for the most-cited prose work and only novel (even so, a short one) to emerge from this movement, *El café de nadie* (No-body's café). Arqueles Vela had been reading this text to colleagues since 1924 and finally published it in a 1926 collection of that title. The extravagant novelty cultivated by *estridentistas* dominates this disjointed, wandering narrative. Only occasionally returning to its theme—that individuals remain opaque to their fellow beings—the novel creates impressive flashes, though not a sustained memorability, through surprising figures of speech and lexical choices, including many items drawn from science and technology.

In addition to these two particularly memorable movements—*ultraísmo* and *estridentismo*—a number of groups and individuals developed Spanish American avant-gardism. For example, the short-lived Mexican *estridentismo* was quickly succeeded by the more politicized and populist *agorismo*, remembered chiefly as a clear example of a social, rather than an esthetic, avant-garde. Xavier Icaza (1892) is best remembered for his experiment in using fragmented vanguardist prose to register social protest and comment on ethnic and regional culture, tasks traditionally approached through realist writing. This effort is the basis of his 1928 novel *Panchito Chapopote, retablo tropical; o, Relación de un extraordinario sucedido de la heroica Veracruz* (Panchito Chapopote, tropical scenario; or, tale of an extraordinary happening in heroic Veracruz). While discontinuously hurtling from scene to scene, the novel pays homage to the African-Hispanic culture of Veracruz and points to the exploitative practices of the petroleum industry.

A number of other avant-gardes occurred in less visible locales than the international centers of literary life and publishing, Buenos Aires and Mexico City. Nicaragua was the site of an intense avant-garde movement that swept up many of the nation's most promising young writers; in this case, verse was really the standard medium for literary innovation, with prose generally reserved for making statements. The Cuban avant-garde was also dedicated to experimentation in verse.

Of Peruvian writers who took up avant-garde concepts and practices, Martín Adán (real name Rafael de la Fuente Benavides, 1908–1984) particularly deserves mention in a survey of prose fiction. His 1928 *La casa de cartón* (*The Cardboard House*) takes to an extreme the contemporary ideal of a plotless narrative; although a few events occur in the course of the text, the narrator prefers to allude to them rather than integrate them into a sequence. *The Cardboard House* is comprised of fresh, witty short sketches or impressions of a seaside resort town that was once the height of style but is now losing its elite chic; the young narrator is fascinated both by its old touches of splendor and its increasing banality. The town is designed to amuse and convenience well-heeled vacationers and offers, as well as its natural attractions, transportation and communication facilities considered excitingly up-to-date for the era. The narrator takes advantage of the town's equipment to experiment, as many 1920s writers did, with incorporating technological terminology into literary language. The description of this self-enclosed ambience appears as the work of a clever adolescent with a sharp, ironic eye on life and an avant-gardist's desire to construct an idiosyncratic language unique to the particular text he is composing. *The Cardboard House* is written in a quirky amalgam that juxtaposes neologisms, surprising metaphors and images, words found only in Peruvian Spanish, archaic terms, and lexical choices that are pleasingly eccentric. The extreme youth of the narrator manifests itself in a hyperexcitable tendency to use one adjective after another and to employ superlatives and a generally hyperbolic expression, giving the effect of exacerbated sensitivity often cultivated in avant-garde writing.

　　　　　Perhaps more significant than these avant-gardes, because they reached a wider public, were the more diverse and far-reaching innovative tendencies that came into being after avant-gardism as such had run its course. The late 1920s saw the rise of a very successful movement of this type, the Mexico City–based Contemporáneos. These "contemporaries," so named after the famous magazine *Contemporáneos* (1928–1931) as well as their eagerness to maintain a culturally up-to-date Mexico, are sometimes classed among the avant-gardes. Yet they based their efforts on a concept broader than avant-gardism; they were less closely knit than an avant-garde and did not issue programmatic statements. They tempered the harsh extremes of avant-garde experimentation; their work was meant to reach beyond the circle of like-minded innovators and appeal to the educated public. Contemporáneos defended the ideal, largely fallen into disfavor since the end of modernism, of a literature whose primary goal was to satisfy readers esthetically, with the making of statements a secondary matter. Unlike the irremediably offbeat *estridentistas*, they sought and achieved a significant, central place in the nation's literary culture. They were able to do so in great measure because the group included some extremely talented writers. Not only did members of this alliance go on to become major presences in Mexican literature, but in the group's heyday associated writers published important texts, most notably, *Muerte sin fin* (Death without end), the influential 1939 book of poetry by José Gorostiza (1901–1973), and many briefer poems by Xavier Villaurrutia (1903–1950).

The Contemporáneos were like the earlier avant-gardists in viewing themselves principally as an alliance of poets, yet producing some of their work in prose. Poets of this group, including Villaurrutia, Gilberto Owen (1905–1952), Salvador Novo (1904–1974), and Jaime Torres Bodet (1902–1974), cultivated the loosely constructed short story or novella (the length varies greatly) well suited to experimental prose. Frequently mentioned examples include the tellingly named 1928 *Novela como nube* (Novel like a cloud) by Owen, Novo's 1928 *El joven* (The young man) and the 1927 *Margarita de niebla* (Marguerite of mist), and the 1934 *Primero de enero* (First of January) and the 1937 *Sombras* (Shadows) by Torres Bodet. Though not often among the best-known work of the Contemporáneos writers, the group's fiction was influential over the long term. It illustrates well the ideal of an urbane writing, sparkling with inventive turns, and the effort to produce a momentary intensity—at best, an insight into human consciousness—through boldly chosen imagery and wording.

One Contemporáneo, Torres Bodet, stands out for his unusual dedication to developing, in prose, the lines of innovation associated with the group. Beginning with *Margarita de niebla*, he created a number of short stories and brief novels (an arbitrary distinction in this case). Sonja Karsen, observing that Torres Bodet abandoned fiction in 1941 "because he felt he was more of a poet than a novelist,"[5] points out that the author's assessment of his talents was by no means that of readers and critics. Karsen insists that Torres Bodet, while he was producing prose narrative, made as valuable and important a contribution to this genre as to poetry.[6]

The following excerpt from *Margarita de niebla* exemplifies the main features of the narrative prose of the Contemporáneos. Individual images, metaphors, and incongruous lexical choices stand out, depending very little on a supporting narrative context. Central to this passage is a specialty of the Contemporáneos: the intense, involving evocation of a character's mind when consciousness has been affected by physiological factors or inner upheaval. The use of a dream narrative, long a staple of antirealist authors, justifies the unstable flux of imagery with which the Contemporáneos replaced sequential storytelling.

> *At night, commingled with the wrinkles in the pillow,*
> *I touched, under the feather of sleep, the shape of the*
> *hours that were bringing me toward dawn. Before*

sunrise, in that peculiar quickening of the shadows that isn't yet light, I found the neighborhood of dawn. I went walking then, beside Margarita, through a white meadow that wasn't a field of snow because it was my sheet, but which immediately stopped being that to change into the page of a book. We were reading The Dance under the Linden Trees, *by Goethe. Margarita was struggling to translate into Spanish the lines of the original, in a prosody full of redundancies. To my left, made out of the curved fragment of a vase, the eyeglasses of the old official of the* Buen Retiro *grew streaked with rage at the abandon with which Margarita underlined the errors in the translation. They would have pulverized her if the headmistress hadn't intervened in time, coming toward me down a microscopic staircase and smiling at me in close-up, with a smile that immediately began to be that of my mother. She had come to open the windows and was saying: "It's very late, Carlos. Yesterday you insisted I should wake you up early to go to San Angel . . ."*[7]

While movements attracted a great deal of attention from the mid-1910s to the late 1920s, writers without any strong affiliation to a group were creating some of the most strikingly innovative texts. These were authors hoping to move beyond modernist principles of composition without sacrificing the unabashed display of imaginative flair that strict realism tends to discourage. Of these inventive postmodernists, two are the previously mentioned "tribal elders" of the Argentine avant-garde, Ricardo Güiraldes, author of the much-read 1926 novel *Don Segundo Sombra* (this character's name also provides the title for the English version) and Macedonio Fernández, whose writing, even when purporting to be the chapters of a novel, almost invariably took the form of miscellaneous fragments.

Before discovering the fusion of elements that brought him success—the celebration of gaucho culture together with a free adaptation of Asian-style mysticism and avant-garde elements—Güiraldes attempted a number of less happy experiments. In a moment of despair he later liked to recall, he threw the remaining stock of his poorly received 1915 collection of poetry and prose poems down the well of his family's country estate.

Gradually Güiraldes weeded out of his literary language the precious flourishes and ornamental touches that were beginning to be widely perceived as an impediment to worthwhile innovation in Spanish American writing. At the same time that he was stripping his expression of its rhetorical encumbrances, he was developing the ideas that undergird his famous novel. These include a cyclical view of existence, a borrowing from the Asian thought the author was then studying, and a belief that Argentines must derive their sense of self and meaning from contact with their country's rural realities, summed up in the landscape of the pampas.

Don Segundo Sombra is an allegory of Argentina's past and recommended future, emblemized by its two protagonists. The gaucho whose name the novel bears is indeed a shadowy figure (*sombra*: shadow). Don Segundo trains a young orphan in stoic self-reliance, fidelity to one's guiding values, and a knowing respect for the pampas and their cyclical rhythms. Over the years, he teaches the boy that, in controlling nature, he can achieve control over himself and thus manhood. The gaucho mentor's mission achieved, he fades out of the picture entirely, very much as gaucho culture was vanishing from a rapidly modernizing Argentina. Don Segundo's disciple narrates his formation by this steely, wise master, which ends when the young man, now seasoned and attuned to the harmonies of the pampas, learns that he is the misplaced heir to a large ranch. Now that he has property and a name (previously he was known as "the orphan"), the young man's upbringing makes him the ideal ranch owner. Unlike the typical landed aristocracy of the times, who considered it elegant to remain distant from their holdings, Fabio brings to his role a year-in, year-out knowledge of the pampas and a willingness to maintain contact with the land. Though he admires the pampas, at times rather effusively, his outlook on the natural world is the practical one of a country dweller who needs the land to make his living. He points out that wild creatures are less healthy and less sightly than members of the same species who have been tended by human owners.

The language in which Fabio tells his story embodies the new union of gaucho toughness and elite outlook: it exhibits a refined lyricism available only to an educated user of the language, but also shows off the oral narrative arts the boy has learned from his master. It is not the language spoken by the gaucho characters, but it shows that Fabio has passed through the gaucho experience and emerged as a new type of landed Argentine.

Throughout *Don Segundo Sombra*, Güiraldes includes extremely detailed descriptions of the work performed by cattle herders, naming the exact equipment and techniques employed. Carlos J. Alonso notes the novel's focus on the condition of "being at work" and "the inordinate attention paid to work and its description as a discipline through the use of a technical rhetoric."[8] At the same time, the idea of material remuneration for work is disdained or even denied. Alonso reconciles the fascination with work and the indifference to its economic value: "This mystified conception of work that is characteristic of *Don Segundo Sombra* is ultimately attributable to the pedagogical enterprise that dominates the novel. Work in this register is not an economic activity but an educational program; not a commodity that circulates but the curriculum of a pedagogical project."[9]

Critics have been quick to observe an obvious point: *Don Segundo Sombra* presents the history of Argentina's vast plains from the point of view of the landed classes. Don Segundo represents gaucho tradition, but the novel distills from that tradition those elements that may most beneficially be assimilated by landowners. The novel elides over the inherent conflict between gauchos, that is, nomadic herdsmen whose way of life demands communality of land, and ranchers holding property claims on the same territory. In this fable, the gaucho, rarified to a set of ethic and esthetic values and a store of knowledge, vanishes from the Argentine scene without rancor and with dignity. Historically, though, gauchos constituted a population with economic needs; they bitterly resisted the conversion of their open range into fenced private holdings and, having lost their lands, declined in status to become ranch hands, servants, and, increasingly, members of the urban underclass.

Though it is no guide to history, *Don Segundo Sombra* is nonetheless a well-composed and original novel. The author's search for a literary language that would give an artless effect had yielded good results, and Güiraldes's novel became for many writers a needed model of simple diction without loss of lyricism. For its poetic transformation of the plain speech of country folk, *Don Segundo Sombra* drew praise equally from the youthful avant-gardists and from the entrenched taste-setter Lugones, who set his seal of approval upon the work from the pages of the establishment *La Nación*. It is also an exemplary modern text in its narrator's reluctance to indicate to readers how to construe it, so granting ample interpretive freedom. Noé Jitrik, admiring the work's tactful reticence about the meanings to be drawn from it, notes that while its view of social history is that of the conservative elite, its nondirective narrator extends to readers a democratic and egalitarian treatment.[10]

The public's fascination with *Don Segundo Sombra* coincided with a great vogue for intuitive explorations of the essence of New World lands. Since the movement for independence from Spain, Latin American intellectuals had tended to perceive in their continent, often in its very earth, an essence distinct from that of Europe. This powerfully new, unsullied land figured as the best hope for a fresh start after Europe's collapse into decadence and stagnation. During the early part of the twentieth century, these long-standing ideas coalesced with a mystical regard for forces emanating from the Latin American earth. The notion of a telluric strength circulating through, and so elevating and distinguishing, Latin America's land and people figures in many contemporary texts, including some to be examined in this chapter.

Macedonio Fernández had long been evolving his ideas on the future of writing, and occasionally putting them into practice, without entering literary life. When Borges returned from Europe, though, he quickly identified this eccentric family friend as a literary experimenter working from a well-conceived set of principles. Borges became Macedonio's admirer and promoter and involved him in the activities of the Buenos Aires *ultraístas*. Macedonio was unconcerned with the publication or even the preservation of his writing, and it was the avant-gardists who published for him his 1928 *No toda es vigilia la de los ojos abiertos* (Not all having your eyes open is being awake), a philosophical essay with features of imaginative writing, and the 1929 miscellany *Papeles de recienvenido* (A newcomer's notes; expanded editions, 1944 and 1966 [posthumous]).

Readers new to Macedonio's work are frequently attracted to the author's one-line jokes, usually based on a violation of generally accepted conceptual categories. Such brief, nonsensical assertions as "He was so ugly that even men uglier than he was weren't as much so,"[11] "So many failed to show up that if one more had come, there wouldn't have been room for him,"[12] and "Autobiography of an author so unknown it's not even known that's who it was"[13] are beyond doubt the most immediately memorable aspect of Macedonio's work. At the same time, though, it is possible to examine the larger set of concepts presented by this author's work; seen in this way, Macedonio's writing reveals a surprising coherence and unity of purpose.

Even when the author half ironically labeled one of his texts as a complete work, as he did with the posthumously published (in 1971) *Adriana Buenos Aires: última novela mala* (Adriana Buenos Aires: the last bad novel), everything he wrote took the form of fragments. Macedonio avoided developing his narratives, citing the principle (later made famous by Borges) that it was futile to amass a bulky text in the hope of saying something new. First, literature had already exhausted the relatively small repertory of propositions it was capable of setting forth, and a new author could only repeat what had been asserted or implied. Rather than add yet more vast stretches to a literature laboring to say something, writers should now strive to remove their texts, insofar as possible, from the entire business of stating—"to make language hold its tongue," in one of Macedonio's favorite phrases. At the point when the author's writing fell silent, the reader's imagination would, ideally, supply what was missing. To illustrate how writing might achieve the ideal of taciturnity, Macedonio would compose narratives that lacked information seemingly essential to their comprehension or that broke off abruptly, the narrator claiming a disinclination to continue.

Macedonio believed that writing should reveal its constructed, artificial nature. For instance, the peculiar character who speaks in *No toda es vigilia* is hyperexplicitly identified, beginning with the lengthy subtitle of the text, as "Deunamor, a Character Created by Art." While many characters appear in Macedonio's work, they are always clearly marked as figures produced through textual strategies. He disdained as pointless the realist struggle to make characters resemble, as closely as possible, human beings: "The Inexpert Novel . . . runs around killing off 'characters' one by one, not realizing that written beings all die at the End of the reading."[14]

Perhaps the most extended—though not continuous—illustration of Macedonio's ideas is his *Museo de la novela de la Eterna* (Museum of the novel of the eternal woman), posthumously published in 1967, though Macedonio was known to be working on it as early as the 1920s. Over half of this work is composed of prologues filled with meditations on the nature of novelistic art and language and the respective roles of writers and readers.

Many of Macedonio's plans to remake the novel and activate passive readers went beyond the feasible. He spoke of transforming Buenos Aires into the setting for a fictional narrative whose readers would be required to be the characters, either by their actions or by writing their characters into literary existence. Participants would thus rouse themselves from the passivity inculcated by fully elaborated novels in which the narrator is all too glad to supply the completion and interpretation that should ideally be the work of the reader.

While a description of Macedonio can give the impression of an easily overlooked eccentric, this thinker and writer has always had admirers among students of literary innovation and had a very considerable impact on Latin American writing. Borges has repeatedly avowed his debt to Macedonio, and Julio Cortázar, who will emerge as a major figure of the

1960s "boom," embedded tributes to Macedonio in his writing. Only after the success of the boom had accustomed readers to many of the innovations Macedonio introduced were his texts widely reprinted or, in many cases, published for the first time.

A different type of highly inventive figure on the 1920s Buenos Aires scene was Roberto Arlt (1900–1942). Arlt scored a great public success as the author of the *aguafuertes* (etchings), a series of short sketches in the newspaper *El Mundo*. While the most famous *aguafuertes* are set in Buenos Aires, Arlt also placed these meditations in Spain, Morocco, and other locations where his travels took him. Many of the *aguafuertes* are complex texts that have attracted literary analysis; nonetheless, critics are drawn primarily to Arlt's novels, short stories, and the experimental theater to which he turned in his last years. Of all Arlt's works, the 1929 novel *Los siete locos* (*The Seven Madmen*, 1984), is the most widely read and influential; its sequel of 1931, *Los lanzallamas* (The flamethrowers), continues the same plot but tends to attract fewer readers, receive less critical commentary, and come in for fewer reissues.

Arlt was a celebrity, and his writing has attracted fervent admirers, among them influential writers and critics, but other readers have found it puzzling or less than fully literary. Some of the difficulties with or reservations toward Arlt's work center on questions of style and language, while others involve issues in the construction of the literary text. Arlt generally manifested a rather rough and unpolished style, though he could change quickly to a lyrical manner, particularly evident in those passages where narrators or characters describe prodigious fantasies. The author's background as a fast-working journalist may help account for his use of a language less elegant than was the norm for literary speech. In addition, Arlt took a dissident's pride in violating norms of stylish expression.

More significant than Arlt's stylistic habits are the options he pursued in the organization of the literary text that mark him as an innovator; these practices are most clearly displayed in *The Seven Madmen*. Readers find it difficult to establish the novel's basic narrative data. Ambiguity and at times outright confusion are engendered by the absence of a central narrator who might appear to be in control of the story. *The Seven Madmen* sometimes reads like a novel, but at other times presents itself as a narrative account of criminal goings-on, as reconstructed out of fragments of information by an investigative reporter with a readily excited imagination. This "chronicler," as he calls himself, occasionally attaches footnotes to the text, adding items not included in the main narration and tantalizing the reader with indications that he knows more than he is telling. In other instances, he is like a reporter in relaying assertions without vouching for their accuracy, as when he notes that the Astrologer said an accident had left him castrated.

The plot that is presented in this discontinuous manner focuses on Remo Erdosain, one of the most thoroughly disaffected protagonists in Spanish American literature. Erdosain is drawn into the sphere of a charismatic, conspiratorial figure known as the Astrologer. The Astrologer continually alters his tactics and personae, at times favoring socialist models and at others emulating fascist leaders; he displays a mystical faith in his mission, then is seen mocking himself and his followers. One constant in his thought is that contemporary life has left many without a sense of meaning; this alienated population, now discharging its dissatisfaction in random ways, could be harnessed as a force for change, if given something to believe in. The Astrologer has his followers setting up brothels, inventing devices of doubtful utility, and spinning tales of gold rush adventures. The characters are pursuing their customary interests, but now the activity is in the service of some vast plan that the Astrologer declines to specify. Since the project never goes into practice—Erdosain's actions attract the police and force the group to disband—it remains unclear whether either the Astrologer or the other characters had the capability to carry it out. The conspiracy may have been a collective delusion or one of the Astrologer's inscrutable jokes.

The novel's fragmentary, disjointed presentation and difficult-to-specify narrative data are features that later distinguish the Spanish American new narrative of the boom years. So is the combination of lifelike detail—one of Arlt's celebrated specialties was the description of grimy eateries, brothels, and bars and their life-battered customers—with passages outstanding for their fantastic or expressionistic qualities. For instance, following a scene in which Erdosain's wife leaves him for being unstable and a poor provider, he experiences an extreme state of estrangement:

> *Searching the earth over, where could one find a man with his skin more withered and furrowed with bitterness? He no longer felt like a man; he was only a barely covered sore that writhed and screamed with each pulsing of his veins. And yet he was alive. He lived as his body stretched away and as it came swinging back. He was no longer an organism with its suffering, but something more inhuman—perhaps*

> *that—a monster furled up tight in the uterine black-*
> *ness of that room. Each layer of dark that came from*
> *his lids was yet more placental tissue forming a wall*
> *between him and the universe of men. The walls rose*
> *tall in climbing rows of brick, and fresh torrents of*
> *darkness gushed into the hole where he lay curled and*
> *throbbing like a snail on the ocean floor. He was a*
> *stranger to himself . . . and he doubted he was Augusto*
> *Remo Erdosain. He squeezed his forehead with his fin-*
> *gertips and the flesh of his hand and the flesh of his fore-*
> *head did not recognize each other, as if his body were of*
> *two separate substances.*[15]

A number of other figures on the contemporary Argentine-Uruguayan scene, though less noted than the above three, are at times pointed out as following similar lines of innovation. For example, Felisberto Hernández (Uruguay, 1902–1964) is frequently mentioned in terms similar to those used to characterize Macedonio. Nonetheless, Macedonio was ahead of his times and his contemporaries. During the same period that the avant-gardists were discovering in Macedonio the possessor of a fully fledged program for the reinvention of reading and writing, Felisberto Hernández was still stuggling to find the idiosyncratically fantastic mode in which, starting in the late 1940s, he would distinguish himself, after winning more appreciation as a pianist than as an author.

During the 1920s, a number of Spanish American writers turned their attention to rural regions—to the land—but with a spirit very unlike that pervading realistic regionalism. Their writing was predominantly allegorical and rested on the premise that the Spanish American land, or some sector of it such as the pampas or jungle, was imbued with an animating spirit. The very earth was seen as possessing a life of its own and emanating powerful forces that influenced human behavior. In some instances, the spirit of the land allows the human characters to develop to their fullest. In others, the irresistible pull of forces generated by the earth drags the characters down to defeat and destruction.

The works most frequently mentioned as exemplifying the novel of the land are three very widely read novels: *Don Segundo Sombra*, discussed above as an extension of the avant-garde impulse, *Doña Bárbara* (1929) by Rómulo Gallegos (Venezuela, 1884–1969), and *La vorágine* (The vortex,

1924) by José Eustasio Rivera (Colombia, 1888–1928). In the first-named of these, nature in its wild, unkempt state is not much valued, but the struggle to dominate the world of the pampas allows the individual to develop new physical and spiritual capacities. In *Doña Bárbara* the land—here the Venezuelan plains—is inherently capable of reducing human beings to savagery, but holds a constructive potential once it has been brought under the control of civilized society. The hero makes some headway in civilizing the plains, but they put him to the test and force him to acquire a rougher, harsher way of being. In *La vorágine* the anthropomorphic plains—the first rural setting the novel presents—are pitilessly harsh, but make their inhabitants resourceful and generate a rough-hewn solidarity among fellow dwellers in such a demanding environment. However, no character can be said to be positively affected by the encounter with the animistic jungle that is the best-remembered and most discussed feature of *La vorágine*.

La vorágine's journey into the rain forest, which is not only teeming with life forms but itself a huge, malevolent living entity, degrades and brutalizes the human characters. The most riveting passages in the novel offer the horror-stricken evocation, by the protagonist and principal narrator, of this environment and its ruinous effects on human beings. Readers tend to recall such scenes as the famous one in which the hero, who has become thoroughly contaminated by the savagery of the jungle, forces his rival into piranha-infested waters and then watches him being reduced to skeletal remains by the voracious fish:

> . . . *millions of piranhas converged on the wounded man, in an earthquake of fins and flashing; and though he tried to fend them off with his arms, they ripped away his flesh in a second, tearing off his soft tissue with each bite, with the swiftness of a hungry flock of chickens stripping an ear of corn. The water all around bubbled infernally, bloodily, churningly, tragically; and, just as an X-rayed body shows up on the negative, there emerged on that moving plate the clean, white skeleton . . .* [16]

After the protagonist's self-account ends, Rivera, posing as the commissioned editor of this character's memoirs, reports just having learned the fate of its author and his party. He reproduces a cabled message that ends with the famous line "The jungle devoured them!" [17]

All three of these novels have attracted readers who examine literature from a Jungian perspective; they have found in the texts an abundance of such archetypes as the terrible mother and various figures associated with spiritual questing.[18] *La vorágine* appeals particularly to such an audience. Its protagonist and principal narrator Arturo Cova, an introspective memoirist who records with care his inner states, produces descriptions of a human being undergoing extreme, turbulent changes in his relation with the world and his sense of self.

Cova, whose autobiography is purportedly being published at the request of a cabinet member, is an exceptionally complex literary figure. His characterization has provided continuing material for discussion among readers and critics of all varieties. Although he is undertaking a spiritual search of some type, Cova is a narcissistic, self-dramatizing type not designed to win the reader's sympathy. It is fairly common to find an almost personal exasperation with the histrionic Cova coloring commentary on the novel. Cova exhibits strongly irrational tendencies in his thought and behavior and is often perceived as out of control. He is given to exorbitant fantasies that seem to seep into his everyday life; he is repeatedly seen committing self-defeating acts; when jungle fevers seize him, he experiences delirious scenes, such as one in which he understands the speech of trees, and later represents these episodes in vivid detail. Yet, as Raymond L. Williams has observed, Cova is the one persistently pointing out and commenting upon his own irrationality. He takes pains to experience extreme states, and then observes himself attentively as the source of raw material for the highly literary treatment he is giving his memoirs, making *La vorágine* less a showcase for a character romantically unhinged by his passions than a novel whose central subject matter is the writer's self and the nature of writing. As Cova draws attention to his unusual states of mind, "The reader observes a patently literary character creating a self-conscious 'literary' text."[19]

Although most critical attention has gone to Cova, in his hard-to-define quest, and to the representation of an overpowering nature eager to humiliate and ruin human beings, *La vorágine* is also a novel of social protest that urges individual responsibility for the state of society. A lengthy section takes place among the ill-used workers of Colombia's massive rubber-growing and -processing enterprises. Their virtual enslavement and exposure to danger are described with unmistakable muckraking intent, seeking to arouse indignation as well as set the reader's hair on end.

Cova, who can unleash impassioned rhetoric when inflamed with the ideal of justice, is eager to denounce cases of exploitation. Yet he himself is deficient in his sense of duty toward the human community. At the end of his memoir, he and his family hide themselves in the depths of the jungle to avoid sharing their food supply with a colony of lepers. The very next thing known of them is that they have been swallowed up by the rain forest in which they have sought escape. This circumstance suggests cosmic retribution for the social sin of failing to help those in need.

Doña Bárbara is the most overtly allegorical of the famous novels of the land. The hero is an urbanized, Europeanized Venezuelan lawyer who leaves Caracas meaning to sell his family's long-neglected cattle ranch. However, the spirit of the land exercises a hold on him, and he becomes determined to reclaim his estate and set it in order following enlightened principles of management. Like the youthful apprentice of Don Segundo Sombra, this protagonist is one of several idealized figures of the landowner, driven by high principles and thoroughly acquainted with his ranch and its operations, that appear in contemporary fiction. In accord with a modern, individualistic notion of private land holding and use, he begins to fence in his estate, thus disrupting the open-range system traditional in the area. He views the native land arrangements as primitive, destructive of the profit motive for improving one's herd, and a source of lawlessness, with wily ranchers constantly laying illegitimate claim to cattle grazing on their lands. The hero's resolve to lay full claim to his property, and the concept of civilization he represents, meets with the opposition of the barbarous antagonist who gives the novel its title.

Doña Bárbara, "The devourer of men!" as an ex-lover calls her,[20] is a figure of mythic proportions who has seized the imagination of readers. She is explicitly identified as a personification of the Venezuelan plains. This character is provided with a number of striking characteristics, including a propensity for sorcery and potent techniques for subjugating men, but the most significant one is the uncivilized brutality with which she treats her fellow beings. She abandons her child, exhausts and humiliates her lovers, exploits her workers, and does her utmost to keep the local population in fear of her magic powers. Her participation in witchcraft and the mythical aura she builds around herself do much to spark the reader's fascination with her. But her irrational forces are not supposed to be believed in; they are rationalistically exposed, both by the narrator's commentary and by the outcome of the novel's events, to rest on nothing more than peasant cunning and a disregard for the rules of civilization. For instance, the omniscient narrator, in one of his loquacious asides, lets readers know that Doña Bárbara deludes herself about her magic hold on others: "She was so extremely superstitious that, believing that she truly was helped by those powers, she didn't keep an eye out and let herself be robbed."[21]

In fact, the seemingly invulnerable Doña Bárbara is handily defeated by her civilized rival, once he has learned to deal with the rough ways of the plain. His early efforts are defeated, not because barbarism is strong, but because the protagonist has not yet learned to include a measure of violence in his civilizing work, thus grounding it in local realities and suiting it to the task of transforming the region. After he naturalizes or acculturates his conduct in this way, Doña Bárbara concedes victory to both him and modern progress. She disappears into the marshy waters from which she is said to have originated, her departure as mysterious and shrouded in rumor as befits a legend. But there is no ambiguity in the letter she leaves behind, conceding to the hero her lands and her daughter's hand. So while the novel at first shows rough, barbaric ways as impressively powerful, it later deflates this very notion. Enrique Anderson Imbert succinctly states the operant principle in the novel: "The civilized man has all the dexterity of the barbaric one."[22] In addition to all the dexterity, the civilizer has the momentum of progress behind him and so will prevail.

The novel is an undisguised allegory pointing the way toward Venezuela's future. Its vision of things to come is most clearly represented in the courtship and marriage of the hero and Doña Bárbara's daughter. The daughter is a wild, unkempt creature when the protagonist encounters her; she is as uncivilized as her mother, but is still young and open to change. Recognizing her raw potential, exactly as he has identified the progressive potential of the backward plains, he civilizes, tutors, and finally marries her. The bride is of mixed Indian and European ancestry, a feature the novel emphasizes as part of its symbolic mapping out of the country's best future course. Gallegos was eager to see greater ethnic mixture. In his outlook, the infusion of hardy Indian and African-Caribbean stock could revitalize the European-descended elite. The latter group, though it possesses the repository of learning and refinement, is seen as in imminent danger of losing its drive and initiative.

At the same time that it urges Venezuelans forward into a progressive era of commingled ethnicity, the novel at moments idealizes the plains as a space of magic purity before European and indigenous cultures ever came into contact. Roberto González Echevarría observes that *Doña Bárbara* often implies that cattle-raising caused the plains to deteriorate and that it expresses "a nostalgia for a past when traditional values prevailed and non-European cultures were true to their historical 'essence'."[23] However, this lost unity cannot be restored by returning to the homogeneous past, but only by progressing on to the hybrid future and developing "a modern, all-encompassing myth that will make whole the disparate fragments of the present."[24]

Doña Bárbara is at times perceived as an embarrassing presence among Spanish America's great novels. In its narrative construction, it is not as innovative as *Don Segundo Sombra* or *La vorágine*, which elaborately present themselves as nonfiction documents and frequently narrate or allude to events in an elliptical, stylized way. Gallegos's famous novel simply offers a story told by an omniscient narrator who frequently interprets events for the reader. The meaning of figures and occurrences is made even more explicit by the names assigned them. For example, the hero's first name is Santos, leaving no doubt that he is the force for good, while his family name is Luzardo, containing the word *luz* (light) and suggesting a neologism for *enlightener*. His ranch, run along fair, modern, rationalistic lines, is named Altamira (Lofty Outlook) while Doña Bárbara's superstition-plagued, feudal domain is called El Miedo (Fear). In addition, the characters are frequently associated with animals bearing similar personality traits; as well as contributing to the novel's overt identification, the human-animal correspondences enhance the text's resemblance to myth and legend.

As John Beverly has noted, the novel is deliberately designed to be overexplicit, and its plot too perfectly tidy, in order to reach a broad public and convince it of the various points it makes about national life: "Gallegos's sense of the possibility of a progressive national history and cultural development is built into the providential logic of his plots where all the contradictory, interlocked elements function to produce the desired 'awakening' or reform."[25]

Additional uneasiness about *Doña Bárbara* stems from the fact that many of its confident recommendations for the reorganization of Venezuela's plains, based on the most progressive side of contemporary liberalism, came to be realities without producing the desired effect. The hero, for example, believes that his reform measures will help fill the plains with industrious ranch workers, failing to foresee the massive migration of rural populations to the cities. In this regard, it seems unfair to fault Gallegos for having the historical vision of the times in which he wrote.

A more reasonable complaint concerns *Doña Bárbara*'s somewhat covert, but nonetheless persistent, favoring of those landowners who can be considered developers. The skew toward educated landowners eager to introduce modernizing improvements is not immediately obvious. *Doña*

Bárbara, unlike the aristocratic *Don Segundo Sombra*, has a liberal look; it is a text marked by populist accessibility and designed to propound a number of democratic ideals. Yet the critical tendency in recent years has been to read it for its ideological agenda. Alonso takes this view:

> Doña Bárbara *enjoyed until the early 1950s an almost universal acclaim in critical circles. . . .* Doña Bárbara *benefited from the fact that it was not subjected to the same ideological scrutiny that was accorded* Don Segundo Sombra *from the start. . . . This is particularly remarkable when one realizes that there is a patently ideological message in* Doña Bárbara *that is virtually identical to the one advanced by Güiraldes' novel: both texts endeavor to shift the grounds for legitimate ownership of the land from a legalistic/genealogical plane into an esthetic realm, where personal involvement and the direct assumption of the responsibilities of ownership become the primary criteria. This is, of course, the entire project of reclamation and final redemption represented by Santos Luzardo.*[26]

Alonso cites a barbed observation by the Cuban novelist Alejo Carpentier, alluding to Santos Luzardo's barely disguised desire to claim land: "All the progress that has come with Santos Luzardo from the University of Caracas is a spool of barbed wire."[27] Alonso may be making the case too starkly by so closely equating Gallegos's outlook with the more strictly elitist one of Güiraldes; yet he does very well to draw attention to the parallels. Even more important, he is correct in making the point that *Doña Bárbara* is a text charged with ideological implications and presuppositions that call for further critical examination.

Substantial and long-lasting innovation in nonrealistic literature fuses the lyrical and at times fantastic writing that flourished during modernism with an examination of the character of human existence and an implicit criticism of society, particularly the elite. The Venezuelan essayist and fiction writer Arturo Uslar Pietri (b. 1906) was especially eager to promote this literary mixture as an exceptional feature of Latin American literature. It was Uslar Pietri who applied to Latin

American writing a term taken from German art criticism, *magical realism*. By the 1960s this phrase would spread dramatically through the discussion of contemporary literature from the region, being taken up not only by critics but by ordinary readers for whom it summarized a quality they had been noticing in recent fiction. In the broadest terms, the phenomenon that seemed to be spreading through a sector of Spanish American writing was the co-occurrence of realism with fantastic, mythic, and magical elements. A secondary trait was the characteristic attitude of narrators toward such subject matter: they frequently appeared to accept events contrary to the usual operating laws of the universe as natural, even unremarkable. Though the tellers of astonishing tales, they themselves expressed little or no surprise.

It is worth noting that Uslar Pietri, in presenting his term for this literary tendency, always kept its definition open by means of a language more lyrical and evocative than strictly critical, as in this 1948 statement: "What came to dominate the story and to leave a lasting impression was the view of man as a mystery surrounded by realistic data. A poetic divination or denial of reality. Something that for lack of a better word could be called magical realism."[28] When academic critics attempted to define *magical realism* with scholarly exactitude, they discovered that it was more powerful than precise. Critics frustrated by their inability to pin down the term's meaning have, in disgust, urged its complete abandonment. Yet in Uslar Pietri's vague, ample usage *magical realism* was wildly successful in summarizing for many readers their perception of much Spanish American fiction; this fact suggests that the term has its uses, so long as it is not expected to function with the precision expected of technical, scholarly terminology.

Uslar Pietri's writing often, though not invariably, exemplifies the mode for which he coined the term. The fiction work that earned him greatest attention was the 1931 novel *Las lanzas coloradas* (The red spears). Set in what is now Venezuela during the wars for independence from Spain, the narrative avoids the expected in presenting historical material. Oblique strategies are preferred. For example, Simón Bolívar never appears in the story of the armed struggle of which he was leader; instead, the novel shows the image of Bolívar that characters carry in their minds.

Las lanzas coloradas is known for scenes that, through impressionistic, heavily metaphorical descriptions, convey the chaos and disruption that accompany a widespead, lengthy war. War-torn tableaux in which confused throngs of people mill about are a recurring and memorable feature.

In the tradition of the avant-garde, the narrative sums up the massive disturbance of war in unpredictable figures of speech all the more eloquent for their irrationalism.

Lyricism, existential considerations, and social commentary come together in the fiction of María Luisa Bombal (1910–1981), a young Chilean writer making her career in Buenos Aires. Bombal produced relatively little: the novels *La última niebla* (*The House of Mist*, 1935) and *La amortajada* (*The Shrouded Woman*, 1938) and a few short stories. However, she has been an important model for Spanish American writers eager to write frankly beautiful prose and to explore fantastic modes without sacrificing literature's ability to comment on real-world conditions.

Bombal's texts repeat the same basic situation. An otherworldly, high-strung woman lives in a large, well-appointed, but rigidly conventional and heartless household, where she has few obligations other than to be elegant and gracious. Though surrounded by family and servants, and in some cases married, the heroine experiences a painful isolation and cultivates an abundant dream and fantasy life. Bombal's women, under their ethereally ladylike and pliant exteriors, harbor strong sexual desires and seek out all-consuming amorous experiences, though they are seldom seen enjoying any fulfillment outside the imaginative realm. The reader comes to know these heroines through a narrative that conveys their subjective outlook and reveals in detail their dreams, fantasies, and other aspects of the intense inner life that remains opaque to most other characters. The exposure of the protagonists' invisible inner drama tends to draw readers' empathy toward these fictional women, whereas their bourgeois families and friends may be unaware of their rich imaginative existence and judge them merely neurotic, languid, or even slightly retarded, as the other characters believe Brígida to be in the much-anthologized story "El árbol" ("The Tree").

The House of Mist, a very short novel that Bombal revised somewhat in translating it into English, features a narrator-protagonist whose central life experience, one that would compensate for the great disappointment of her marriage, may well have been a fantasy. Her intense, consoling memory of time spent completely absorbed with a lover becomes contaminated by doubts as to its veracity. Particularly after the only person who witnessed them secretly together dies, she has no way of substantiating the scenes that are nonetheless engraved on her mind. By the end of the novel, she appears passively resigned to a loveless marriage and routine existence, but her passionate memory, even if now flawed by her awareness of its probable falsity, has added to her life an otherwise absent excitement and meaning.

The Shrouded Woman, which the author also rewrote while producing the English version, has as its heroine a woman at her own wake, reflecting over her life, which has come to its end without providing her any fulfillment or contentment. She is visited by the people she has had most to do with, and each new visitor provokes a fresh set of memories. The heroine reveals herself to have been an extraordinarily frustrated and dissatisfied woman who communicated her troubled outlook to those close to her. But neurotically unhappy as she is, she retains the ability to analyze and assess herself, others, and the situations they lived through, all with penetrating acuity. Though the emphasis of her remarks always appears to be on individual and personal issues, her account of her life and her relations with others offers a decidedly negative vision of the existence of the Chilean bourgeoisie, and in particular of the role assigned to women of this social class, who appear excluded from most types of activity that might allow them a sense that they are taking the initiative in causing events to occur or participating in a significant way in the world's, or even their households', real business.

One great attraction of Bombal's works is their ability to generate a universe charged with myth and magic. Bombal's women are ethereal-looking beings; frequent mention is made in the texts of their thick, dark braids, which when unloosed seem to become powerfully animated entities. Copious rains, along with various streams, pools, and puddles, provide a fluid background to the protagonists' dramas and hint at a world losing its solid contours. In "The Tree" the heroine has for company a sonorous rain, while in *The House of Mist* a vaporous dampness envelops the main character as part of her alienated condition. In *The House of Mist* deep waters, sensed to contain the secret of the characters' unhappiness, work a fatal attraction. Trees and forests become personified; the title entity in "The Tree" establishes a more intimate bond of communication with the heroine than do any of the human figures surrounding her.

Critics have correctly observed that many such elements in Bombal are transformations of staple features of folk legends,[29] and students of this author's texts often refer to dictionaries of symbols and myths. However, the utilization made of these long-existing elements may be original and run counter to tradition. Gabriela Mora analyzes the way this process operates in "Las islas nuevas" ("New Islands"). This is one of Bombal's stories that most overtly relies on a magical phenomenon, for the heroine has sprouted the beginnings of a wing. After citing analyses that reduce this protagonist to a feminine archetype, Mora rereads the evidence to show a woman evolving away from the standard mode: "This woman represents a half-developed, incomplete being. Yolanda would need to incorporate 'masculine' principles to become fully a person. Some of these principles, predominance of reason, action, independence, are exactly what has been drowned out by the cultural model of what is feminine that has held sway for so many centuries."[30] Mora's reading, which at first looks paradoxical, is in line with the current tendency to see in Bombal's works a half-submerged vein of social criticism that stops only a little short of a feminist critique of society.

Bombal enjoyed the enthusiastic backing of many Argentine literary intellectuals as well as a wider public fascinated by her lyrical prose and mysterious fictional universe. In contrast, the literary experiments of her contemporary Juan Filloy (Argentina, 1894–1967) were known to a select few; he was a writer's writer whose impact was disproportionate to his readership. Although commercial publishing houses have since issued texts by Filloy, for some time his novels were available—those that had been published at all—only in small private editions. Filloy was a forerunner of the fondness in the 1960s and 1970s for playing with novelistic language and construction. His novels are for the most part short, rely minimally on plot, and have in common, among other idiosyncrasies, seven-letter titles. Filloy was an aficionado of palindromes and in his odd spare moments (he held posts in the judicial system) devised a great many of these sentences and phrases that read identically forward and backward. He embedded in his novels not only notable specimens of this figure, but a number of types of structures manifesting a similar left-right, backward-forward symmetry.

The 1934 *Op Oloop*, whose title and protagonist's name are almost a palindrome, is probably Filloy's most cited novel. It displays to best advantage the author's playful experimentation with language and novelistic form, although it does not exemplify his ability, manifest in several other texts, to infuse social protest into an innovatively designed narrative. *Op Oloop* records the last nineteen hours and forty-nine minutes of Op Oloop's life, the time being carefully noted at the left margin. When the novel's clock starts up, Oloop, presumed to be a cool-tempered Finn, appears to enjoy an orderly mind and the satisfaction of seeing a logic to life. He feels a special affinity for numbers, associating them with mental discipline. To hear the subject matter of a discussion quantified, even if it is a question of pimps enumerating the distinctive features of their prostitutes, provides him with a sense of well-being. But his systematized mind becomes invaded by the evidence of irrationality, originating in the world, coming from within his own thought processes and inherent in language itself. The resulting loss of clear organization leads to his suicide.

Surprising and often playful treatments of language are a major source of the book's interest. Filloy utilizes typographical aberrations, which resemble bizarre printer's errors, yet upon inspection prove to be metaphors for the unraveling of Oloop's tidy mental scheme. A segment of the narration is presented as if it were the transfer into an approximate written equivalent of what is some type of extrasensory, extralinguistic communication between Oloop and the woman he loves. In the midst of his crisis, Oloop hosts a dinner party where the guests reveal themselves to be sophisticated practitioners of linguistic games, particularly the violation, for playful effect, of semantic categories. Their inventive and irreverent amusements, which give the novel a witty, intellectual appeal, also demonstrate the arbitrary character of linguistic systems and patterns of mental organization. While Oloop discovers many varieties of disorder once he has been awakened to the chaos all around him, illogic and randomness are nowhere more evident than in language, the prime vehicle for organizing information and experience. *Op Oloop* can be read as showing a person destroyed by the recognition of arbitrariness while encouraging readers to acknowledge but enjoy this very feature of language and human personality.

Throughout the 1930s and 1940s, stories and novels with a fantastic component enjoyed special support from the publishing industry and reading public of Argentina. Their popularity was in part the work of a few powerful taste-setters who regarded realistic fiction with distaste and favored elegant texts that relied heavily on stylization. Especially influential was Victoria Ocampo (Argentina, 1890–1979), who in 1931 founded the journal *Sur*. Many writers in Ocampo's stable gained considerable renown. She discovered Ernesto Sábato (Argentina, b. 1911) when he was still a youthful surrealist, and published several chapters of a wildly irrationalistic novel he would never complete; Sábato would later grow famous for a very different type of fiction. Silvina Ocampo (b. 1903) became as distinguished a short story writer as her sister was an editor; she steadily favored the fantastic mode. Adolfo Bioy Casares (Argentina, b. 1914), married to Silvina Ocampo, was another talent in the circle of *Sur*. He attracted both critical acclaim and good sales with highly imaginative texts tending toward the allegorical, as in his 1940 novel *La invención de Morel* (*The Invention of Morel*). But of all the authors Ocampo promoted, the great luminary was Jorge Luis Borges.

Borges, who had won his first fame as an avant-garde poet, during the early 1930s began edging toward the form for which he would attain worldwide renown, a variant of the short story incorporating features of the essay. Toward the end of the 1920s, Borges began to express publicly his revulsion with avant-gardism. The usually prolific author ceased to publish poems and, as Martin S. Stabb notes, from summer of 1929 to spring of 1931 stopped publishing new material entirely.[31] He then resumed his usual level of activity, but was an all-purpose man of letters with no creative genre in which to work. By his own account, he admired the short story but was too insecure to attempt this form. Instead, he did all types of literary jobs, editing, translating, reviewing books, and collecting and retelling unusual plots for a newspaper supplement. This last activity brought him close to short fiction with the retold tales collected in 1935 under the title *Historia universal de la infamia* (*A Universal History of Infamy*). These are accounts of criminal activities as told by a narrator who is curiously indifferent to what would seem to be the natural subject matter of the book, evil and its consequences. Disregarding the ethical meanings of the cases he summarizes, the historian of infamy is preoccupied with the style and flair demonstrated by his misbehaving protagonists as well as with his own self-consciously baroque narrative manner. The same volume contains "El hombre de la esquina rosada" ("Streetcorner Man"), undeniably a short story though not in Borges's distinctive mode.

Borge's 1936 *Historia de la eternidad* (History of eternity), otherwise a collection of essays, included the first full-blown example of what would become recognized as the Borgean short story: "El acercamiento a Almotasim." ("The Approach to al-Mu'tasim"). As do many of the author's stories, "The Approach to al-Mu'tasim" presents itself as if it were a non-fictional document, in this case, a review of a detective novel. Soon it is clear that the narrator is gripped by some mental uneasiness that distracts him from his reviewing duties and involves him intensely with the novel. Although he presumably possesses a copy of the novel under discussion, he appears unable to specify the proliferating details of the plot and expresses uncertainty with increasing frequency. The story that so seizes the reviewer has to do with a secularized Bombay law student who unexpectedly abandons his rational existence to undertake a mystical quest for al-Mu'tasim, the source of radiance in the world; the tale breaks off just as the long-sought encounter is about to occur, leaving it unclear whether the protagonist's search was fulfilling, self-destructive, or deluded.

"The Approach to al-Mu'tasim" is one of many Borges stories in which characters become convinced that possession of some information, whether a cold fact or a revelation, will make sense of the world. Such a conviction leads them to pore through research materials, devise theories and systems of thought, undertake journeys, and scrutinize seemingly random phenomena in hopes of discerning a significant pattern. Borges is a skilled mimic of the thought and speech of those in the grip of a belief. The elaborate means the characters devise to find meaningful order at times appear ridiculous, with ingenuity displacing common sense. Yet the drive to discover or invent a system to the universe is seen as fundamentally human and worthy of consideration, all the more so as it may be an urge impossible to fulfill.

By 1941 Borges had produced enough stories in this vein to publish *El jardín de senderos que se bifurcan* (*The Garden of Forking Paths*). In 1944 this collection became a subsection of an expanded volume bearing the now famous title *Ficciones* (called *Ficciones* in the British edition and *Fictions* in the United States). Nearly every story in *Ficciones*, which Borges reissued in 1956 with the three additional texts, and in the 1949 *El Aleph* (*The Aleph;* the English volume bearing this title is actually a Borges anthology), of which an expanded version was published in 1952, has earned major status. These tales have been subjected to a multiplicity of interpretations, translated, anthologized, imitated, and in some cases adapted to other media.

When readers speak of a Borgean story, they refer to a number of thematic, stylistic, and structural traits common to the texts in *Ficciones* and *The Aleph*. (In the short stories Borges published late in his career, following a twelve-year absence from the genre, these features occur with much less frequency.) The manner of the narration is baroque, both in the complex syntax of individual sentences and in the overall organization of the text. It is easy to feel overwhelmed by the proliferation of diverse items of information, only some of which prove relevant to the main plot. By supplying a bewildering overload of detail, the stories give the reader a taste of the dilemma faced by the protagonists, who cannot order and utilize all the input assailing their minds. The characters generally commit two cognitive errors. Some try to hold everything in the mind simultaneously, as with the Aleph, a fatuous mystical device that allows every constituent of the universe to be seen at the same time, thus obliterating all meaningful design. Others attempt to eliminate all but the most vital issue.

One of the most famous of the Borges characters consumed with all-inclusiveness is Irineo Funes of "Funes el memorioso" (English, "Funes the Memorious"), from *Ficciones*. The narrator is recalling his encounters with the pathological prodigy of the title. Funes is an Uruguayan country boy who, after being thrown from a horse, undergoes curious changes in memory and perception. While most observers might conclude that Funes has lost the ability to forget and his mind is succumbing to a clutter of useless information he cannot even organize, the individual affected is certain that he has attained a breakthrough in human consciousness. The narrator remembers the self-account Funes gave him in an all-night conversation: "For nineteen years, he said, he had lived like a person in a dream: he looked without seeing, heard without hearing, forgot everything—almost everything. . . ."[32] Though his neurological injury has also produced a good deal of paralysis, Funes considers this latter side effect a small price to pay for his perfect recall. The narrator then struggles to reconstruct Funes's world:

> *We, at a glance, perceive three wine glasses on the table; Funes saw all the shoots, clusters, and grapes of the vine. He remembered the shapes of the clouds in the south at dawn on the 30th of April of 1882 and he could compare them in his recollection with the marbled grain in the design of a leather-bound book which he had seen only once, and with the lines in the spray which an oar raised in the Rio Negro on the eve of the battle of the Quebracho. These recollections were not simple; each visual image was linked to muscular sensations, thermal sensations, etc. . . . He told me:* I have more memories in myself alone than all men have had since the world was a world.[33]

While Funes's memory is as all-retaining as he claims, other mental abilities are substandard. Funes cannot make a hierarchy or subcategories for information; for instance, he proposes an asystematic mode of numbering in which each number would bear a unique name. While Funes and characters like him are a reminder of the need to edit knowledge and to select certain items to bring sharply into focus, the Borges characters who do these things incur another set of problems as fixed ideas seize their consciousness. Among Borges's talents is the creation of notable monomaniacs whose minds are riveted either on some belief or system which is apt to strike the reader as unsound, or on some person or object, such as the obsession-provoking coin named in the title of "The Zahir" ("El Zahir").

In addition to these cognitive problems, the Borgean tale is marked by allusions to a typical repertory of items. Many texts refer to labyrinths, either constructed mazes or such metaphorical labyrinths as the desert, library stacks, treatises, gardens, houses, philosophy, time, memory, and human awareness. Borges's searchers often find themselves in red enclosures and accidentally acquire objects with hidden powers. Certain everyday articles prove treacherous, especially mirrors, masks, coins, maps, and reference books. Characters offer a showcase of curious neurological aberrations, ranging from paralysis to syndromes affecting memory and language. Indeed, human consciousness seems inherently to predispose to, or to constitute, a form of cognitive disorder. Unusual scripts or other writing systems often absorb the narrators' and characters' attention, as do books with oddities of format or irregular bibliographic information. A Borges specialty is the description of shabby, dilapidated environments, ranging from rundown houses and overgrown gardens to an entire universe in the process of losing the principles that have held it together.

During the period that Borges was just winning notice as a short story writer, the late 1930s and 1940s, the leading figure in Spanish American literature was Eduardo Mallea (1903–1982), who worked alternately in the essay and the novel. Though his fame has dimmed with unusual rapidity over succeeding decades, in his prime Mallea was influential enough to set the issues for discussion in Argentine intellectual life. He occupied for many years the editorship of the then highly influential literary supplement of the newspaper *La Nación*. During the 1930s and 1940s he was awarded a number of literary prizes and saw his work widely translated. The Alfred A. Knopf publishing house made Mallea one of the few Spanish American writers to attract a U.S. readership as early as mid-century.

Mallea enjoyed international attention for his meditative, symbolically laden narratives whose solitary, sensitive protagonists were given to brooding on certain problems, the same ones treated in the author's essays. Characters and events often lose their realist outlines to become allegorical figures of Argentina and the forces within it. The narrator and characters are accorded ample space to discuss their ideas, a strategy Mallea recognized and defended as *narrar definiendo* (to narrate by defining). The form of the novel takes on features of the essay by including these disquisitions. A recurring issue is the attainment of an authentic existence as an Argentine. Mallea's protagonists experience lengthy periods of anguish and self-scrutiny in their search for the genuinely Argentine. These characters at times pursue pilgrimages through Europe, and Mallea's fiction contains admiring descriptions of European high culture and the cosmopolitan style of European women. Yet the inevitable conclusion is that European civilization is inadequate to nourish the Argentine being struggling to take form. A further evolution, a spiritualization of Argentina not amenable to rational explanation, is needed to bring the nation fully into its own. The 1940 novel *La bahía de silencio* (*The Bay of Silence*) best represents Mallea's fiction in this vein. The protagonist, addressing a woman he admires from a distance, is less engaged in telling his life story than in scrutinizing his own and Argentina's sense of being who they are.

Mallea launched a concept that gave rise to much discussion. He postulated that the nation contained within it both a visible and an invisible Argentina. The term and concept *visible Argentina* is associated with the active commerce, ambition, and entrepreneurial spirit that, while often hailed as evidence of the nation's forward-looking character, in Mallea's vision testify to a misconceived, meaningless way of life. The Argentina that remains hidden from view, however, is composed of individuals who have little concern with advancing their own careers and status or building up the material nation. These invisible Argentines feel isolated and alienated; if they find a genuinely worthwhile way of being Argentine, it is not through the undertaking of projects, but through coming to a special, somewhat mystical acceptance of their condition and place in the world. For example, the hero of *The Bay of Silence* is repeatedly unsuccessful when he embarks on active plans to rechannel the nation's destiny. Toward the end of the novel, he appears as paradoxically successful when he abandons such striving and resigns himself to being what he already is, a passive but alert and sensitive observer of his country and of himself.

Not only has Mallea's work become dated with the passage of time, it has also been the target of adverse criticism. The solution Mallea proposes to the problem of Argentine national culture and identity is a passive one, and his readers receive the message not to attempt projects to reshape the nation. The ideal is to let oneself undergo a distinctively Argentine process of spiritual transformation.

Mallea postulates the invisible Argentina as an aristocracy strictly of the spirit, but many characters who embody it would be defined, by real-world standards, as members of the leisure class. While Mallea's protagonists are tormented by problems of a spiritual or existential nature, they appear loftily above all material concerns. They are free to spend hours wandering the streets of European capitals or Buenos Aires and sitting in bars, cafés, and restaurants, lost in reverie or discussion, untroubled by the need to earn a livelihood. The idealized females who recur in Mallea's works, including both women who figure significantly in *The Bay of Silence*, are quickly identifiable as members of the upper class. Mallea's women tend to be taller and lighter in coloring than the general population, aloof and even haughty in bearing, cosmopolitan, casually elegant, and sure of their entitlement. Mallea disparages the ostentation of prosperity, the mark of the newly rich; his writing reveals a fascination with the signs of long-standing wealth, such as heirlooms used with apparent disregard for their material value.

Readers who find Mallea's narrators and characters too talkative are more apt to appreciate his atypically brief, spare novel of 1941, *Todo verdor perecerá* (*All Green Shall Perish*). Here the protagonist and representative of true Argentine values is not especially educated or articulate. In the early chapters she is married to a bitter, uncommunicative farmer; later she is taken up by the chic set of a small city, but among the socialites she remains almost as silent and isolated as beside her hermetic husband. The novel relies more on allegory and metaphor, frequently evoking biblical associations, than on exposition of meanings. Its emphasis on showing and suggesting rather than telling, together with its relatively tight organization, gives Mallea a better opportunity to display his grasp of the novelist's art than in his more essaylike novels.

Perhaps more than any other factor, Mallea's idealization of a genteel, dignified, quietistic approach to life has made his work seem stuffily out of date. He has been retrospectively displaced as the major Argentine writer of mid-century by Borges, whose narratives are characterized by violence, betrayal, cognitive disorders, and a vision of human existence as both terrifying and ridiculous.

Borges's stories, with their great complexity, have proven endlessly absorbing to critics and to readers in general; yet there is one area in which their innovative power seems to make little headway. Of Borges's many original inventions, none is particularly effective in strengthening literature's ability to comment upon real-world social conditions, except in an oblique and implicit manner; for example, Borges can be cruelly funny in portraying unintelligent political beliefs and rhetoric. But during the same period in which Borges was publishing his famous baroque tales, other writers more concerned with social protest were developing similarly imaginative modes. The long-standing association between social criticism in literature and realistic representation began to be questioned by writers who found stylized, mythical, and magical modes the best vehicle for their artistic statements about society.

Foremost among these nonmimetic yet socially conscious writers is Miguel Angel Asturias (Guatemala, 1899–1974). He was one of the first authors to win a wide audience with the hybrid mode of representation that would later win recognition as magical realism, even if critics did not apply the term to Asturias's work until both had been in circulation for some time.

(Although *magical realism* has proven a term and concept notoriously difficult to specify, the phrase will appear at times in this survey. As noted in the discussion of Uslar Pietri, the term is a handy and recognizable way of drawing attention to the fusion of realism with myth and fantasy that distinguishes a sector of modern Spanish American fiction. Less used will be the often-heard *new novel* or *new narrative*. The latter is a vague term applied to any Spanish American fiction from the 1940s or 1950s onward that displays novelty in narrative design and in the handling of time and space. To speak of a *new narrative* often entails the suggestion that only from mid-century forward did Spanish American fiction become innovative in form, while in fact there had been a long line of Spanish American writers experimenting with the construction of narrative.)

Asturias's *El señor Presidente*, which retains in English translation its Spanish title with its resonances of ceremonious power, was in the writing as early as the 1920s but appeared in 1946. It had a great influence and is now regarded as the first widely read example of the novel of the dictator, a subgenre that has since been practiced by a number of celebrated Spanish American authors. The dominant presence in the novel is that of the dictator. His existence is all-pervasive and threatening because of, rather than in spite of, the fact that he is only rarely seen; he makes six appearances in the novel he dominates. Despite his title, the president is not seen or heard of presiding over any governmental activity; as head of state, he appears to have no real business other than to maintain his own authority through intimidation. Rumor and conjecture about this shadowy ruler are constantly proliferating, serving to strengthen his hold over those who might otherwise oppose him. Though these features of the fictional dictatorship are based on observable dynamics of real-world regimes, the mode of representation is stylized and hyperbolic rather than realistically lifelike. In descriptions of *El señor Presidente*, the word *nightmare* frequently appears, and justifiably so. Not only does the text generate a general atmosphere of nightmarish fear and uncertainty, but it replicates certain spatial and temporal distortions characteristic of uneasy dreams, such as the perception that all motion is paralyzed when urgent action is necessary and the sense that threatening elements loom unusually large and prominent in the field of vision.

The novel's portrait of the powerless shows the same distortion for sinister effect. The first characters to appear in the narrative are the homeless who inhabit the public spaces at the center of the city. These wretched beings are recurring figures throughout the novel; despite efforts to drive them from the downtown area, one of them still lurches dementedly onto the scene in the novel's epilogue. Between them, they present a gallery of grotesques, showing off the varieties of deformity and mental and physical malfunctions. As well as being a matter of indifference to the government and the church, both of which appear exclusively preoccupied with the conservation of their own influence, these outcasts are cold to one another's welfare and fight over their miserable holdings. Their interaction suggests the breakdown of the patterns that give human society its coherence. While features of naturalistic representation enter in, the portrayal of the thieves and beggars is characterized by grotesque caricature rather than any effort at verisimilitude.

Asturias drew upon the resources of avant-garde experimentation to give his novel its distinctive linguistic texture. In the much-noted opening passages, a voice of unknown origin is overheard, appearing to utter, from out of a trance, a ritualistic invocation addressed to fire and light. The incantation at first seems more focused on the rhythmic repetition of certain sounds, bordering on speaking in tongues or ecstatic babbling, than on the communication of semantic content. On closer examination, this supplication divulges several possibilities of meaning. Phonetically, it mimics the tolling of the cathedral bells, while its reiterated allusions to light and its naming of Lucifer hint at the struggle between the forces of enlightenment and evil in the novel. Other potential interpretations may also be derived from this enigmatic opening discourse. Only gradually does the ambiguous opening give way to a description of the everyday life of the homeless.

At the time of its publication, *El señor Presidente* aroused alarm among supporters of a more straightforward manner of writing when social issues were involved. Their fear was that the introduction of techniques cultivated by the avant-garde would weaken the critical force of the social novel and reduce it to just another showcase for authors' technical virtuosity. This concern today sounds old-fashioned because, in the polemic between defenders of verisimilar social realism and proponents of a more stylized, openly literary variety, the artistic vision of the latter has become the majority viewpoint. Spanish American prose has been strongly affected by the belief, of which *El señor Presidente* is an outgrowth, that artistic distortion and narrative innovation can enhance critical awareness of social injustice. This principle, though it has always continued to draw bitter opposition, motivates some of the most accomplished works of modern Spanish American fiction.

Though its Central American setting is clearly established, *El señor Presidente* is the most urbane and cosmopolitan of Asturias's novels. The president may be feudal-minded in some respects, but he is skilled in utilizing such manifestations of modernity as telephones and rapid transportation to maintain widespread apprehension over his probable actions. The 1949 *Hombres de maíz* (*Men of Maize*), Asturias's other great novel, is by contrast rooted in a premodern, largely pre-Hispanic world charged with myth and magic. The author had long been a passionate student of indigenous mythical narrative, particularly the Mayan book of the *Popol-Vuh*. As well as having lived in an area with a substantial Indian presence, he undertook formal studies and accumulated a great deal of information. Yet he was not an actual speaker of any indigenous language, which necessarily kept him at a remove from Indian life, and not a scientific researcher into Mesoamerican writing. The use he made of native myth, as of all his knowledge of Indian lore and culture, was creative literary reinvention. His 1930 *Leyendas de Guatemala* (Legends of Guatemala) was his own free adaptation, in a highly lyrical manner, of narratives of Indian origin. The mythic tales Asturias had so far treated either as a rapt student or semipopular reteller received a very different use in *Men of Maize*. Now Asturias took unprecedented liberties with his indigenous raw material, transforming and reshaping various elements to incorporate them into what was unmistakably a twentieth-century text by a novelist adept in innovative narrative techniques. The imaginative fusion of ancient source material with state-of-the-art novelistics proved fascinating both to readers and critics and to other writers eager to draw upon their region's rich stores of myth without appearing to be simply regional folklorists and antiquarians whose fidelity to sources precluded the full utilization of the modern artistic imagination.

Men of Maize is a story of loss; at the novel's end, the Indians have suffered a significant erosion of their culture, their vision of the universe and its workings, and their approach to agriculture, seen as a collaborative endeavor between the earth and the human collectivity. But even though they are losing ground, literally and metaphorically, the indigenous characters of *Men of Maize* possess an imaginative resourcefulness that sets them apart from the suffering, downtrodden masses that had become a staple of novels of Indian life. The Indians of *Men of Maize* retain in their shared consciousness the image of Gaspar Ilom, a figure of indigenous rebellion whose revival is perennially expected. As well as signifying resistance against the encroachment of non-Indians and their ways, Gaspar Ilom provides the highest standard of an Indian in full command of the complete, intact legacy of Mayan culture. He can enter into communication with—indeed, effect virtual fusion with—the natural world. He is knowledgeable in the art of self-transformation and can assume a physical shape consonant with the experience he is undergoing at any moment. In comparison with this exemplar, the present-day indigenous characters have a scant familiarity with their traditional culture and must struggle to use it as a source of power. Nonetheless, at the same time that the Indian characters are losing portions of their once-extensive cultural repertory, the whites are involuntarily acquiring features of indigenous thought. In *Men of Maize* the mythic outlook of the Indians is so powerfully stimulating to the imagination that even whites who consciously reject indigenous ways absorb some aspects of the Indians' vision.

Two Indian characters recapture something of the legacy of Gaspar Ilom by reasserting their ability to draw upon what remains of indigenous lore and magic knowledge. The recovery of mythic power is signaled, above all, by the ability to turn into the alter ego from the animal world that all human beings are presumed to possess. One of the self-transforming characters is an unlikely symbol of rebellion, for he has allowed himself to become not only Westernized but banalized and incorporated into the state bureaucracy as a mailman. Yet one day, abandoning his undelivered mail, he runs away in the shape of a coyote. Another character changes into the form of an opossum, cures himself of a longtime case of blindness with the help of a traditional ritual healer, and then sets out in search of his runaway wife. The wife, as the magically unattainable object of his search, suggests a figure of the once-intact indigenous cultural world. These and other events make the point that native myth and magic have not lost their potency as sources of strength for the Indians; these forces can still sustain the native characters in their efforts to heal and transform themselves and to put up resistance. Yet the indigenous figures find it increasingly difficult to recall and utilize their reservoir of myth.

Play with language, which distinguishes *El señor Presidente*, also gives *Men of Maize* much of its originality. The narrator (as well as the Indian characters) gives the impression that his speech, both the syntax of individual sentences and the overall organization of his discourse, is being influenced by an Indian language with which he is more comfortable. Yet the apparently indigenous patterning of the novel's Spanish is an effect that Asturias has generated through imaginative literary mimicry. The lyrical prose of the narrator by no means displays a linguistically accurate adaptation of features of any particular Indian language.

The characteristic of *Men of Maize* that brings it closest to Native American discourse is the way that the novel is organized along the lines of indigenous myth. When compared with, for example, *El señor Presidente*, *Men of Maize* does not appear to have a unitary plotline or to exhibit any clear progression from one set of events to the next. The focus of the narrative shifts unexpectedly and the previous characters seem to be somewhat abandoned in the last events, concerned with the renegade mailman turned coyote. Nancy Gray Díaz has proposed an analysis of *Men of Maize* that would account both for this apparent discontinuity and for another much-noted feature of the novel, its debt to the *Popul-Vuh*. Her analysis shows that *Men of Maize* has a narrative logic to it. The case she makes for the novel's overall organization has as its point of departure correlations between Asturias's novel and the *Popol-Vuh*. Her argument may be too strongly stated, since many readers have found *Men of Maize* satisfyingly intelligible in itself, without considering parallelisms to the Maya-Quiché sacred book.[34] Yet Díaz is right to point out that the narrative of *Men of Maize* does not follow the linear progression generally held to be the contemporary standard mode of Western storytelling; its discourse is organized according to different principles.

The other figure often pointed out retrospectively as an early practitioner of magical realism is the Cuban Alejo Carpentier (1904–1980). Carpentier, like Asturias, was an enthusiastic student of a New World culture that stood distinctly apart from European tradition, and he freely adapted items from this repertory in the creation of his novels and stories. In Carpentier's case, the cultural development thus brought into focus consisted of the heterogeneous African-American variants that flourished in the Spanish- and French-speaking Caribbean.

Carpentier had an investigative and theoretical turn of mind as well as a creative one; he was a musicologist and a cultural journalist and essayist. The issue that most engaged his scholarly curiosity was the unique quality which he perceived as inherent in all aspects of Latin American reality and which he characterized as fundamentally baroque, at times calling it surrealistic. In his vision, this attribute is already present in such naturally occurring phenomena as tropical rain forests, with their luxuriantly complex life forms; however, it comes into focus as the object of analysis in its cultural and artistic manifestations. Carpentier acquired a great deal of information about such forms as Caribbean music, treated in his 1946 *La música en Cuba*, and the architecture of Havana, the theme of his *La ciudad de las columnas* (The city of the pillars; appeared as a discrete book 1970). He displayed his expertise in essays, often as support for his theory of a Latin American expression, and in his novels, which generate a wealth of significance through informed and well-chosen cultural allusions.

In his discussion of literature Carpentier devised a term and concept that has competed with *magical realism* to describe the co-occurrence in Latin American literature of realism and (broadly speaking) the fantastic. His notion of the *marvelous real* rests on the assumption that Latin American writing stands out from other literatures, particularly European ones, because Latin American writers have as their raw material a reality that is innately marvelous. Carpentier also characterized the special quality he perceived in Latin America as *baroque* and *surrealistic*, but using these terms in a way in which they could not be employed in the discussion of European literature. While European writers strove to manufacture features of the baroque and surreal by means of literary invention and technique, Latin American authors had only to reproduce faithfully the astonishing exuberance of their home continent or islands. This argument is in tune with the contemporary search for traits and properties occurring exclusively in Latin America.

From Carpentier's statements it is clear that he found his own concept stimulating in the composition of his 1949 novel *El reino de este mundo* (*The Kingdom of This World*) and several of the short stories he wrote and published during the 1940s, collected in 1958 as *Guerra del tiempo* (*War of Time*). (Carpentier's 1933 *Ecue-Yamba-O* is, of his novels, the least successful in giving a worthy literary form to his vision of African-Cuban culture; though students of his writing have examined it, the author tried to disavow this early effort.) Of Carpentier's oeuvre, the fiction of the 1940s most stands out for the fantastic and magic strain that runs through its recreation of Caribbean social history.

The Kingdom of This World has as its basis a series of events taking place in what is today Haiti, with passages set in Santiago de Cuba and (briefly) Rome, in the latter half of the eighteenth century and the early 1800s. The time period appears to have particularly drawn Carpentier's imagination, as he set other contemporary fiction works in this same era. The first two sections are dominated by two slave uprisings, followed by an inefficacious Napoleonic invasion meant to quell the disturbances. When the third part begins, it is already the postcolonial period, and slavery as such has been abolished. This section opens during the curious reign of Henri Christophe, in which Haitians gain a leader and an elite of African descent, only to find a despot who sets about reproducing, down to its most superficial details, the wasteful, sumptuous irresponsibility of the prerevolutionary French aristocracy. The black-dominated regime is followed by one in which mulattos occupy posts of power. The mulatto government fills the gap left in the economy by abolition, instituting a system of forced labor. As does Christophe's rule, the government of mulattos shows liberation to be a more difficult achievement than leaders of uprisings tend to assume. While a good deal of the novel centers on issues of ethnic groups in the social hierarchy, by its end *The Kingdom of This World* poses hard questions about the prospects for human progress generally.

Although the voice is that of an educated-sounding third-person narrator, in most portions of the novel this narrator conveys the outlook of Ti Noel. Ti Noel is a physically and mentally robust character who has fathered more children than he can remember and lived through perhaps eight decades of turbulent changes. He manages to be on hand for a number of key historical moments, though he is more a witness to and occasional participant in history than a leading actor. Despite being born in slavery, Ti Noel has absorbed a good deal of African oral history and myth from his mentor, a charismatic abolitionist warrior who instills in his followers an Afrocentric vision of history. Ancient stories of gods, kings, and wars shape Ti Noel's understanding of the contemporary history he witnesses and interprets. He offers a grassroots participant's perspective on historical occurrences and can enunciate the mythic outlook of the African-Haitians, sharpened by his own exceptionally powerful imagination. In his old age, Ti Noel goes through a period of self-transformation, assuming the forms of a bird, a stallion, a wasp, an ant, and a goose; while he eventually abjures this form-changing, his prowess at the magic art shows the power he draws from the African myth and magic in his consciousness.

Carpentier had been part of a widespread intellectual movement toward a greater appreciation of the African element in Cuban culture. A number of contrasts in the novel suggest that African-Cuban life has a vigor lacking in Europe and its derivates. Such an implication furthers the contemporary view of European civilization as in decay. African-derived religion, rituals, and healing practices are a vivifying force capable of rousing spirits and creating bonds of community. A common faith fortifies and unites the slaves in their uprisings. Even a Bonaparte princess becomes a devotee of African-Caribbean medicinal magic. The energetic, resilient Ti Noel, with his powers of literal and imaginative fecundity, emblemizes the vitality of African-Caribbean culture. The novel sets him in contrast to less hearty European males, beginning with the opening passages in which he makes his French master look effete by comparison.

The author's own prologue to his novel, a reworked version of which appeared among his essays in *Tientos y diferencias* (Gropings and differences of opinion, 1964), has become a much-cited manifesto in favor of the concept of the marvelous real.[35] In it, he comes close to disclaiming responsibility for the magical and astonishing qualities of his novel, which he attributes to Latin American historical realities already marvelous without the benefit of artistic elaboration. This sets him and others like him in a category apart from, particularly, surrealists (Carpentier knew this movement from his time in Paris), who resort to artifice to devise an effect of the marvelous with no basis in the real world.

González Echevarría observes that Carpentier relies on Caribbean history to provide the raw material of his novel, but on his own imagination to elaborate this subject matter in a significant way. The historical sequence of events requires selection and reorganization. This circumstance disproves Carpentier's contention that the marvelous element in his writing, as in much Latin American literature, arises unmediated from historically produced realities of the region. González Echevarría raises the question: "In other words, what Carpentier claims is perfectly consistent with the rest of his theory—the marvelous that emerges spontaneously from American historical reality is ciphered onto his text. But who establishes the links between events, who selects?"[36] Here González Echevarría has touched on the flaw in the notion of a marvelous real—a flaw, at least, if one expects logical consistency from the concept. Whether or not Latin American reality possesses a special quality, any significant marvelous element in literature is brought into being through textual organization, not through faithful copying of real-world phenomena. Though discounting Carpentier's claims about the marvelous real for their truth value, González Echevarría sees in them another type of worth: "Carpentier's prologue may lose the assertive status that it claims and assume a more strategic position within his writing."[37] The faultily constructed concept is useful in motivating and driving forward the development of Carpentier's literary innovation. Readers and writers other than Carpentier have also taken inspiration from the term and concept, which provide a sense that Latin America enjoys qualities found nowhere else and that its inhabitants benefit from a special perspective denied to Europeans.

One of the most notable novels to emerge from 1920s avant-gardism did not appear in print until 1948. This work is *Adán Buenosayres* by the Argentine Leopoldo Marechal (1900–1979). While most avant-garde novels are brief and strung together in a loose and casual way, *Adán Buenosayres* is a massive work of over six hundred pages, and the elaborate system governing its construction is one of its most prominent features. While hardly an obscure work, it has earned more appreciation from critics and writers than from the wider public. It is a novel with characteristics of the epic and the allegory. Virtually inviting interpretation, it gives clues to its possible significance through elements borrowed from Homer, the Bible, and the *Divina Commedia*, to name only the most prominent sources.

The text, which follows an intricate organization scheme, is subdivided into seven books. In the first five a third-person narrator relates three days, sometime during the 1920s, in the since-concluded life of the schoolteacher and poet Adán Buenosayres. The sixth, "The Notebook with Blue Covers," is Adán's spiritual diary; this segment has particularly attracted critical discussion. In the seventh book, the protagonist tells of his descent into a city that is both a modern version of Dante's hell and the megalopolis Buenos Aires, identifiable by very concrete and specific landmarks and inhabited by the characteristically diverse population of that city.

Adán is in some senses a metaphor; he can be seen as a figure of man at the outset of life, or a representative of the human quest, and he incarnates the Argentine, the man of Buenos Aires, or the city itself figured in human form. But even though he stands for these composite entities and abstractions, Adán manifests a number of decidedly realistic characteristics. In many other regards as well, the novel moves back and forth between verisimilitude and a more stylized, abstract mode of representation. Certain of the characters have names that are symbolic or cultural allusions, like Circe and Polyphemus, while others bear names that might easily occur in 1920s Buenos Aires; the duality is present in the events and settings that appear in the novel. Adán's beloved becomes doubled into two alternative versions. The novel alternates between two variants of Adán's girlfriend Solveig Amundsen, "the earthly Solveig" and "the celestial Solveig." Created by Adán out of frustration with his beloved's imperfections and trivialities, the latter is a Beatrice-like figure of perfect beauty and spiritual orientation, yet she retains traces of her more prosaic original.

While many Spanish American novels offhandedly commingle lifelike realism and the nonmimetic, *Adán Buenosayres* runs to an extreme in fluctuating between an exact, street-smart recreation of Buenos Aires and a soaringly symbolic mode. The language of narration, accordingly, brings together local colloquialisms with meditations expressed in a much more elevated register devoid of regional markings. The novel develops philosophical concerns, neo-Platonic and Christian, that Marechal considered of the greatest significance. Yet the weight of its subject matter does not preclude an irreverent treatment; of features that identify *Adán Buenosayres* with its country of origin, its distinctively mocking style of humor is one of the most instantly recognizably Argentine traits.

Students of the avant-garde period are particularly fascinated by those portions of *Adán Buenosayres* that satirize the Argentine *ultraísta* movement. Adán falls in with the avant-garde, several of whose best-known members appear caricatured in the novel, and accompanies the group on an expedition to find the prehistoric essence of Buenos Aires. The search is judged to have been a fulfilling one when the avant-gardists satisfy themselves that the remains of a horse are eloquent witness to a primeval Buenos Aires underlying the modern city.

The year 1948 is also the date of publication of *El túnel* (first translated into English as *The Outsider* and then, more literally, as *The Tunnel*), a short novel by Ernesto Sábato. Sábato had been winning attention during the 1940s with his brooding, introspective essays. His writing was based in part on his unusual personal experience. As he frequently explained, he had thrown himself into activism before suddenly and traumatically losing faith in Marxism. He then transferred his devotion to science, becoming a promising young nuclear physicist, but the erosion of his confidence in scientific thought led him to abandon a postdoctoral fellowship at the Curie Institute. As well as citing the authority of his experience, he drew upon his wide readings to discourage readers from trusting reasoning and science and from perceiving human beings as essentially rational. In his vision, reliance on logic and rationally argued doctrines had led Western culture into its present condition, characterized by anomie, poor communication, and violence on a massive scale. As part of his effort to cultivate an unashamedly irrational expression, he had published chapters of a surrealist novel, *La fuente muda* (The mute fountain), before turning to the more straightforward narrative of *The Tunnel*.

Coinciding with the contemporary fascination with existential themes and alienated protagonists, *The Tunnel* claimed a good deal of attention; it is the clearest single example of existential fiction in Latin America. Over the years, it has also attracted critics with a psychological outlook on literature. The novel presents itself as a confessed murderer's account of the events that led to his crime, which he considers a defensible and even rational outcome of the story he tells. Consequently, the reader has access only to what transpired as it is filtered through the consciousness and words of a narrator determined that the story support his outlook and justify his actions. The protagonist, a well-recognized painter, has gone through life convinced that he lives in extreme isolation from other human beings. He suddenly meets a woman who, by appearing to see an aspect that only he has seen in his work, offers temporary relief from the oppressive certainty of his solitude. He enters into an adulterous affair with her, but when the relationship fails to fulfill the promise of empathy that drew the painter into it, he kills the woman.

The Tunnel earned admiration for its intense and involving recreation of a mind governed by powerful, disturbing beliefs that the narrator vigorously defends with his logical faculties. This ceaselessly reasoning individual has no sooner begun to experience an exceptional feeling of closeness to the woman than he destroys his enjoyment by imagining scenarios of betrayal and rejection. While in some passages his reasoning seems relatively sound, at other moments his outlook is decidedly abnormal, as when he expresses outraged revulsion toward the blind. Even though the novel is told from the perspective of the obsessed lover, who is convinced that he knows the woman well, it is obvious that he has very little verifiable information concerning her and that most of the ideas he harbors about her are his own conjectures. The lack of clearly established facts strengthens the novel's effect of offering a glimpse into a maelstrom of obsession, suspicion, and jealous anxiety.

By the end of the 1940s, many characteristics of avant-gardism, which had begun as a movement apart from the literary mainstream, had gained a more central and visible role. Even the novel of social protest had made a place for elements derived from surrealism (in the case of *Men of Maize*), although there was by no means universal approval for the move away from straightforward realism in socially conscious narrative.

The spread of avant-garde, fantastic, or at least highly imaginative features into what would otherwise have been realistic writing produced highly original results. Early practitioners of such a mixed mode include Bombal, Asturias, Carpentier, and Borges. This fusion is the characteristic of Spanish American narrative that wins greatest admiration as, in coming years, an international audience comes to this literature.

Four # REALISM AND BEYOND, 1930–1960

Realism—verisimilar realism that seeks to represent social and individual realities with a relatively low component of artistic distortion—has been steadily present throughout the history of Spanish American literature. Looking only at those twentieth-century Spanish American writers who have won the largest international readerships in translation, it is easy to perceive fantastic, magical, and mythical elements as occupying a more dominant place than they do in this literature as a whole. There is no doubt that fantastic literature and magical realism in its many variants are the sector of Spanish American literature that has most fascinated foreign readers. In addition, critical studies of Spanish American fiction tend to be more abundant in the case of highly imaginative, stylized works than when strictly realist writing is involved. This critical skew away from unalloyed realism becomes more pronounced as the century progresses, and there is a growing belief among critics of Spanish American literature that purely realistic strategies of presentation have lost their efficacy. At the same time, the definition of what constitutes realism is growing more flexible and inclusive. By 1960, a revised concept was emerging that allows greater latitude for stylized representation and formal experimentation in fiction that is nonetheless regarded as predominantly realistic.

Nonetheless, unabashedly realist writers have produced texts of considerable impact, some of which are also successful as literary art. Beyond affecting the way that certain types of subject matter were dealt with in literature, the most prominent realist writers succeeded in influencing the general climate of social thought. Particularly in the case of the long-standing, intractable dilemmas facing Latin American society, discussion of these problems frequently drew on the work of creative writers as well as that of essayists and social scientists.

The impact of realistic fiction is especially evident when the subject matter is one that tormented Spanish American intellectuals of the 1930s and 1940s: the status and well-being of indigenous peoples in the modern era. During the mid-1920s, fresh attention had gone to issues of indigenous rights. The New World's native peoples were the principal focus because of new threats to their amply demonstrated capacity for physical and cultural survival. Certainly the Indians had suffered great disruptions in the way they lived, but in many cases they had remained on the same territory, or some reduced portion of it, either as communal landowners or as serfs or sharecroppers. Now economic pressures were resulting in greater commercial penetration of predominantly Indian areas and displacement of the native groups from their ancestral, or at least long-held, lands.

Indigenismo, a renewed interest in Indians and issues affecting them, swept through the intellectual and artistic world. The resurgence of indigenous matters as literary subject matter was most marked in the Andean countries, where approximately 75–85 percent of the population could be considered Indian. (A contemporary flowering of *indigenismo*, to be discussed shortly, developed in Mexico.) There was a great fascination with the idea, whose most eloquent exponent was the earlier-discussed essayist José Carlos Mariátegui, that the governance of the Inca empire had been an early form of socialism. Mariátegui argued that the current-day Andean countries had, in this system antedating the Conquest, a model of socialism well suited to the historical situation of their region. The Indian population retained down to the present day a stronger sense of collective decision making, group action, and shared ownership than did the white group. But, to make sense in its historical and cultural context, socialism in South America could not be a European import; it would need to develop as a natural outgrowth of the social pattern the Incas had established.

Mariátegui's ideas were given a more applied and practical treatment in the political party APRA (Alianza Popular Revolucionaria Americana), founded by another charismatic contemporary figure, Raúl Haya de la Torre. While it has since become a standard political party, APRA originally had a daring conceptual program, some but not all of which had been freely adapted from Marxism, and proved extremely attractive to intellectuals. Haya de la Torre, like Mariátegui, posited that the New World's indigenous peoples were predisposed to accept socialism because of their communal outlook. The pragmatic problem, though, was that Indians still immersed in their traditional culture were unprepared to initiate or join social movements of the type needed to cause change. For the latter to occur, Indians needed to be brought into contact with modern social thought and means of protest. Intellectuals now pondered how the often-isolated Indian population, justifiably distrusting of whites, might be reached, radicalized, and mobilized for social action.

Beyond the striking concepts Mariátegui had expounded, there were a number of other reasons for the renewed preoccupation with indigenous groups. Anthropology, and the social sciences generally, were on the rise. While there had always been observers collecting indigenous history, narrative, and poetry and documenting folkways, and this information had made its way into works of fiction, now it became more common for students of indigenous peoples to acquire a systematic grounding in the principled study of cultures.

Although *indigenismo*, properly speaking, centers on Indians and their cultures, the same general impulse motivated researchers and writers to examine ethnic groups of less strictly indigenous background. Populations whose ethnicity was a mixture involving some combination of European, Indian, and African ancestry also attracted both scientific study and literary treatments. Persons of mixed ethnic background were more likely than Indians to be literate, to be in contact with modern currents of social thought, and to have a strong concept of self-assertive individual action. For these reasons, leftist intellectuals often perceived them as riper for radicalization than the more insular indigenous population.

Of the many works of fiction that arose from *indigenismo*, the one that most electrified readers was the 1934 *Huasipungo* (an indigenous term for a sharecropper's plot of land; translated *The Villagers*) by Jorge Icaza (Ecuador, 1906–1978). This short text exemplifies one variant of the *indigenista* novel in its unswerving concentration on the sufferings of exploited Indians, who are first reduced to virtual serfdom and then displaced even from the undersized plots allowed them for subsistence farming. All other features of indigenous life, including any that would make Indians appear to possess a rich and appealing culture, become obscured. The narrator describes scene after scene of corruption, conniving, abuse, and suffering. While the episodes he recounts might well appear in a naturalistic novel, *Huasipungo* lacks the typically explanatory narrator of naturalism who is ready to comment on events and draw explicit conclusions. *Huasipungo*'s narrator relies largely on detailed descriptive accounts, playing up the re-

pulsive nature of matters for shock value; nonetheless, a good deal of editorializing still occurs through such means as the selection of value-laden
adjectives.

The one individualized character to emerge from the otherwise indistinct Indian masses that populate *Huasipungo* is an exemplary victim of
injustice, Andrés. When his wife must breastfeed a white child, his own
child dies. He is disabled while doing exploitative labor, under hazardous
conditions, in one of several worksite accidents that the narrator recounts
in horrifying detail. When Andrés loses his *huasipungo*, he has no means
of sustenance; when, out of desperation, he feeds his family rotten meat,
his wife dies; finally, the revolt he leads is repressed with violence.

Huasipungo is unashamedly a novel of social protest, and it is crudely
blatant in identifying the villains. The villagers are forced off their *huasi-
pungos*, the remnants of their ancient lands the white owner has agreed to
leave them in exchange for their work on what is now his land. Their
expulsion results from a deal the white title holder has struck with a foreign company seeking access to the interior in order to exploit the country's mineral wealth. The local priest is well aware of these cruel proceed-
ings, but unthinkingly acquiesces to the designs of those at the top of the
social hierarchy. In the anticlerical manner typical of social reformers,
Icaza makes the priest a caricatured figure of lechery and immoderation as
well as of capitulation.

The subordination of all other aspects of the novel to the didactic function brings *Huasipungo* close to the ideal of socialist realism encouraged by
many committed intellectuals of the era, including the widely heeded
Mariátegui. Icaza was, in fact, one of a number of Spanish American fiction writers who attempted regional variants of socialist realism, casting
the indigenous peasantry, or one of mixed ethnicity, in the role of the
proletariat. Also in line with this tendency is one of the most striking
features of *Huasipungo*, the blurring of the Indian characters (with the notable exception of the more fully characterized Andrés) into what often
approaches an undifferentiated mass entity. In the best of cases, this technique makes the Indians into a collective protagonist, relying on communal effort rather than individualistic striving. But the negative side to the
same form of depiction is the risk of dehumanizing the Indian characters.
Beyond any doubt, *Huasipungo* succeeded in drawing attention to the
plight of dispossessed Andean Indians, but subsequent generations of
readers often feel uneasy when they consider its presentation of the indigenous population. While *Huasipungo*'s treatment of white exploiters is

certainly damning, the novel's portrayal of Indian victims is, on close inspection, less than optimally respectful of the population in question, both as individual people and as members of a cultural community.

Ariel Dorfman sums up the late twentieth-century view, preferring more recent fiction in which Indian characters show their special strengths, not their vulnerability, when they band together to resist oppression, drawing force from the magical thought and myth present in their culture. *Huasipungo* and other similar works, in Dorfman's summary, "devoted themselves to documenting the violence *done to* our continent, to photographing its social dimensions, to denouncing in the public forum the brutal, inhuman conditions in which the inhabitants of these lands struggled. The emphasis is placed on *suffering*, on the social-economical-legal state that permitted such exploitation, on a nature that swallowed up man, who appears as a *passive* being who receives the blows that social and natural forces rain down upon him. The essence of America, as far as this literature was concerned, lay in suffering." [1]

In Dorfman's assessment, it is more productive for writers to provide their Indian characters with a cultural and historical basis for maintaining resistance than to show them as the tatters of a devastated culture, only able to muster desperate flurries of quickly suppressed rebellion. The downtrodden, faceless, inarticulate Indians of *Huasipungo* have little to distinguish them beyond the inhumane treatment they receive. In the course of the novel the Indians manifest no special knowledge or talents worthy of admiration. The cultural universe of indigenous peoples is scarcely glimpsed in a novel like *Huasipungo*. Though Icaza makes a vigorous attempt to ensure that the reader perceives the Indians' experience with horror and indignation, he shows no curiosity as to how the events might have appeared from the point of view of the Indian characters.

When authors return to Indian themes in later years, *Huasipungo* often figures as the old model of *indigenista* writing needing to be superseded. It becomes important to show Indians as part of a living culture and to seek ways of exploring their personal and collective lives.

Icaza's successors also sought to improve on his techniques for representing the language of Indian characters. *Huasipungo*, like many *indigenista* narratives, intersperses Quechua words here and there in the dialogue, then defines them in a brief lexicon following the ending. In subsequent decades this practice came to be regarded as a facile and mechanical convention, and writers developed alternative ways of infusing Spanish-language dialogue with certain properties and features of Quechua. In addition, the Indians in *Huasipungo* do not appear competent to express themselves linguistically, whether they are speaking among themselves or to non-Indians. Their utterances very often consist of only one word. Even when they produce more extensive statements, their words tend to refer to aspects of their situation that are already plainly observable, revealing very little of themselves. Later writers would try to correct this tendency by writing narratives that emphasize special communicative skills unique to Indians, such as the ability to produce oral narratives, songs, and poetry.

A particularly troubling feature of *Huasipungo* is the narrator's practice of characterizing Indians in a way that arouses repulsion and disgust. For example, the narrator reveals that the Indians are utilizing human urine in the preparation of medicine; the other ingredients that accompany the urine are nearly as disquieting. When the main character injures his foot, first one Indian proposes treating it with what the narrator queasily refers to as "stinking, greenish mud,"[2] then another applies "filthy cobwebs."[3] After the wound becomes infested with parasites, the narrator describes the affected site in detail, then gives an account of a healer's oral suctioning of the vermin and inflammation. The hero's ignorant, fumbling efforts to care for his food-poisoned wife are also narrated in a manner almost certain to inspire revulsion. No one can doubt that such details strengthen the novel's much-noted crude, jolting power and in so doing provoke greater indignation and alarm over the Indians' situation. Yet there is also the disturbing implication that indigenous folkways are disgustingly unenlightened. Native healing arts are one of the few aspects of indigenous tradition seen in the novel, and they appear in a thoroughly negative light.

During the 1930s a vigorous realist movement arose in the coastal Ecuadorean city of Guayaquil. The writers involved were young when they made their names and tended toward a Marxist outlook. They possessed a considerable knowledge of the region's populations, in some cases producing descriptive accounts of local ethnic groups as well as literary treatments of the same subject matter. Guayaquil writers had, as their most original and distinctive subject matter, Ecuador's *montuvios*, the peasants living in areas near the coast. The *montuvios'* mixture of Indian, European, and in many cases African ancestry, their complex history in the New World, and their ways of dealing with their tropical habitat gave them unique ethnic and cultural traits. Guayaquil authors took an interest in isolated, local units smaller than ethnicities, living hidden away in the least populated areas of Ecuador.

The Guayaquil group includes one author whose work has had success in translation, Demetrio Aguilera Malta (1909–1981), and two writers known throughout the Spanish-speaking world, José de la Cuadra (1902–1941) and Alfredo Pareja Diezcanseco (1908), while Enrique Gil Gilbert (1912–1973) and Joaquín Gallegos Lara (1909–1947) enjoy nationwide fame in Ecuador. The group was identified about equally with a mode of writing in which a fictional narrative also served to present a descriptive ethnographic account of a given population and with the literature of social protest. The Guayaquil writers' work caught the public's eye when it appeared showcased in the famous short story collection of 1930, *Los que se van* (Those who go away), featuring texts by Aguilera Malta, Gallegos Lara, and Gil Gilbert. Characteristically, the subtitle of this volume announced it as "Tales of *cholos* and of the *montuvio*," alluding to the sectors of the Ecuadorian population that the young authors had claimed as the raw material of their stories. (*Cholos* refers to a population that is only partly of Indian descent, and usually designates an Indian-European mixture.) The collection caused a stir, not only for its successful working of a little-treated subject matter, but also for what struck many contemporary readers as excessive crudity and violence and the freely expressed sexuality of the characters. While the Guayaquil group first presented itself as a strictly realistic movement, as its members developed their literary programs their realism frequently became commingled with an unmistakably mythic strain.

De la Cuadra's short novel of 1934, *Los Sangurimas* (The Sangurimas), violent, terse, and dynamically paced, is one of the strongest works to emerge from the Guayaquil group. It bears the name of the family upon whom it focuses; the name looks as if it is formed from *sangre* (blood) and might well be a variant form of "bloody" or "bloodthirsty." The Sangurimas, taking advantage of the remote, near-wilderness qualities of the sparsely populated region they inhabit, isolate themselves from their fellow human beings, forming a unit that resembles a clan as much as it does a family in the modern sense. The Sangurimas exhibit no awareness of being under the authority of any type of government. Instead, their insular little society is ruled by a patriarch who cultivates and rewards those of his descendants who most clearly display the violent, ruthless behavior he most values. Though they deal almost exclusively with one another, the Sangurimas are not a united group; factional strife comes to obsess the family's members, and they devote their time and energy to carrying out vendettas. Finally, with an excessive act of vengeance including incest, rape, and murder, the Sangurimas provoke such a sense of outrage that the police, who have hitherto tended to treat the family's domain as an autonomous fiefdom, intervene. As a result of overstepping even the ample bounds of behavior accepted in the rough region, the Sangurimas bring themselves down, and the patriarch finds the era of his dominance at an end.

De la Cuadra's work shows more complexity, both in its concepts and its novelistic art, than one might usually expect from socially committed writing. In a well-displayed paradox, the elder Sangurima represents the type of authority most injurious to society, yet the novel assigns him a positive esthetic value. Through juxtaposition and association, this patriarch is likened to such beautiful natural forces as a powerful river coursing through the region he dominates. *Los Sangurimas* frequently makes the melancholy point that things beautiful in their wildness and unchanneled power can be destructive and harmful, and may deserve to be suppressed by the more banal and tedious forces of social order. The mythic dimension of the author's writing tended to be obscured by the contemporary perception of the Guayaquil writers as crude realists given to portraying raw violence. More recent students of De la Cuadra's fiction, such as Humberto Robles, have drawn scholarly attention to the current of mythic thought this author worked through his texts.[4]

Los Sangurimas fulfills the Guayaquil program by providing a gripping narrative and vivid description while unobtrusively supplying the reader with a substantial amount of information about the population group to which the characters belong. However, it is less a work of social criticism and more a work of art than is much writing by Guayaquil writers. It is worth considering that De la Cuadra, three years after presenting his favored raw material in the highly artful novelistic form of *Los Sangurimas*, published *El montuvio ecuatoriano* (The Ecuadorian *montuvio*). The latter is an unadornedly informative and sociological study of the same theme— Ecuador's ethnically mixed people concentrated near the coast—that he had earlier treated with an all but lurid creative imagination.

Aguilera Malta, who also became a repository of information about Ecuador's special ethnic and regional populations, first stood out as an individual talent with the publication of his novel of 1933, *Don Goyo* (identically entitled in English), named after the ancient, wise, and lusty leader who is its hero. *Don Goyo* enjoys the advantage of showing a human group unfamiliar to most readers and one that Aguilera Malta specialized in depicting: the inhabitants of the islands of the Guayas Archipelago near Guayaquil, with their extensive mangrove swamps.

Despite a mysterious early appearance, the title character emerges only halfway through *Don Goyo*. The first sections follow a younger, unformed character as his wanderings take him away from the mountains and through a panorama of life in the humid, low-lying areas of Ecuador. In accord with the Marxist literary ideal of focusing on workers and labor, the novel highlights this character's experiences in the workplace. He is subjected to one form of exploitation after another until he loses his health. Don Goyo then comes into his life and adopts him as a member of the older man's personal workforce. The men under Don Goyo's patriarchal leadership are by tradition fishermen; however, in an attempt to keep pace with the changing economy, they have recently taken up the practice of cutting wood in the mangrove swamps where they fish.

Though he appears in a novel full of realistic detail, Don Goyo is a larger-than-life character. The narrator presents him as a case of exceptional vigor: "Don Goyo Quimi—the forebear of those people—must have been some one hundred forty or fifty years old, as he himself said. His children and grandchildren looked liked brothers of his . . . He handled the fishing net like any of his great-grandchildren." [5] Neighbors attest to Don Goyo's tireless sexual activity; the new wife he acquires in his last years produces yet further proof of his fertility. Besides being the most skillful and knowing of fishermen, he is an expert in folk healing, here seen as superior to Western medicine, and serves as a storehouse for the oral traditions of the locality.

The ability to establish communication and to unite oneself with nature is one of the traditions Don Goyo most cultivates. He knows sharks well enough that he has nothing to fear from them. The oldest of the mangrove trees appears to be Don Goyo's counterpart in the vegetable world. In a half-dreamed episode, the tree convinces Don Goyo that the cutting of mangrove is a greedy white man's ploy to exploit and despoil nature, after which the leader forbids his men to harvest this wood.

By the sheer strength of his personality and knowledge, Don Goyo has become the head man among a little group of fishermen and mangrove cutters. Although he has too little exposure to the wider world to become a labor leader or agitator in the usual sense, Don Goyo nonetheless assumes an informal, folk-level equivalent of this role. He is sharply aware of white outsiders' desire to turn to financial profit the natural world with which the coast dwellers, with their semi-indigenous background, enjoy cooperative relations of long standing. To honor these relations, Don Goyo is determined that he and his men not contribute to this unacceptable exploitation. Those who rally around the iron-principled Don Goyo manage to achieve, despite their poverty, a certain autonomy in the conditions of their work.

Guayaquil-style realism edges over into a mythic mode following Don Goyo's death. In the form of a shadow, he continues to make himself present among the islanders whom he organized and led during his lifetime. Aguilera Malta's concern with legendary figures and with magic thought grew increasingly prominent in his later writing, which included a good deal of work in theater and film as well as the fiction in which he had first made his name. In this respect he resembles a number of 1930s practitioners of realist fiction who remained basically faithful to this mode while bringing the mythic dimension of their writing increasingly to the fore.

Spanish American writers continued to seek solutions to the extreme difficulty of representing Indian characters with a reasonable degree of justice. Ciro Alegría of Peru, with his novels of Indian and *cholo* life, made significant progress toward showing indigenous and semi-indigenous characters both as members of a culture and as complete persons in their own right, reacting to and moving along the events of the plot. Alegría was one of the most prominent intellectuals involved in the APRA party, and it is frequently noted that his novels illustrate the ideas propagated by Haya de la Torre and his followers. He was particularly concerned with displaying to best advantage the communal and collective tendencies that had been retained through the generations by the descendants of the Incas.

This writer's first two novels, *La serpiente de oro* (*The Golden Serpent*, 1935) and *Los perros hambrientos* (*The Hungry Dogs*, 1938), are set in remote areas of northern Peru. The author's ability to turn to best literary advantage his longtime familiarity with little-known northern regions is part of what makes his novels stand out among *indigenista* texts.

The first of these novels shows a group of *cholos* resourcefully making their living in the valley of the Marañón River. *The Golden Serpent* particularly impresses itself on the memory by means of scenes in which the characters, though pitted against the great powers of nature, most of all the river itself, draw upon their quick wits and tenacity to win well-deserved victory. Here is one such scene, in the widely distributed English version that Harriet de Onís first published in 1943:

> *When Roge was swallowed up by the river, Arturo fell over senseless on the raft. His last thought was to thrust his hands in the cracks between the poles of the raft. How long was he there, hours, days? Who can*

*say? He felt a bump and the raft sort of straightened
out, and inside his breast he heard a voice that was like
his own say to him: "Save yourself." He managed to
sit up, drawing strength from he knew not where and
saw that the river had risen. The water came by very
black, so he took hold of his paddle, throwing himself on
the mercy of the Virgin . . . The water roared like a
maddened herd of cattle. The raft rushed past sharp
rock points on one side and the other. Here was a
whirlpool, there an outjutting rock in the middle of an
eddy. Now they were rounding the curve with its pro-
jecting outcropping of stones. He tried to steer toward
the other side, but a boatman is a poor thing at best,
and besides there was no strength left in him. So the
raft went headlong into the cliff. Would the jolt tear
it apart? "Virgin of help, beautiful patroness," and he
commended his soul into her hands. He raised his paddle
toward the cliff to break the force of the blow. The impact almost knocked him off into the water, but it tempered the blow to the raft and it only came apart a
little.[6]*

After the hero of this struggle has endured other trials, including the
seemingly insuperable one of being caught in a whirlpool, his persistence
suddenly earns him safety:

*Raft, good stout raft! Now they were to one side again.
And once more they began spinning around. "Here's
where I am going to die," said Arturo. Until, finally,
as the raft made a broad turn, a huge, black log came
along. It passed to one side but he managed to reach it
with the paddle and steady himself against it. He held
on hard, hard. There was a moment of doubt in which
it seemed as though the log were going to follow them
into the whirlpool, but the current straightened it out
full length and it started downstream dragging them
after it. Now they were free. As the river comes out of
the narrows it spreads out to its two broad banks, and
he let go the log. The sight of the banks was like life*

*itself. Stroke by stroke . . . He must save himself. But
the raft kept on down the middle without respond-
ing to his feeble strokes. Until he saw the valley of
Calemar . . . His valley . . . And then he began to
cry out.*[7]

In the second work the principal focus is upon Indians in the sierra.
The characters here are more neighboring sharecroppers than members of
an intact community, but nonetheless they maintain bonds of solidarity
with one another. They are not always successful in coping with their
circumstances, including the devastating drought that provides the novel
with its plotline, but exhibit an admirable perseverance. The groups Alegría shows in both novels are notable for the degree to which they have
maintained a core of tradition centuries after the Spanish Conquest and
despite a number of inevitable changes in their way of living. The traditions that Alegría most emphasizes reveal a sense of collectivity and communality; this feature particularly concerned the author, given his socio-
political vision.

Alegría's fiction exhibits an effort to display Indian culture as fascinatingly complex, in contrast with those narratives in which the indigenous
characters appear as the last tatters of an unraveled cultural fabric. At the
same time, this author's texts work to present the Indian or *cholo* experience from an insider's vantage point; yet this latter task proves fraught
with problems. In *The Golden Serpent* Alegría attempts what might seem
an obvious remedy to the external treatment of indigenous and *cholo* characters: the narrator is a member of the community, but was not born into
it and so understands what must be explained as he speaks to an outsider.
Yet this solution brings its own problems. James Higgins summarizes the
difficulty in making the narrator speak from inside the Indian community:

> *Technically, the novel* [The Golden Serpent] *high-
> lights the major problem confronting the regionalist
> writer, that of communicating to the urban reader a
> reality very different from his own. . . . The narrative
> perspective is that of the* vallinos [*valley dwellers*]
> *themselves, in that we are given what purports to be
> an inside view by one of the group, who introduces the
> reader into his world as if he were a visitor from out-
> side. Unfortunately, the impression of authenticity that*

this approach achieves is offset somewhat by the incon-
gruity it leads to. Not only does the narrator recount
events he could not possibly have witnessed, but, more
importantly, the demands of comprehensibility oblige
him to narrate in a literary Spanish which jars with
the popular speech reproduced in the dialogues. Ulti-
mately, what the novel reveals, therefore, is the impos-
sibility of achieving an authentic inner expression of
one culture in a literature aimed at a public belonging
to another.[8]

In his subsequently published novels, Alegría abandoned this particular experiment, returning to the standard mode for *indigenista* fiction: an
omniscient third-person narrator whose register of speech is much more
formal and elevated than that of the characters. It should be noted that,
so far as the texts indicate, the Indian characters in Alegría's novels utilize
Spanish as their medium of communication. The use of Spanish is plausible given the regions and populations that Alegría depicts. At the same
time, it exempts him from having to seek solutions to the problem, with
which many *indigenista* writers struggled, of finding a convincing strategy
for representing Quechua speech in a work of fiction written in Spanish.

Alegría continued to develop strategies for conveying some of the properties of local, grassroots expression. Perhaps foremost among these is his
practice of placing within each of his novels a number of folk narratives,
sometimes in the voice of a central narrator and sometimes told by one of
the characters. One of Alegría's most evident talents is a gift for recreating
oral narratives in a written form without sacrificing their lively qualities.
The inclusion of tales, song lyrics, and other items of oral lore also provides Alegría, whose novels always emphasize the strengths of regional
ethnic cultures, with an opportunity to exhibit the richness of Andean
oral traditions.

It is with Alegría's third novel of northern Peru, *El mundo es ancho y
ajeno* (*Broad and Alien Is the World*, 1941), that he demonstrates a significantly new approach to the subject matter by bringing together his detailed recreation of rural indigenous culture with the theme of exploitation
by the dominant society. *Broad and Alien Is the World* focuses on the experiences of exploited and abused Indians, but makes every effort to do so
while recreating the Indians characters' interior landscape. It proved of
enormous interest both to readers and to other writers who had felt dis-

satisfaction with the existing range of options for depicting indigenous characters. Readers have often been struck by the fact that Alegría's novel has the same fundamental story as *Huasipungo*. Suddenly more aggressive in the drive to exploit the countryside, white-owned enterprises lay claim to traditional Indian lands and force the native population out. The Indians' situation worsens until they are pushed to the point of rebellion. The parallelism is surprising because the two novels are so disparate in their treatment of indigenous peoples.

The Indians of *Broad and Alien Is the World*, in comparison with those of *Huasipungo*, have enjoyed success in maintaining the cohesion of their traditional community, though the events of the novel eventually destroy them. At the outset of the narrative, they inhabit an intact cultural universe, which Alegría portrays in an idyllic manner. Unlike the serfs of Icaza's novel, Alegría's villagers in *Broad and Alien Is the World* are found living in a communal settlement on their original, undivided land. They have adopted many European traits, but have been flexible enough to integrate them into the distinctive system shared by, and clearly understood by, all members of the group. The backbone of this system is the communal social arrangement inherited from the days of the Incas; land is jointly held, and the *comuneros* herd their cattle together and mark them with a single brand. Although their mayor is technically an elected official with a Spanish-style city council, his interaction with members of the collective shows that he receives a treatment more befitting a respected elder or wise man. His authority derives from his good judgment and his expert knowledge, handed down through the generations, of agriculture and community governance. The group still knows how to conduct a hearing and administer punishment according to native law, although its inherited methods for dispensing justice must now compete with the state-run judicial system. In an especially strong tradition, the villagers identify themselves and their collective existence with their land; a move to another area initially seems inconceivable.

In the opening passages, the mayor's wife has just died. The successful performance of mourning and funerary customs, efficacious in comforting the survivors, shows to best advantage the community's well-functioning cultural system. Shortly after this reassuring episode, though, the Indians encounter a threat to and a violation of the community lands that they have managed to maintain through the years.

The events that deprive the indigenous community of its holdings unfold at the rate at which the Indians perceive them. The narrator is usually scrupulous not to give out more information than has yet become accessible to the indigenous characters. While the story is seen primarily through the perceptions and thoughts of a central character—first the wise old mayor, then the adopted son who succeeds him as community leader—the narrator also reveals the thoughts of other members of the group, providing a collective portrait. Readers follow the Indian *comuna* through a painful, disillusioning process of learning. The indigenous collective first hears of its impending displacement when it receives a seemingly irrational order to leave its long-held lands. The villagers at first make a straightforward effort to resolve matters by setting forth the basis of their claim to the village. They consult a lawyer, who plies them with glib assurances, and the mayor testifies earnestly and lengthily in court. Only gradually do they grasp the principle that the judicial, police, and ecclesiastical authorities will always favor wealthy, influential, unscrupulous whites seeking to develop land over Indians plainly stating their traditional claims to the same territory.

The first part of the novel deals with Indians still fully part of a traditional, communal life. It ends with an unplanned, disorderly rebellion, the imprisonment of the mayor, and his death. The novel shows the failure of the impromptu revolt as inevitable, given the insular life the Indians have led. The novel represents, and to some degree idealizes, the indigenous characters, who appear faithful to powerful concepts of justice, propriety, and cooperation. They find it difficult to understand the hierarchical social structure of white society, in which individuals strive for supremacy and domination over others. Straightforward and sincere, they are caught off guard by the devious tactics of the white landowner. The novel's Indians are easily bewildered by bureaucracy and do not know how to organize resistance against the type of aggression that has driven them from their lands.

In the second part, the novel moves from portraying a seemingly timeless and static life to showing the effects of change. The Indian community, contrary to its own expectations, has succeeded in settling most of its members on new lands. Even so, a number have left and are floundering in their attempts to function outside the group. The community is now ready to begin developing a modern awareness of the flaws in society's structure. The focal character in this portion is the old mayor's adopted son, a worldly young man who has returned from his extensive travels to find the old communal settlement destroyed. In comparison with his stately father, dedicated to tradition and to collective thought and action, the son has absorbed a more Europeanized outlook and so exhibits greater willingness to take aggressive, individual initiative. He is literate and grasps the workings of bureaucracy. Though he understands the nuances of indigenous dress, he wears white man's clothing so as not to be at a disadvantage in his dealings with non-Indians. Alegría has made the younger figure of leadership half white and half Indian. It will be recalled that a number of leftist intellectuals viewed the *cholo* population as easier to radicalize than the more tradition-bound Indians and hence a potential spearhead of progressive ideas into the hard-to-reach indigenous population.

During this latter portion of the novel, the Indians, who have begun to adapt to new lands, face a second expulsion order. Again rebellion arises, but this time in the form of a modern movement of resistance, with the old mayor's modernized son at its head. The Indians receive a good deal of instruction in dealing with their oppressors, including a lesson from a labor leader that appears transcribed in the novel, to rather didactic effect. Nonetheless, the second rebellion is defeated and the members of the community massacred. There is a certain contradiction in the logic of the novel: the Indian community suffers less damage from its first, unthinking rebellion than from the second uprising, in which there has been a principled effort to lay the conceptual and logistical groundwork. This conflict points to an inherent limitation of realism in the fictional treatment of the indigenous population. So long as the narrative events must give the effect of being possible under real-world conditions, a successful Indian rebellion cannot appear plausible, since readers had never known Indians to have any but the most fleeting success in reclaiming their ancestral lands. The only solution to the impasse seemed to be to go beyond realism and depict Indian resistance as achieving triumph on some more abstract and mythic plane, as in the case of *Men of Maize*, discussed in the previous chapter. The concept that Indians might win subtle victories by disseminating their outlook into the dominant culture came to have a considerable fascination for writers and the reading public.

During the same years that Alegría was publishing his three novels to general acclaim, a contemporary Peruvian fiction writer began his publishing career without drawing nearly as much notice; yet, by the late 1960s, the less heralded author would become at least an equally studied and respected figure. This second Peruvian is José María Arguedas (1911–1969). Though his most significant innovations would not show up clearly until his 1958 novel *Los ríos profundos* (*Deep Rivers*), to be discussed later in this chapter, Arguedas published an early collection of stories and a novel that deserve some consideration. These are, respectively, the 1935 *Agua*

(Water) and the 1941 *Yawar Fiesta* (Blood festival; the bilingual phrase refers to an Andean festival centered on bullfighting).

Agua contains three short stories whose primary theme is the exploitation and ill treatment of Indians by whites. While this subject matter hardly constitutes a fresh contribution, *Agua* introduces a feature that would be one of the great strengths of Arguedas's later, more strikingly original fiction.

The narrator in the stories is a child who occupies an anomalous and difficult place in the cultural scene he describes. This unhappy young person, variants of whom were to recur in the author's work, has been born into a white family, but has come to feel alien in the white culture, which he perceives as cold, harsh, and characterized by an excessive rivalry and reliance on coercion. Both through circumstances and by preference, the child has acquired a speaking knowledge of Quechua and an extensive knowledge of indigenous folkways. The Indians' beliefs and ceremonies offer him some consolation, since he finds in them an involving sense of collectivity that he cannot obtain in the individualistic, atomized white culture. Nonetheless, the young man is unable to enter fully into Indian culture, and in his own mind stands out clearly as an outsider and even as an inauthentic replica of an Indian.

Yawar Fiesta centers on a controversy over the bullfighting ceremony that is the showpiece of an Andean village whose population presents a complex ethnic mixture. In a paradox that demonstrates the extreme intricacy of the village's cultural configuration, the bullfight has been so thoroughly woven into the fabric of Andean Indian ceremonial life that it is one of the quintessentially indigenous forms of expression in the area. When a ban is imposed on the festival, it polarizes opinion in a way that shows up the contradictions of cultural politics in the Andes. For example, a progressive group supports the ban in the wrong-headed belief that the festival allows the local whites to exploit the Indians.

His early writing shows Arguedas struggling with the difficulty of rendering indigenous characters' linguistic expression in Spanish. Arguedas had a native competence in Quechua, and his narratives leave no doubt that this is the language of his characters. In *Agua* and *Yawar Fiesta* he still follows the *indigenista* writers' custom of placing an occasional Quechua word in the speech of his characters and that of the narrator. In an unusual experiment, he makes certain modifications in the Spanish syntax of his narrative, following patterns that occur in Quechua. This early line of innovation is of greater interest for the idea than for the actual results, which were at times ungainly. In the later narratives on which his reputation rests, the author abandoned for the most part his system of syntactical alterations, preferring more subtle, and esthetically much more satisfactory, strategies for conveying in Spanish certain properties of Quechua.

Scholarly concern with native groups was also strong in Mexico. This country had an indigenous population larger than those of many nations. Yet groups that still retained a sharply Indian identity accounted for a relatively small portion of the national population, which was heavily *mestizo*. In addition, many believed these communities to be fragile, and even predicted their cultural extinction. The idea of making the often quite isolated pockets of Indians a major force in the nation's political life, strong as it was in Andean social thought, was difficult to sustain in Mexico. Much discussion went to the best way to preserve remaining Indian cultures, or at least a record of them. There were campaigns to help native peoples maintain themselves, their languages, and their way of life. But, partly because Indian cultures appeared doomed to disappear, anthropologists were eager to write ethnographic accounts and create museum displays that would show posterity what indigenous life had been like. Perhaps needless to say, the practice of despoiling the small, fragile Indian population of its lands and resources aroused indignation in Mexico as elsewhere; yet the activist concern with protecting Indians had to compete with the work, more characteristic of the researcher, of discovering and recording data on native populations.

The 1936 novel *El indio* (English version also entitled *El Indio*) by Gregorio López y Fuentes (1897–1966) is one of the two works most often cited as exemplifying the *indigenista* novel in Mexico, in which social criticism is commingled with descriptive passages that reveal a dispassionately ethnographic intent. The predominant plot concerns the depradations made by aggressive non-Indians upon the holdings of an indigenous community. The outsiders force the Indians to work as guides in the search for exploitable resources; they fish with dynamite, a practice forbidden to the native population; and, finally, they move to possess the Indians' ancestral lands.

The narrative of exploitation by outsiders alternates with a secondary story of conflict internal to the Indian community. This plot arises from a painful and complex case in courtship and marriage laws. A council of elders gathers and decides that a betrothed man who has become disabled must cede his claim on the bride to an able-bodied suitor who will make a better provider. While the community accepts the logic of the decision and the elders' authority, the sacrifice of humane to practical considerations generates a lasting unease as well as resentment by the disabled fiancé and his family. Soon the village believes itself to be suffering from the results of witchcraft. Since there is no indication that the injured party resorted to sorcery, and since the successive misfortunes attributed to magic are all realistically plausible occurrences, the narrative appears to be treating the belief in witchcraft as a phenomenon in social psychology.

The novel's vision of Indians as victims of injustice and objects of study was more appreciated by contemporary readers than it is likely to be by today's. Joseph Sommers, who mapped out in several studies the mid-century changes in Indian-theme novels, has characterized the fiction exemplified by *El Indio* as taking an external approach to Indian subjects, with relatively little effort to explore the subjective experience of members of indigenous groups.[9] *El Indio*'s narrator refers to Indian characters, not by their names, but by their roles in the community, as "the disabled man" or "the elder"; he frequently appears to regard them as subjects in a case study in community conflict.

The decline in *El Indio*'s critical reputation since its publication derives, not simply from its external view of Indian culture, but, as important, from its author's unimaginative use of the resources available to a novelist. For example, when López y Fuentes wants to air the proposition that Mexico's Indians share a common cultural heritage that transcends tribal divisions, he introduces into the narrative a professor of ethnology who lectures in support of this point. Though *El Indio* appeared at a time when there was intense concern with producing ethnographic accounts of Indian life in Mexico, none of this new scholarship can be detected in the novel's descriptions of native folkways. *El Indio* focuses on colorful rituals of the type that might attract tourists and renders them following the well-worn conventions of *costumbrismo*, the local-color writing popularized by nineteenth century Spanish language writers.

El resplandor (1937; English version *Sunburst*) by Mauricio Magdaleno (1906–1984) is the other Mexican novel often referred to in discussions of literary *indigenismo*. *Sunburst* goes only a little farther than *El Indio* in probing the inner experience of its Indian characters, in this case, the inhabitants of an Otomí village. Yet critics, for whom *El Indio* provides little material for analysis, have found *Sunburst* more amenable to discussion as a literary work. Magdaleno typifies not only the *indigenismo* of his era but also the contemporary excitement over twentieth-century narrative experimentation. The technical innovations of such novelists as Joyce,

Faulkner, and Dos Passos had stimulated Spanish American writers to begin integrating modern narrative strategies into their own work. In Magdaleno's dual concern with the Indians' plight and with the renovation of narrative prose, he anticipates later Mexican writers who skillfully combined the making of literary statements about social conditions with the creation of artistically complex texts.

Although Magdaleno is at times a surprisingly old-fashioned novelist for 1937, making his narrator voice opinions baldly, in other cases he tries out the repertory of new techniques. In introducing the Otomí community to the reader, he forgoes linear chronology, instead shuffling together present-day narration and flashbacks from different eras of the Otomís' long history of exploitation. The prose of *Sunburst*, which calls attention to itself throughout, utilizes features pioneered in the avant-garde era: descriptions that depend on unexpected metaphors and lexical items employed in an unfamiliar way. Stream-of-consciousness writing makes an appearance in the novel, as do dream sequences that reveal the dreamer's subjective world. The point is not just to utilize new techniques, but to bring to the reader the Otomís' own vision of their situation. These and other similar elements are somewhat unevenly integrated into a writing that is in large part straightforward, didactic realism. One of Magdaleno's specialties is the evocation of his characters' experience during states of drunkenness, febrile hallucination, or mental confusion resulting from overstimulation. As well as providing an opportunity to display his experimental prose, these situations offer a rationale for the insertion of aggressively modern writing in what is fundamentally a social protest novel. For example, after a political rally in which a *mestizo* candidate bamboozles the Indian community in which he was raised, the politician and his entourage ply the entire village with free liquor. The narrator then abandons his factual manner to speak of the night of drunkenness in the startling prose of a linguistic experimentalist: "Down the main road, San Andrés de la Cal was sleeping off its drunkenness. The shadow of the diffuse light of the stars puddled itself and on the skyline a great bloody bruise was bludgeoned out, from which there emerged, slender and macabre, a last surviving moon, a dislocated crest of moon. Packs of dogs tolled a mournful weeping, answering the invective from shack to shack." [10]

Chile had a strong tradition of realistic writing; as noted, it was in Chile that the regional literature known as *criollismo* flourished. As the century progressed, realism continued to be a mainstay of

Chilean prose fiction, but both the raw material and its narrative treatment underwent significant transformations.

In Chile, as elsewhere in Spanish America and indeed worldwide, the population was moving from rural to urban areas. In the specific case of Chile, urbanization brought diverse groups into greater contact. Whereas before there had been some degree of separation between a peasantry with a more Indian background, concentrated in or near the Andes, and city dwellers whose outlook and ancestry were more European, internal migration created the now-familiar phenomenon of peasants in cities. Chile was one of the most industrialized of Spanish American nations and quickly developed a true proletariat, a matter of no small interest to authors eager to attempt the types of realist writing that had been possible only in countries with considerable industrial development. Some second-generation *criollistas* were able to remain within the tradition of Chilean realism, yet make it evolve to produce literary accounts of a more complex, urbanized, and internationalized society. Marta Brunet, discussed in Chapter 2, was such a neorealist. By now she had become an important figure on the literary scene, respected for her own work and able to wield influence through her editorship at the Zig Zag publishing house and other posts. Brunet drew into her writing a strong implicit current of gender analysis and an acute look at the class structure in an era when the white-collar class had reached unprecedented numbers and importance. At the same time, her often lyrical prose style moved her texts away from unalloyed realism and gave them a more twentieth-century texture.

Yet however flexible realism proved to be in dealing with the new thematic issues raised by social change, there was growing discontent among younger writers with the very concepts that guided realistic writing. The Chilean writer who effected the most outstanding transformation in the fictional treatment of social problems went entirely beyond realism. This figure was José Donoso (b. 1924), to be discussed in the next chapter.

In 1947 Agustín Yáñez (1904–1980) published an outstanding novel that would become a point of reference in the subsequent development of rural-theme fiction in Mexico. This work is *Al filo del agua* (*The Edge of the Storm* in Ethel Brinton's 1963 English version), whose title hints that it takes place in the years immediately preceding the Mexican Revolution and shows how that historical event came to be necessary. Its setting is a small town that has long remained out of the reach of modernizing currents. When first seen, the village is still largely in the grip of severely restrictive customs preserved from the Spanish colonial era, although their hold will loosen by the novel's end. The most generally accepted mode of thought in the town, propagated by the Catholic church, focuses on the interrelated issues of sin, particularly sexual sin, penance, suffering, and death. Individual characteristics appear, in this light, as shameful indulgences; every parishioner is expected to subsume personal traits into a collective and uniform obedience to shared standards.

The parish priest, Don Dionisio, the novel's most central character, accepts as his responsibility the maintenance of this ideology into the twentieth century. The novel shows his mission as both impossible and undeserving of success. Yet he is a sympathetic character because the ascetic, conscience-ridden priest assumes his task disinterestedly and devotes himself to it unstintingly. By the novel's close, the priest has so exhausted himself that he stands in a condition of imminent collapse in front of his fascinated parishioners, struggling to say one more of the masses that he hopes will stave off change.

The vehicle for the town's ideology is a Christianity from which the element of festivity has been, in great measure, deleted. The very church calendar that regulates communal life seems to have been skewed to support a joyless vision. Solemn, mournful, and remorse-filled church holidays receive a prominence denied celebratory ones, and penitential exercises come in for especially scrupulous observance. Lent, the prime season for guilt and repentance, is being elaborately honored as the novel opens. The narrator suggests in the "Overture" that in that village a Lenten season is virtually redundant: "The whole existence of the village is a never-ending Lent."[11]

Even under stable circumstances, the village is constantly generating conflicts and tensions, owing to the inherent impossibility of holding an entire community uniformly within norms of thought and behavior that run counter to natural human impulses. At any moment one or another of the parishioners is likely to break out of this rigid framework in an effort to establish his or her individuality or assert the drive for pleasure. Despite his earnest efforts, Don Dionisio proves unable to maintain control even over those young people whose upbringing he has personally supervised, his two nieces and the town bell-ringer. Even the ritual apparatus of the church may provide the occasion for such an escape. The bell-ringer, whose task it is to mark the routine imposed by religious duties, moves from gaining proficiency at his job to finding in it an outlet for his own original artistic expression. This deviance sets Gabriel on a path Don Dionisio regards as perdition; the young man's enrapturement with his music is one with his fascination with a pretty widow, one of the exciting outsiders to the town, and the bell-ringer is nearly destroyed by the resulting conflict with his background and his mentor.

As the novel opens, the tension intrinsic to the town has been exacerbated by influences from outside. The mass media bring reports of crimes of passion, leaving the townspeople in a suggestible state of excitement. Even more disruptive is the return of townspeople who have experienced a freer way of living, either in Mexico City or the United States, and who now expect more leeway for the expression of their sexuality and unique qualities as individuals. Together with the new demand for a more open sexuality, the town's hegemony sustains the blows of a renewed campaign for social justice.

Plot is not the most important element in *The Edge of the Storm*. The novel develops several plots, each centered on the conflict between repressively uniform tradition and the desire for individual expression, enjoyment, and justice. None of these subplots is pursued at a vigorous pace. Readers unsympathetic to Yáñez's approach have judged the novel slow-paced, and indeed it often exhibits a deliberate, ponderous quality, especially notable in the first half. The narrator at times leaves the various story lines in suspension to concentrate on evoking a mood or tone, so that lengthy segments appear in a poetic discourse without a narrative thread running through it. Interior monologues reveal the villagers' tension, torn as they are between a desire to remain faithful to the beliefs and behaviors with which they have grown up and a need to try out the possibilities of freedom they have now glimpsed. Much more central than the specifics of the plot is the novel's success in conveying the atmosphere and climate prevailing in the town, charged with repressed desires and rebellion. In the prologue, a prose-poem entitled "Overture," which has become one of the most famous passages in Mexican literature, an anonymous incantatory voice speaks of the town, not so much giving out narrative data as reeling out a long string of sensory and affective impressions. Using cadences reminiscent of liturgy, the novel, in Brinton's translation, opens:

> *Village of black-robed women.*
> *At night, at the first stir of dawn, throughout the*
> *long course of the morning, in the heat of the noonday*
> *sun, in the evening light, they may be seen—strong,*

> *radiant, colorless, long-suffering—old women, ma-*
> *trons, maidens in the bloom of youth, young girls; they*
> *may be seen on the church steps, in the deserted streets,*
> *inside the shops, and glimpsed through a few, the very*
> *few, furtively open doors.*
> *People and streets absorbed in their own thoughts.*
> *The smooth, straight walls present a blank surface,*
> *broken only by doors and windows. Doors and win-*
> *dows, set in plain stonework, and fastened with heavy*
> *beams of good seasoned timber; there is no varnish or*
> *glass and all have the appearance of having been fash-*
> *ioned by the same craftsman, primitive and exact.*
> *Time, the sun, the rain, the daily touch of hands have*
> *given a patina to the panels of the doors, to the lintels*
> *and thresholds. From these houses no sounds of voices,*
> *no laughter, no shouts, no cries escape; but above them*
> *hovers the fragrance of fine wood, burned in ovens and*
> *kitchens, wrapped like a gift from heaven in clouds of*
> *blue smoke.*[12]

The prologue, which offers readers their first look at the village, also provides a mark against which one may measure the change and progress that occur between the opening and ending of the novel. While *The Edge of the Storm* may appear slow-moving, the village has undergone a great transformation in its pages. The novel opens in 1909, the last year before the outbreak of the Mexican Revolution, and closes in November of 1910 with the Madero revolt, which signaled that the revolution was unstoppably underway. The "Overture" presents a static, timeless scene. As the novel moves along, it becomes increasingly obvious that change is coming even to this tranquil backwater, and by the end, revolutionary bands have made a sweep through the town. In the novel's early passages, it is Lent, and this season is the ritual, changeless, cyclically recurring event by which the townspeople orient themselves in time. The revolt that closes the novel is a new and unprecedented social phenomenon. It belongs to a time that is historical and progressive in nature. Joseph Sommers has observed that while the novel's treatment of time is chronologically linear, it is far from uniform throughout: "The structure of *The Edge of the Storm* converts the progression of time into a more complex phenomenon than mere lineal sequence, even though the narrative follows a defined chronological order . . . the tempo of the novel builds up—the whole of the 1910 portion being treated in one long, fast-moving, final chapter."[13]

With the 1950s decade, realism as such was in retreat. The works that most successfully treated the standard themes of realism now, more and more, took on a magical and mythical tinge, following to various degrees in the wake of Miguel Angel Asturias. The narrative of Asturias had already demonstrated that the tendency that would later be designated as magical realism could give a new impetus to the languishing Indian-theme novel. Still, Asturias's innovations left a good deal for future writers to explore. The Guatemalan author's powerful imagination frequently outstripped the precision of his information about indigenous life and culture. Ethnographic accuracy received lower priority than poetic truth. Asturias's explorations had proven successful from a literary point of view, but anthropologists were fond of pointing out areas in which the novelist had not been faithful to ethnographic fact in his depiction of Guatemalan Indians. Asturias conveyed a mythic outlook that was Indian, but not much sense of the intimate experience of the native group. There was clearly an opportunity to be seized by a writer with a vision of Indian myth as strong as that of Asturias, but with more of an insider's familiarity with the indigenous characters' world.

The missing component of ethnographic factuality, though not that of intimate, lived experience, was abundantly supplied by *Juan Pérez Jolote; biografía de un tzotzil* (translated by Lysander Kemp as *Juan the Chamula: An Ethnological Re-Creation of the Life of a Mexican Indian*), a half-documentary, half-fictionalized text by the Mexican social anthropologist Ricardo Pozas A. (b. 1910). The text first appeared in 1948 in the specialized series *Acta Antropologica* and was reissued in 1952 by the more general-interest Fondo de Cultura Económica. The topic of much discussion in its day, *Juan the Chamula* is the best-known example of the ethnographic current in indigenist writing. The 1949 *El callado dolor de los tzotziles* (The unvoiced pain of the Tzotziles), a novel consisting of rather loosely strung-together scenes, by Ramón Rubín (b. 1912), was second in importance. While Pozas's experiment was well worth undertaking, the facts-above-all tendency it represents was a dead end for Indian-theme literature. Pozas worked with native informants to produce a ghost-written autobiography by a composite man of the Tzotzil group, the descendants of the Mayas found in the highlands of Chiapas province. This figure exemplifies the problems facing the Indian, from culture shock on encountering a wider world to alcoholism. The principal complaint about the work is that it seems to reduce the Indian to a subject matter about which readers should become well informed.

More typical of the new tendency that Indian-theme writing would take is the 1957 novel *Balún Canún* (English version *The Nine Guardians*) by Rosario Castellanos (1925–1974). Castellanos had grown up in highland Chiapas, where Tzotziles and whites lived in necessarily close and inter-dependent, if uneasy and unequal, contact. As a result of her background and her involvement in outreach programs to indigenous communities, Castellanos had a detailed knowledge of Tzotzil life. But the most admired feature of *The Nine Guardians* is not its ethnographic precision, which only experts could fully appreciate, but the intimate, personal treatment it accords indigenous culture and interethnic relations. More than a composite or collective characterization, it presents individual characters. The portion of the novel narrated by a girl child is the strongest in this respect. The girl's mother shows scant concern for her daughter, undisguisedly preferring the family's male heir, while a Tzotzil nanny cares for her and reveals to her aspects of indigenous culture usually hidden from whites. As a result, when her landowning family enters into conflict with the surrounding Tzotziles, the child identifies with the Indians.

Castellanos continued to examine situations of difficult, but unavoidable, Indian-white contact in her short stories of the 1950s and 1960s and in her 1962 novel *Oficio de tinieblas* (fragment published in English as "Tenebrae Service"). She set much of her "Chiapas cycle" of fiction in the late 1930s and early 1940s. This was the time of the most vigorous campaign to implement the reforms of the Mexican Revolution and also the period when landholders dedicated their strongest efforts to blocking and evading measures for change. *Oficio de tinieblas* is unusual among Indian-theme novels in having as a protagonist an Indian woman who is portrayed as a unique, individual character. Recovering from a loss of status owing to her sterility, the woman rebuilds her importance as a charismatic oracle, attaining enough power to spark a catastrophic Indian revolt. The construction of the novel follows a plan in which the events are simultaneously developing forward temporally, as in the unidirectional Western concept, and cycling back to reiterate past happenings, as in the indigenous vision of time.

Castellanos's Chiapas fiction exhibits, in addition to the more obvious concern for indigenous life and Indian-white contact, a preoccupation with the relations between men and women. Though women are officially subordinate in the societies she depicts, her women characters often learn to take advantage of their situation by exercising covert and devious power. By the 1970s, the issue of women's role and status became predominant in Castellanos's writing. An English-language sampling of both her Chiapas fiction and her later work in a frankly feminist vein may be found in *The Rosario Castellanos Reader*, edited by Maureen Ahern and *Another Way to Be: Selected Works of Rosario Castellanos*, edited by Myralyn F. Allgood.

José María Arguedas, whose uneven, early Indian-theme novels were discussed above, finally made a breakthrough that enabled him to fill the space Asturias had left. His 1958 novel *Los ríos profundos* (*Deep Rivers*) supplied an intimate sense of knowing an indigenous culture, including a native knowledge of the language. Here Arguedas was able to make fine literary use of his bilingual, bicultural upbringing and to find a satisfactory solution to the problem of suggesting qualities of a native language while writing in Spanish.

The novel's narrator is an autobiographical, reminiscing "I" who, by the age of fourteen, has developed a painfully anomalous cultural identity. As a small boy, though not himself an Indian, he comes into contact with several indigenous communities as he accompanies his lawyer father, who works with Indians seeking legal assistance. The disruption of his family of origin and the warmth, communication, and plenitude of meaning he perceives among the Indians lead the motherless Ernesto to identify with the indigenous group. As he moves toward adulthood, though, this transfer of loyalty proves to have given him an unworkable sense of who he is.

Ernesto's dilemma becomes evident when his father places him in a clerically run boarding school. In the school, as in a microcosm of the Peru shown in *Deep Rivers*, whites, Indians, and persons of mixed background are all present, yet white values invariably receive the highest recognition. The child is disturbed by the rigidly hierarchical organization of mainstream society, which the students replicate in miniature by bullying and intimidating one another. Racism and the subjugation of the lowest members of society impinge on his awareness with unsettling impact. At the same time, a return to the indigenous world is impossible, although he continues to admire this culture and attain a degree of participation in it. As the novel progresses, the child must approach an admission that he is no Indian.

Partly because of his impossible identity, which precludes his entry into any major group in his society, the child becomes magically attuned to such natural forces and phenomena as the rivers of the title, mountains, wind, trees, and bushes. Supposedly inanimate objects may be for him eloquent with significance. One of the most intense communicative contacts he remembers occurs between himself and a stone wall. The child encounters the wall on a visit to Cuzco, where he is vividly aware of standing in the heart of the Inca empire and, indeed, in the center of the universe. It is the remnant of a palace erected by the Inca emperor Sinchi Roca. In the child's mind, the Incas still seem to govern the region. Transfixed by the wall, the child envisions the stones flowing and swarming with life and insists that every stone is speaking to him. Later, isolated in the boarding school with its domination, pettiness, cliques, and one-upmanship, the child takes a measure of consolation from escaping human society for the natural world. The passages in which the narrator nostalgically recreates the contact he experienced with the natural realm are among the most memorable and often-cited ones in the novel.

Perhaps the most-praised feature of *Deep Rivers* is its ability to convey an outlook on the world that the reader will accept as stemming from indigenous thought. Unlike the *indigenista* novel of the 1930s and 1940s, sprinkled with exotic-looking lexical items, *Deep Rivers* makes sparing use of the Quechua language. Nonetheless, the narrator's way of relating and visualizing events has a magical coloration to it that readers are quick to identify as non-Western. For example, in the boarding school a demented female servant is sexually exploited by a priest and a number of the students. While this situation is realistically plausible, Ernesto's narration of it suggests the intrusion of diabolical forces. Though victimized, the deranged servant has a sinister capacity to trouble and unhinge the boys.

The living culture currently maintained by native groups is often neglected in indigenist novels, where it may appear as a depleted reminder of formerly great civilizations. For this reason, *Deep Rivers* has been particularly valued for its detailed and sympathetic recreation of such cultural aspects of indigenous life as music, verse, handcrafts, and storytelling. While best known internationally for his fiction, Arguedas was also a professional folklore scholar specializing in orally transmitted narratives and an aficionado of Andean music and musical instruments. His ability to speak knowledgeably of Andean culture becomes one of the great strengths of *Deep Rivers*. The solitary Ernesto, alienated from life in his school, consoles himself by recalling native instruments and their sounds. An Indian top that hums as it spins, brought by a fellow student, restores some of the magic that school life has drained from Ernesto's existence. Stories he has heard among the Indians give him a consoling glimpse of a universe in which phenomena make more sense and hold more meaning than in the fragmented mainstream society.

The language in which Arguedas composed *Deep Rivers* has been admired for its ability to reflect, in subtle ways, certain features of Quechua. While there is general agreement that Arguedas's language is successful in convincing readers that there is a Quechua presence hidden in the Spanish, the exact nature of the borrowing has proven difficult to characterize specifically. Alberto Escobar, the linguist who was the architect of Peru's Spanish-Quechua bilingualization program, has turned his scholarly attention to Arguedas's expression. Escobar considers Arguedas's fiction to exemplify the nuances and complexities that can arise only in a bilingual and multicultural context such as that of Peru. In seeking to identify what is indigenous in Arguedas's works, Escobar does not limit his inquiry to purely linguistic aspects of this author's discourse. Andean social history, the linguistic situation of Peru, myth, conventions of orally transmitted narrative, and many other factors enter into the production of the heterogeneous, hybrid Arguedas text.[14]

In subsequent decades Spanish American writers working in exclusively realist prose would find themselves upstaged by colleagues more given to formal experimentation and to a freer use of novelistic invention and imagination. The realist tendency by no means disappeared from Spanish American writing, but it would no longer enjoy the prominence it once had. Consider that in 1941, Carlos Luis Fallas (Costa Rica, 1909–1966) was able to make a great impact with his novel *Mamita Yunai* (*Ma United*, i.e., the United Fruit Company). This work, in the vein of Upton Sinclair's *The Jungle*, relied on effectively horrifying descriptions of unsafe and exploitative labor and editorializing on the part of the narrator. By the 1950s, it would have been difficult for such artless muckraking, showing little concern for narrative construction, to gain much ground except, perhaps, as a popular best-seller.

The movement away from unmodified realism shows up even in the fiction of writers generally regarded as upholding the principles of social realism. Writers dedicated to making a statement about real-world society eventually began to introduce narrative innovations that deviated significantly from the *modo standard* of Spanish American realism. The widely acclaimed Paraguayan novelist Augusto Roa Bastos (1917), winner of the Cervantes Prize, is certainly a case in point. Roa's central subject matter has been the long history of social repression in Paraguayan life, along with the resistance it has aroused. His 1960 novel *Hijo de hombre* (*Son of Man*) features the type of themes and historical raw material that have characteristically attracted realist treatment. But in its narrative design and mythic substratum, *Son of Man* is far from what would have counted as "social literature" in the 1920s. There is a complex interplay between two alternating varieties of narration. Roa shows Paraguay's history as driven not only by social forces but also by mythic ones, and is frankly lyrical in his evocation of the latter. The mythifying tendency in the novel transforms all of Paraguay into one struggling, suffering collective entity. Roa's narrative shows how eclectic and inclusive realism had become by mid-century. By the time he published his next novel, the 1974 *Yo, el Supremo* (*I, the Supreme*), on dictators, Roa would have moved beyond what could reasonably be called realism, though he continued to be the type of socially critical writer who in earlier decades would have opted for a social-realist approach.

Other examples of a diversifying realism are the charismatic Marxist intellectual José Revueltas (Mexico, 1914–1976), Mario Benedetti (Uruguay, b. 1920), best known for his short stories of white-collar life, David Viñas (b. 1929), a signal figure on the Argentine intellectual left, and Marta Lynch (Argentina, 1925–1985), noted for her ability to combine an intimate story of personal experience with observations on the political scene. The writers who were most skilled in mixing realism with myth, magic, and fantasy and in utilizing twentieth-century narrative strategies would be the ones to attract a contemporary public.

Five

THE BOOM
AND ITS
ANTECEDENTS,
1950 – 1970

U ntil the decade of the 1950s, very few Spanish American authors, however highly esteemed by readers and critics, had been able to attract an audience outside the region. In a familiar pattern, authors well respected in their home countries were unable to arouse substantial interest beyond national borders. As the 1950s began, the only Spanish American fiction writer to enjoy international renown was Eduardo Mallea. (Brazilian writers had been faring somewhat better in the English-language market, owing in part to the enthusiastic backing of Alfred A. Knopf.) Borges had already written most of the stories that would make him a creative innovator of worldwide impact, but he had yet to come in for general recognition. Asturias and Carpentier had also been producing powerfully original narrative without arousing the acclaim they would later enjoy when retrospectively hailed as practitioners of magical realism and the new novel (i.e., formally innovative Spanish American fiction of mid-century onwards). For one reason or another, Spanish American writing remained unable to claim its place among the literatures regarded as centrally important. This situation persisted despite the presence, in many U.S. publishing houses, of editors who possessed a knowledgeable appreciation of Spanish American writing and the dedication of such translators as Harriet de Onís. A number of Spanish American prose writers, such as Ciro Alegría, had been published in good English translations by well-established houses, but had never attained widespread importance. Spanish American writing was apt to be viewed as a regional literature. Such an outlook was not altogether unfair, since a great many of the works available in translation actually were, like Alegría's novels, first-rate examples of the regionalist tendency in Spanish American literature.

The 1950s in Spanish American literature were marked by the start of a new phenomenon: the appearance of works that would reach larger and farther-flung literary publics than had previously been attainable. Although these works, in great part prose fiction, began to be written and published in the 1950s, the upsurge of attention paid to Spanish American writing was not really well underway until the 1960s. With the spotlight turned on the genre of the novel, the newly increased interest affected both Spanish-language readers and those who relied on translations. Spanish American writing until only recently had been at a perennial disadvantage; it was often perceived as limited in comparison with the prestigious work of European and English-language authors. Now it acquired a special luster for many readers. Spanish American fiction became associated with imagination, innovative narrative construction, and original treatments of fictional time and space. From the 1950s onward, even before the boom, the terms *new novel* and *new narrative* began to be applied to originally structured fiction from the region. These phrases carried the exciting, if exaggerated, suggestion that fiction was being reinvented in Latin America. Such associations were reinforced by the tendency of publishing houses outside Latin America to bring out in translation those works most distinguished by their memorably fantastic touches and complex, unusual narrative design. The realism and regional descriptions earlier appreciated as a hallmark of Spanish American writing lost prestige; realist authors had less chance of achieving an international public. The flourishing sales enjoyed by a number of Spanish American publishing houses and the favorable attention reaped by certain Spanish American authors gave rise to the term *el boom* to describe these unprecedented indices of success.

One major complaint about the boom is that it focused attention too narrowly on a limited number of Spanish American writers who fit a certain profile. The authors who most benefited from the new attention were cosmopolitan in culture and often skilled in English and French, aiding their "discovery" by the most widely influential critics and the largest and wealthiest book-buying publics. In many cases, they spent considerable time living in Europe or as visiting faculty at universities in the United States. They performed well in interviews and public appearances. Most typically, they made their impact by publishing large, ambitiously sweeping novels whose construction was full of technical innovations. It was often observed, with some unease, that the primary measure of their success was the fate of their writing abroad and in translation, rather as if foreign critics and readers were necessary to validate the work of Spanish American authors.

To a certain extent, the spectacular fame of the boom authors spread, piquing interest in Spanish American writing generally. For example, Borges, who long before the boom had written the work that won him his place in literature, appears to have won a wider public during the period when Spanish American writing was internationally "hot." Rediscovered innovators from earlier eras, such as Roberto Arlt and Felisberto Hernández, were published internationally in large measure because the boom had convinced publishers that there was a market for Spanish American fiction in translation. The more diffused effect of the boom still tended to be most beneficial to writing in which experimental techniques stood out clearly and fantasy and imagination enjoyed a prominent role.

Still, literary fame is often unfairly distributed, with certain types of authors favored over others. One cannot dismiss the boom as entirely a product of publicity and marketing. More important than the sales figures are the original, influential narrative works that marked a golden age of Spanish American fiction. The "new narrative," marked by experimentation with narrative structure and the treatment of time and space, begins as early as the 1940s with Carpentier and Asturias, though many examples of structural experimentation occurred in earlier decades. The prosperous 1960s are the prime years of the boom, which, it should be remembered, is defined by unprecedented sales and publicity as well as by the characteristics of the texts that enjoyed this bonanza. In all fairness, the great novels of the boom should not be seen as a sudden new development, as they appeared to the international public, but rather as a continuation of an experimental tendency that had long been gathering force in Spanish American narrative.

The fiction of the boom represents, in a number of ways, the continuation of the avant-garde tendencies that arose in Spanish America in the 1920s. It is not at all unusual to find boom authors expressing their admiration for the 1920s wave of innovators. Julio Cortázar, for example, avowed his debts to Roberto Arlt and Jorge Luis Borges and embedded many homages to Macedonio Fernández in his writing. A number of earlier experimental writers, such as Juan Filloy, were rediscovered as a result of the new appreciation for innovatively constructed narrative that the boom had created.

The continuities between the avant-garde and the boom bring back the question of modernism, in the European and Anglophone sense, and the terminological issue discussed in the Introduction and the chapter on avant-garde tendencies. Though in Hispanic letters *modernism* is almost exclusively used to refer to the turn-of-the-century movement that originated in Spanish America, *modernism* as a general, international public understands the term is unmistakably recognizable in certain portions of Spanish American literature. The writing of the avant-garde period and that of the boom are the most evident cases.

Boom writing is *modern* in its ambitious drive to create major works of fiction whose innovative force would drive art forward into the future and secure a place in the history of narrative. It is not very surprising that an admiration for the modernist fiction of William Faulkner, each of whose most-noted works constitutes a distinct narrative experiment in the treatment of time, space, and narrative voice, was widespread among boom authors. The boom authors shared the modernist confidence that art was making unprecedented progress during the twentieth century. In their robust vision, literature, and particularly Spanish American narrative, had a future full of the promise of significant new advances. They often referred to the writing of their generation as superseding previous Spanish American narrative, moving far beyond its stodgy predecessors in style, language, and textual construction.

Yet as the boom continued and shaded into the post-boom era, the program of modernism, based on a belief that groundbreaking experiments were waiting to be realized, was becoming eroded worldwide. Writers and literary publics were losing their confidence that literature could still produce masterworks that would stand as authoritative watersheds in the history of esthetic innovation. The postboom, to be discussed in the next and final chapter, is in certain senses a manifestation of *postmodernism*, to use the term popularized by Jean-François Lyotard and developed by many subsequent discussants. At least one well-known critic of recent Spanish American narrative, Raymond Leslie Williams, has been identifying the boom generally with modernism, though he recognizes that boom authors, highly conscious of contemporary literary theory and cultural studies, also began to participate in the postmodern era. Williams associates many postboom writers and texts with postmodernism. Speaking of the prime example of the boom novel, he asserts: "For García Márquez and Latin American writing, *One Hundred Years of Solitude* represented a culmination, in 1967, of a modernist project . . . ," which rapidly lost its impetus following the boom years.[1] Any substantive consideration of *postmodernism*, which has eluded clear definition despite extensive discussion, would be well beyond the scope of the present survey. Still, the parallels between *postboom* and *postmodernism*, in the late twentieth-century sense, are important enough to deserve being briefly pointed out in the chapter on the postboom.

Since the 1930s, the Uruguayan Juan Carlos Onetti (b. 1909) had gradually been winning a small reputation as the author of somber narratives whose isolated, dispirited protagonists were perceived as embodying, in an extreme form, the existential condition of the contemporary urban individual. His emergence as a novelist was often faltering; he was slowly developing what would become his celebrated repertory of themes and narrative procedures, and he hesitated to complete and publish his work. In a pattern of loss that would plague Onetti's career, the manuscripts of two early novels were misplaced. *El pozo* (The pit) was lost; Onetti reassembled it largely from memory and published it seven years later in 1939. *Tiempo de abrazar* (A time to embrace) existed as a completed manuscript as early as 1934; it was a finalist in a competition in 1941, but then disappeared and only surfaced in complete form years later, to be published in 1974. *Tierra de nadie* (No man's land) appeared in 1941, but failed to make a wide impact at the time. Although Onetti eventually acquired an international readership, he never enjoyed the sales and fame of the boom novelists. He is generally seen as a precursor of the boom, whose innovations helped make possible the massive success of Spanish American fiction in the 1960s and 1970s.

As Onetti became a surer-footed novelist, a wider range of readers and critics began to be impressed by the originality and expertise with which he constructed his narratives. His breakthrough novel of 1950, *La vida breve* (*A Brief Life*), was his first consistently mature work and offered readers a full appreciation of what would become readily recognizable as Onetti's fictional world. *A Brief Life* develops the city of Santa María, which would appear in nearly all of Onetti's subsequent narratives. This desolate, rundown city, isolating and alienating to the human being, resembles both a more provincial version of Buenos Aires and Montevideo and a disturbing dream. Onetti presents it as a creation of his protagonist and first-person narrator Brausen, a disaffected advertising copy writer. Brausen eventually flees Buenos Aires for Santa María, and the latter city, with a fictional character as its founder, increasingly manages to supplant Buenos Aires as the setting of Onetti's novel. In a move that would become one of his trademarks, Onetti has empowered a character to bring fictional settings and other characters into existence. In the case of *A Brief Life* this secondary creation begins during Brausen's desultory efforts to become a hack screenwriter. Running possibilities through his mind in odd moments, he invents Santa María and peoples it with characters. Brausen subtly acquires the ability to insert himself into his invented landscape, and one of the inhabitants of Santa María progressively becomes a supplement to his creator's original, deficient self. At the same time, he eavesdrops and spies on the adjoining apartment, where a prostitute lives an existence whose drunken disorder fascinates the routinized, rule-bound, and cautious Brausen. Assembling his fragmentary knowledge, Brausen constructs in his mind an image of life next door. He then enters the apartment and introduces himself under a pseudonym, becoming a lover and abuser of the semidemented prostitute. In his incursions into the chaotic space of her apartment, he creates for himself another alter ego, full of a sexualized violence.

While the characters' ability to project new settings and selves gives complexity to Onetti's literary writing, the new creations do not offer regeneration to the beaten-down protagonists. No sooner has Brausen begun to imagine Santa María than the freshly created reality is contaminated by an unhappy echo of the problem—his wife's mastectomy—that is throwing its inventor's household into a drearily prolonged crisis: a woman enters a doctor's office and bares her breasts for examination. While his alter ego Arce presents an obvious contrast with Brausen—the created self is dissipated and irresponsible, while his originator is monotonously respectable—the supplementary identity does little to refresh its creator's dismal outlook. Even murder and its consequences fail to provide more than temporary stimulation. The human figures that spin out of the imaginations of Onetti's characters are as embittered, jaded, disappointed, and flattened by life as Onetti's own creations. Fantasy lives become corroded by the same tedium and meaninglessness that had made the fantasy necessary.

Nor does the shift into fiction generated within fiction fundamentally alter the linguistic style and general tenor of the novel. Onetti's third-person narrators, his protagonists, and the latter's projections are all apt to speak in the same morose, disgusted vein. (A persistent complaint about Onetti is that the speech of his narrators is not differentiated from that of his characters.) The dividing line between the original characters invented by the author and their once-removed or second-hand counterparts remains blurry and difficult to trace.

One of the most memorable aspects of Onetti's work is his representation of the urban scene. His vision is frequently realistic and even natural-

istic. Scenes set in Buenos Aires convey the grime, delapidation, and un-
manageability of a giant city, and those placed in Santa María, the forlorn
quality of a backwater town in decline from a former period of flourishing
growth. Yet commingled with this realism, the dreams and imaginings of
his perennially dissatisfied characters occupy a major place in his urban
vision. An Onetti specialty is the rendition of the urban night as an eerie
dream, with harsh, intermittent electric lights and human figures whose
proximity only highlights their mutual isolation. The protagonist wanders
through this oneiric, but also grimly realistic, landscape without becoming engaged in the surroundings. The ability to mesh realism and nightmare in a fictional city had earlier been one of Roberto Arlt's eccentric
skills; it is not surprising that Arlt was one of Onetti's earliest advocates.

Many thematic and structural features go into the making of the distinctive Onettian world. There is a persistent link between the reaching
of middle age and the loss of buoyancy and hope, qualities associated with
youth. Young people seldom make any direct appearance. The quality of
youth seems to be fading from Onetti's described world, and his characters and the shabby settings they inhabit provide an exhibition of the
signs of aging and decay. Middle-aged characters are described in cruelly
sharp detail, while younger people are not very clearly visualized. Yet the
vaguely remembered images of an earlier, fresher time persist as a remem-
brance that further embitters the characters; their insistence on situating
hope and happiness in the past implies that they have nothing to look
forward to in life. Though Onetti's characters generally have little to bring
them together, they manage to share fantasies and longing dreams. In
Tierra de nadie the characters imagine an island that one of them might
inherit, while in *A Brief Life* Brausen takes another character with him
when he escapes into his fictional city of Santa María.

Onetti's narrators and characters exhibit an uneasy relation with the
human body, of which they have an unshakable awareness. They often
express revulsion over relatively common bodily imperfections that betray
the human vulnerability to deterioration. For example, in *A Brief Life*
Brausen's thoughts return with obsessive disgust to his wife's otherwise
unremarkable mastectomy incision. Both Onetti's third-person narrators
and his narrating characters manifest a horrified fascination with such
everyday features as distended veins, protuberant abdomens, enlarged
joints, stubble, sagging flesh, dandruff, wrinkles, exudate, and residue on
skin. For all their squeamish sensitivity to the sordid and degraded aspects
of the life of the body, several of Onetti's male characters feel impelled to
participate in the lives of prostitutes and become procurers.

Critical commentary on Onetti tends to draw attention to certain features. The novelist's manner of narration has often been called cinematic, in that his texts at times rely on the juxtaposition of quick scenes, sometimes presented so briefly as to be virtually static. The manner in which fiction is seen being generated and constructed within a work of fiction has been the topic of extensive commentary, particularly Josefina Ludmer's essay "Homage to *A Brief Life*." [2] Close examination of an Onetti text reveals a complex network of symmetries and reiterations. Both Ludmer and Roberto Ferro, concentrating on *A Brief Life*, discover many intricate lexical, thematic, and structural echoes within the relatively brief novel. [3] For example, Ludmer finds the amputated breast of Brausen's wife, which he visualizes as a proffered wineglass, metaphorically replaced by the wineglasses that are forever being filled and drained in the prostitute's apartment. [4]

During the 1950s Alejo Carpentier continued to move away from the exuberant magical realism for which he had earlier been noted. Carpentier was now emerging as a novelist careful to create complex narrative designs. Driven by curiosity, Carpentier had accumulated an erudition that marked his novels. Caribbean social history and ethnomusicology were his primary concerns, but he also gathered a miscellany of expertise in such diverse areas as manufacturing processes and botany, favoring information with a specifically New World reference. Highly ornamental architecture, with its intricate vocabulary of moldings, cornices, turrets, and various other outcroppings and adornments, particularly fascinated Carpentier; he read in the often lavish decoration of Latin American architecture the signs of the baroque vision he attributed to the region. Carpentier turned his reservoirs of specialized knowledge into a novelistic resource. One of the hallmarks of his narrative is the appearance of unusually technical, erudite terms for both cultural artifacts and natural phenomena found in the Americas.

Los pasos perdidos (*The Lost Steps*), his novel of 1954, centers thematically on the complexities of cultural identity. To its hero, the world presents two fundamental options: impersonal, urbane societies and those characterized by communal organization, face-to-face interaction, and a shared body of still-living myth. These extremes are represented by New York City and a jungle community; somewhere between them lies a nameless Latin American capital in which he spends a few chaotic days. At the outset, the first-person protagonist exemplifies the Latin American intellectual perennially troubled by a sense of uprootedness. He is based in the United States; like Onetti's Brausen, he is in advertising, apparently seen as the epitome of numbing and meaningless work. Yet he nurtures the hope of making a great name for himself as a composer and musicologist, and broods over the composition that will stand as his monument. As his field, he has unreflexively chosen the presumably neutral tradition of European art music—simply *music*, as opposed to the forms marked off as belonging to *ethnomusicology*. As the hero becomes increasingly expert in maintaining an international self, he develops an irrepressible urge to seek out what is homegrown, vernacular, and distinctive to his native region. For Gustavo Pérez Firmat, the protagonist of *The Lost Steps* exemplifies the *criollista* movement, in which cosmopolitan Latin American intellectuals sought out and valued whatever most spoke of their land. The quest for connections with home begins in their absence or attenuation: "There is something profoundly *criollo* in the fate of Carpentier's protagonist, living in a North American city, forced to express himself in a native language that is not his own."[5] The hero's suppressed eagerness for a Latin American rootedness comes to the fore at the suggestion he defraud a university by selling it falsified native musical instruments. Instead, he undertakes an authentic, arduous journey into the Venezuelan jungle, where he finds the desired instruments and takes a questioning look at the culturally homeless, sophisticated self he has hitherto cultivated. Pérez Firmat sees the novel as "the closing episode in the Cuban criollist project . . . the protagonist's search for primitive instruments . . . [is] a moving emblem of criollism's search for a vernacular culture. The plot of the novel *is* the criollist adventure."[6]

The quest that gives the novel its plot at first appears to be of highly doubtful value, beyond the hero's obvious success in locating the instruments that are the purported object of his search. Roberto González Echevarría states unequivocally: "The protagonist's quest ends in failure."[7] In fact, the hero does fail in the romantically grandiose and all-embracing projects he sets for himself, partly because they have mutually exclusive goals. He hopes to become a major name in the history of music but also to disappear into a village that he sees as standing outside history. Just as he imagines himself on the verge of seamless integration into a jungle community, he must break off his stay in order to commit to paper the new musical composition with which he hopes to win the world's recognition. Writing, and through it the chance to leave a permanent mark, is the one thing he cannot sacrifice for the fullness of meaning he perceives in preliterate societies that rely on immediate, in-person, and therefore quickly lost communication. Subsequently, as if paying for his defection, he is unable to make his way back to his village and his native woman, and realizes that he has lost any chance at absorption into timelessness. The writing of his envisioned masterwork also eludes him. One could add that the hero's "return to civilization" degenerates into the ridiculous; at first hailed as a rescued captive, he is soon vilified by the irate competing women in his life and reduced to selling his story to a cheap magazine.

While the protagonist is unable to bring to reality the grand ambitions on his agenda, he inadvertently begins projects that are likely to sound more interesting to a current-day reader than the creation of a towering musical monument. These are conceptual undertakings that by their very nature resist resolution and termination. In his thought and expression, the hero is a practitioner of the very type of open-ended, questioning creative work that characterizes the innovative art of the twentieth century and of which Alejo Carpentier's *The Lost Steps* is an example. His quest provokes him to think about certain perennial problems, such as the relations between technically advanced societies, with their displaced inhabitants, and those societies where communal, local cultures remain intact. Among the results of this reflection, which is still in process at the novel's end, are the essaylike meditations that appear in *The Lost Steps*. These include a partially developed theory to explain the origin of music and several attempts to specify the difference between cosmopolitan societies and those still close to tribal organization. Even though the hero never completes his *Threnody*, he appears to have composed a thoughtful, insightful memoir, for the text of *The Lost Steps* presents itself as his own version of his troubled actions and thoughts. González Echevarría is "inclined to believe" that the text of *The Lost Steps*, while it might be construed as a travel journal or journalistic account, should be viewed as representing the novel the protagonist says he is writing.[8] However, in line with his outlook, the hero continues to grieve over the frustration of his composition and the greatness it would have brought him, and obtains little if any compensatory satisfaction from the writing of this complex, uneasy, ambivalent account. Though practicing a creative activity well attuned to the twentieth century, which favors the inconclusive, questioning, in-process text, the hero retains the belief that the only creation that matters is the masterwork that makes a single, unquestionable statement.

Carpentier took pains to construct each of his narratives according to a complex pattern, especially evident in the elaborately artificial treatment of time and space. Attentive reading uncovers intricacies whose exact nature and purpose prove fascinating questions to students of Carpentier's work. One of the most famous of these is the lost day in *The Lost Steps*. Many of the short sections within the novel have dates as their headings.

Section X bears the heading "Tuesday, the 12th" (of June). However, Section VII is headed "Saturday, the 10th." (Section VIII is "June 11" and Section IX is "Later.") To pass from "Saturday, the 10th" to "Tuesday, the 12th," one day must have dropped out of the progression of time. Despite the divergent significances that readers have attributed to the deletion, there is widespread recognition that the disappearance of the day constitutes one clue to a highly artful pattern at work in the entire novel. Not only the lost day but also the critical speculation that it has stimulated force recognition of the artifice and invention necessarily present in any work of fiction, by virtue of its fictional character. (Not only time but space has been rearranged by art, since the hero's journey does not correspond to the geography found on any real-world map.) By making the element of contrivance more salient than usual, Carpentier drives home the principle that art is not life.

The Lost Steps is not entirely representative of Carpentier's mature production, since, unlike several of his most noted works, it does not fictionally recreate events from real-world social history. Yet it exhibits many features that quickly identify a text as Carpentier's. Among these are the enthusiasm and precision with which the narrator describes not only the exact features of architectural work—one of the author's famous passions—but all manner of decor and embellishment. One of Carpentier's unusual pockets of expertise was processes of decay and putrefaction, and his narratives contain evocations of bodily deterioration that stand out both for their artistry, expressive of a luridly gothic esthetic, and for their exactitude. In *The Lost Steps*, for example, the hero records in detail his observations of a decomposing crocodile and a man in an advanced stage of leprosy.

The author's preoccupation with the baroque mode is evident in all his writing, but the term *baroque* could only quite loosely be applied to his own language and style. Carpentier does not attempt to rival in syntactic complexity the baroque texts of seventeenth-century writers, and his narrative is not particularly difficult to follow, with the obvious exception of the rare lexical items. While his language is not baroque in any very technical sense, he does favor sentences so constructed that the reader must take a moment to reexamine them and determine how their constituent elements, an accumulation of clauses and phrases, fit together. González Echevarría refers to this type of construction when he says: "This lack of center generates the baroqueness of Carpentier's style—the excessive accumulation of predicates attempting to define an ever fleeting subject."[9]

Carpentier is eager to describe already existing phenomena that exemplify his concept of the baroque, but not so quick to generate fresh occurrences of the baroque in his literary language. His fiction, like the essays in which he associates the notion of *baroque* with Latin America's expression,[10] seeks to point out to readers the marks that betray the continent's baroque nature, thus preparing them to recognize these signs on their own.

Harriet de Onís, translating *The Lost Steps*, recreates these qualities in her English version of the hero's description of the city that the novel identifies only as the Latin American Capital:

> *I looked out through the blinds again. Beyond the Governors' Palace, with its Grecian columns supporting a baroque cornice, I recognized the Second Empire façade of the theater where, for lack of more popular entertainment we had forgathered, under great crystal chandeliers, with the draped marbles of the Muses flanked by busts of Meyerbeer, Donizetti, Rossini, and Hérold. A curving stairway with rococo urns on the balustrade had led us to the red velvet salon, with golden dentils edging the balconies, where, under the lively chatter, the orchestra could be heard tuning up. Everybody seemed to know everybody else. The laughter ran along the boxes, from whose warm shadows emerged bare arms, hands putting into motion such survivals from the past century as mother-of-pearl opera glasses, lorgnettes, and feather fans. There was a kind of soft, powdered abundance to the flesh emerging from the décolletages, the uplifted bosoms, the shoulders that evoked the memory of cameos and lace corset-covers.[11]*

One of the specialties with which Spanish American writers would surprise and please an international public was the extremely short prose piece, usually ironic, often fanciful or even fantastic, and relying for its effect on a clever, insightful twist. Such terms as *microcuento* and *minicuento*, invented to designate the brief prose writing cultivated by a number of Spanish authors, cover only those pieces that have a definite narrative strand running through them. However, the exceptionally brief prose pieces for which Spanish American literature is famed also include aphoristic statements and descriptive vignettes. Among the first to make his name as a contemporary practitioner of these abbreviated forms, although he also wrote outstanding stories of more standard length, is Juan José Arreola (Mexico, b. 1918).

The now-famous neologism that Arreola created as the title for his 1952 miscellany *Confabulario* (expanded into *Confabulario total*) indicates a desire to try out new possibilities within the tradition of the fable. (The English-language volume of Arreola's work, *Confabulario and Other Inventions*, retains the same made-up word.) Indeed, Arreola draws upon such familiar conventions as animals endowed with human attitudes and the satirical illustration of failings inherent in the human character. Yet his short pieces are less simple, straightforward, and timeless than fables. His worldly, intellectual style of joking requires a reader with a good fund of knowledge and an appreciation for the ridiculous and absurd. The humor, in many cases, rests on fairly sophisticated cultural and literary allusions.

Arreola has built his success not only on his skill as a literary writer but also on his strong and markedly eccentric personality, which he has been well able to display both in his written work and in his unpredictable public appearances. He has impressed himself on the public's imagination with his distinctive sense of humor. Arreola is at times curmudgeonly, even misanthropic. He manifests a great apprehension about all women, whom he tends to view as a collectivity who might easily make common cause against all men. In his satirical vision, when women and men come into contact, desperate misunderstanding and conflict break out. Still, even when his judgment on humankind would seem to be a condemnatory one, his overall tone is leavened by sudden escapes into carefree playfulness and clowning.

In 1953 and 1955 the Mexican writer Juan Rulfo (1918–1986) published two very brief books that would constitute almost his entire creative oeuvre and exert a great influence on the development of Spanish American narrative. His short story collection of 1953 is *El llano en llamas* (*The Burning Plain*). It produced a stir of excitement in great measure because Rulfo had invented a new approach to writing about peasants and rural life, an area of literature especially in need of renovation and new options. Rulfo avoided the usual conventions, established by realistic regional writers, of identifying characters and scenes as belonging to a specific local reality. He had developed new solutions to the problem of how to represent the speech and thoughts of peasant characters. Regional realists were likely to depend heavily on educated-sounding central narrators whose precise, knowledgeable explanations cast the peasant characters, by contrast, as inept rustics. In Rulfo's stories, narrators and characters speak a common language not closely resembling any real-world variety of speech. Their form of expression occurs nowhere except in the fiction of this particular author. They speak with what seems to be uncalculated artlessness; yet their highly metaphorical language is undeniably the product of lyrical stylization. The extent of Rulfo's innovation became even clearer in his novel of 1955, *Pedro Páramo*, carrying the name of the local boss, or *cacique*, whose near-feudal rule has profoundly marked his region. (The setting common to all of Rulfo's narrative, a parched, scorched desert marked by outcroppings of rock, has widely been perceived as a literary version of the author's home state of Jalisco, though this identification is never made in the fiction.)

Juan Preciado, the protagonist of *Pedro Páramo*, is one of Páramo's many offspring. It is essentially from Juan's viewpoint that Pedro Páramo is encountered. Juan has come to Páramo's town, Comala, in fulfillment of a deathbed promise to his mother, who wants the *cacique* to pay for a great wrong he once did to her. The discovery that the object of his search has been dead for some time does not impede the mission. Juan now strives for an informed understanding of Páramo and his brutal reign by making inquiries throughout the town. The implication is that possession of knowledge of Páramo will constitute a posthumous form of revenge. Juan's first-person account of his quest for Páramo is predominant during the first part of the novel, though an omniscient narrator supplements Juan's statements and relays to the reader the thoughts and words of other characters, including those of Páramo himself.

The text of *Pedro Páramo* consists of short fragments that do not form chapters. Particularly in the first half of the novel, the relation of one block of text to adjacent sections is often difficult to identify, as is the voice that is speaking. These textual segments supply pieces of information that eventually accumulate into a portrait of Pedro Páramo and his relations with the inhabitants of his domains. The narrative data appear not only out of chronological sequence, but also in an order that delays the discovery of information needed to make sense of the story. For example, only after the novel is well underway is Juan Preciado's name ever mentioned. The name, in turn, is the clue that Juan's mother is the Dolores Preciado that Pedro Páramo induced to marry him, then cast off after despoiling her of her fortune. This link in turn explains why Juan's mother sent him questing for revenge.

Even more surprising is the delayed revelation that marks a great turning point in the novel, virtually dividing it into two halves. One learns that Juan Preciado is himself among the many characters in the novel who have already died, but are driven to continue their unfinished tasks. This circumstance comes to light when Juan matter-of-factly narrates his own death and burial. He survived only two days after his arrival in Comala, suggesting that he could not live in a town where death has come to dominate. The reader now discovers that all the segments Juan has narrated have been spoken from the cemetery and have been addressed to a woman buried in the same grave with him. Following this revelation, the narrative becomes less difficult to make sense of. Its progression, with some interruptions, follows the career of Páramo up to the *cacique*'s violent death at the hands of yet another aggrieved son. His murder is the last event narrated, and his killer is the same muleteer who at the novel's outset met Juan and served as his guide to Comala; so the end of the text reflects back to its beginning. In the novel's second half, Páramo's story is told through, among other types of narration, dialogues between Juan and his gravemate and monologues by another inhabitant of the same cemetery, a woman who was the great obsession and frustration of Páramo's life.

   Pedro Páramo is often cited as an instance of magical realism. The construction of the plot allows both realistic and magical or mythlike elements to co-occur throughout the narrative. The story of Pedro Páramo encapsulates boss rule in rural Mexico, showing the pressure that built up to the Mexican Revolution of 1910. At the same time, though, both the figure of Páramo and certain of the events of the plot manifest a strong legendary strain. Páramo is like real-world *caciques* in utilizing guile, violence, and intimidation to dominate an ever-larger area of land. His realistically brutal methods are out of place, though, when he employs them to win the hand of Susana San Juan. The passages referring to or spoken by the mysteriously pure Susana, and those concerned with Páramo's consuming love for her, represent a move away from the verisimilar mode. After Páramo has lured her to his domain and had her father killed, Susana goes mad. Páramo experiences continual frustration trying to reach the now-remote Susana. At Susana's death, public revelry breaks out over Páramo's misfortune, and the *cacique* reviles the community, saying he will let it die. In effect, Comala turns from the green, flourishing place Juan's mother remembers to a wasteland. Pedro spends the rest of his life isolated in bitter mourning, but without relinquishing his hold over Comala and its surrounding lands.

   Some elements of this narrative are clearly quite lifelike, such as Páramo's devious and violent methods of securing lands and power. But others belong more to myth and magic. Obviously reminiscent of myth is the theme, familiar from ghost stories and other folktales, of the dead who can know no peace in the grave and return to haunt the scenes where they were scarred in life, attempting to pay retribution for their sins or avenge wrongs done to them. Guilt and anger impel the dead characters to speak of, and in many cases arise from their graves to act upon, the business they left incomplete at the end of their lives. Joseph Sommers says of the topic, running through *Pedro Páramo*, of the unquiet dead: "Such popular beliefs are such a great part of the structure and are so important to Rulfo's conceptions about existence, that they constitute the living reality of *Pedro Páramo*, superimposing magic elements upon the 'realist' narrative process."[12]

Most mythic of all is the figure of Páramo, whose name means "barren plain" or "wasteland," and who in his wrath is able to lay a curse on formerly fertile lands, which quickly degenerate into desert. There is the reiterated suggestion that the patriarch has so marked his region that everyone there is at least figuratively the offspring of Pedro Páramo. Sommers states: "Pedro Páramo . . . attains vast proportions because he incarnates the elementary nature of myth, because he is an abstraction, an entity."[13] The characters themselves are quick to point out that Páramo is something larger than a human individual. A much-quoted line from the novel is the answer Juan elicits from his guide by asking, concerning Páramo: "Who is he?" The guide responds by summing up Páramo as "He's hate. He's just pure hate."[14] Páramo's death is consistent with his ambiguous representation. The cause of death is prosaically likely; Páramo is attacked by a knife-wielding peasant, one of his many abandoned offspring. But the ways he dies is not that of a man of flesh and blood. It is not clear how figuratively the narrator is speaking when he says, in the often-quoted last words of the novel, that Páramo "crumbled to pieces as if he were a heap of stones."[15]

Rulfo's innovations in style and language have won the admiration of readers and critics. His accomplishment has been to develop a type of speech that, at least within the fiction, seems plausible in the mouths of uneducated characters, yet is unmistakably poeticized. Both in the speech of the omniscient narrator and in that of characters, which are not sharply different from one another, Rulfo prefers to limit his lexical choices to words that are likely to occur frequently in day-to-day exchanges. The characters tend to use few words and often speak in short sentences. Although they inhabit an isolated rural area, there is nothing to mark their speech as typical of a regional dialect. Instead, their expression exhibits a timeless, unplaceable neutrality that imbues it with a classical or mythic quality. Nonetheless, the characters' speech draws attention to the fact that they are country dwellers of the peasant class. The many clues include the spareness and simplicity of their language and their allusions to such typically rural preoccupations as anxieties over livestock, crops, and weather. After noting how difficult it is to single out the features that make Rulfo's language both peasantlike and elegant, Brushwood sums up the issue: "The closest I can come to describing this style is to say that [Rulfo] captures and uses the essence of rural speech so that we accept his language as authentic, but allow it to remove us from a folkloric plane to a mythic plane where we observe not customs but symbols of customs." [16] Exemplary of this quality is Dolores Preciado's recollection of Comala: ". . . You'll see why I loved it there, my son. The village I loved. Where the dreams made me thin. My village, raised up over the fields. Full of trees and green leaves, like a money-box where we kept our memories. You'll feel that you'd like to live there forever. Daybreak, morning, afternoon, evening, always the same except for the difference in the air. The air changes the colors of everything . . ." [17]

After the publication of *Pedro Páramo*, Rulfo never again published a substantial new creative work. For many years he spoke of a longer work in progress, which he referred to as *La cordillera* (The mountain range). He tantalized interviewers with the suggestion that he was occupied in the creation of an important new work, but was hoarding it away or destroying what he had written without showing any of it to his public, by now grown extremely curious. Rumors circulated that the new novel was about to appear or even had appeared with one Mexican publishing house or another. After Rulfo's death, though, it became clear that no manuscript of *La cordillera* was extant, if indeed one had ever come fully into being. Rulfo's oeuvre, apart from the celebrated narratives of the mid-1950s, consisted of his work as a screenwriter, interviews and miscellaneous occasional pieces, and some photography, of professional quality, that perfectly matched the desert images conveyed in his fiction.

Marco Denevi (Argentina, 1922), who, like Arreola, would establish himself as a practitioner of the *microcuento*, made his debut with a novel. Denevi has identified the 1955 *Rosaura a las diez* (*Rosa at Ten O'Clock*) as his first literary effort. It was rewarded with the Guillermo Kraft Novel Prize and excellent sales. *Rosaura* is an elegantly conceived and realized detective novel, much admired for the ingenuity of its plot. The novel's central puzzle arises when an introverted, melancholy art restorer living in a boardinghouse appears to have created an imaginary woman out of his longings and succeeded in drawing his credulous fellow boarders into his fantasy. Later a woman materializes on the doorstep and asks for him;

the boarders greet her as the heroine of the painter's great romance. Clearly stupefied by events, the boarder marries the woman who seems to have stepped out of his dreams, although she has become coarser and more vulgar than when he invented her. Shortly afterward he becomes the obvious suspect in her murder. Of course, the simple and evident explanation is incorrect. The ending of the novel exemplifies the rigorous construction much admired in detective fiction. An unearthed letter, although it breaks off suddenly in the middle, provides the information to account for every single element hitherto unexplained in the plot. The solution is logically possible, but not realistically very likely, relying as it does on some staggering coincidences. The rational justification of the events of the plot does not prevent the narrative from taking place in great part in the realm of the characters' fantasy and imagination.

The mode of narration Denevi employs in *Rosaura* is elaborate and clever. The pieces of information needed to resolve the puzzle must be culled and sifted from the accounts provided by several different narrators. These are characters with varying degrees and types of involvement in the story. Most of the narratives take the form of depositions given to the investigating officer, though the fragmentary document that answers the novel's questions is a long-lost letter from the murdered woman. Denevi, showcasing his talent for mimicry, has created for his witness-narrators the most widely divergent linguistic styles and approaches to the giving of information. The boardinghouse owner is a garrulous busybody who inundates the detective with gossipy detail. In a cruelly accurate satire of the fashionable cult of psychology, Denevi makes one of the boarders a self-appointed expert in the criminal mind. For his deposition, this pseudointellectual insists on subjecting the detective to what he advertises as a flawless exposition of the case. The art restorer proves to be the most unforthcoming witness. To obtain his account, the detective must speak for the first time in the novel, teasing information out of his withdrawn, morose subject.

Rosaura is one of the works most often cited as evidence that, on the Spanish American literary scene, detective fiction has enjoyed unusually high prestige and benefited from the most skillful efforts of literary talents. It should be remembered that Borges, an important arbiter of literary tastes, had long been promoting the belief that narratives of detection should not be seen as a cheap and easy genre because they are so rigidly governed by conventions. In Borges's judgment, the rigorous completeness required in the plotting of detective fiction, where nothing should be left unaccounted for, and the need to satisfy the highly conventionalized expectations of detective-fiction readers challenged writers to display to the fullest their technical virtuosity. To innovate while complying with the subgenre's many rules was more of an attainment than to experiment in free forms. By the late 1960s, the tale of detection would go out of fashion, subjected to persistent criticism for its tenuous relation to social realities. Even so, narratives centered on criminal activities and their investigation remained a Spanish American specialty. The hard-boiled crime novel now became the popular subgenre that Spanish American writers reinvented, at times adding in a fantastic strain, reaccommodating its conventions and formulae to their expressive needs.

A novel that appeared in Mexico in 1958, *La región más transparente* (*Where the Air Is Clear*), succeeded in establishing internationally the name of its author, Carlos Fuentes (1928), already well known in Mexico. It provoked a great deal of discussion even before its publication date, since extracts had been appearing in magazines. Yet much of the talk ranged well beyond the novel itself to involve the then-heated debate over Mexican national identity.

Polemical exchanges over the nation's collective sense of self had been carried on for years, but the late 1940s and 1950s saw many Mexican intellectuals, especially those known as the Hiperión group, devoting substantial thought to formulating the issues involved. The highly original and influential book-length essay of 1950, *El laberinto de la soledad* (*The Labyrinth of Solitude*) by Octavio Paz (b. 1914), was the best of the many contemporary essays treating this set of issues. It brought the debate to a new level of complexity and sophistication. Paz had achieved a focus broader than the question of national character through his ability to weigh issues universal to humankind along with those specific to Mexican culture. His heterogeneous, intergeneric *Labyrinth* drew freely upon anthropological and sociological styles of discourse as well as existential thought, popular culture studies, and literary criticism. Though it gives many signs of its author's vocation as a creative writer, *Labyrinth* could not without exaggeration be called a work of imaginative literature. Rather, it was widely read and discussed among writers and provided many of them with ideas to which they gave a literary elaboration. As Fuentes began his career, he was closely associated with the older writer, and *Where the Air Is Clear* is thematically in the vein of discussion that Paz had begun. Fuentes's detractors have complained that he drew too heavily on Paz for his ideas. The complaint is somewhat irrelevant to the evaluation of *Where the Air Is Clear*, since even if there is overlapping of themes, the novel is elaborated in a completely different way from Paz's essay.

Fuentes has been well able to retain the public's attention after this early success. As the son of a diplomat, Fuentes had lived in Washington, D.C., and become virtually bilingual; one of his special knacks throughout his career has been explaining Mexico to the United States. He is urbane, articulate, and amusing in Spanish, English, and French; he is a good interview subject and has a flair for composing all types of occasional pieces. He has enjoyed a great advantage in that Margaret Sayers Peden, one of the most skilled English-language translators of Spanish American literature, came to work with his writing on a regular basis. All in all, Fuentes is the Mexican writer who most fully incarnates the boom.

Where the Air Is Clear is a panoramic novel of life in Mexico City. At the time of its publication, it seemed daringly experimental in its technique, although the subsequent appearance of many formally innovative Mexican novels has diminished the extreme novelty of Fuentes's 1958 work. The narrative cuts rapidly from scene to scene across the city; its construction has often drawn comparisons with John Dos Passos's *Manhattan Transfer*. In addition to the scenes with action and characters, the loosely organized *Where the Air Is Clear* includes monologues that resemble essays interspersed into the fiction. It ends with a lengthy, allusive, ruminative essay on Mexico City, past and present. Fuentes is successful in transforming his store of factual knowledge of Mexico City into a literary vision, giving a human and experiential aspect to the abundance of information set forth in the course of the book.

The scenes include life in all social classes represented in the city's population. Fuentes lays special emphasis upon the indigenous element, which he sees as a pervasive subcurrent in Mexican life, likely to manifest itself at any moment even in the most genteel social context. The novel frequently draws attention to the omnipresent evidence of this component of national life, such as the traces of Indian ancestry in characters' features, the marks the pre-Colombian past has left on Mexico City, the use of Nahuatl words in Mexican Spanish, and, most subtly, certain behaviors and attitudes whose origins lie in pre-Hispanic times. The most prestigious and august constituent of Mexican culture, the Iberian heritage, must compete not only with the robustly persistent indigenous past and present, but also with the graceless modern commercial culture currently invading the city through the media and consumer goods.

Where the Air Is Clear shares certain features with the realistic novel, especially in the depiction of the most prominent of its many characters.

The aging, crisis-ridden protagonist is Federico Robles, who rose from provincial poverty, fought in the Mexican Revolution, and subsequently made a stellar corporate career for himself by benefiting from the changes that revolution occasioned. He is now a powerful corporate magnate. A spokesman for the business world's ethic of efficiency and up-to-date techniques, Robles is a vigorous exponent of the idea that Mexico must discard its past, and the legacy of its past, to enjoy its full share of the rewards of the modern era. Although in public he speaks the rhetoric of ambition and upward striving, the form his success has taken disgusts no one more than himself. By the novel's end he has abandoned his career and fled Mexico City to restart his life, this time as a farmer.

Other aspects of the work, though, range well outside the conventions of lifelike representation. Time and space change and move about, with the cutting from scene to scene typical of much innovative twentieth-century fiction. In line with his vision of Mexico as constantly living its past in its present, Fuentes interjects material from earlier eras into the current-day scene. Moving among the novel's more or less verisimilar characters is an indeterminate, mysterious figure, Ixca Cienfuegos, who is able to change his social class and ethnic identity at will and who somehow materializes all over the city, integrating himself seamlessly into the most diverse cultural environments. Ixca is not designed to resemble a believably human figure. He enjoys a telepathic omniscience with regard to the other characters, asking them searching questions that presuppose a knowledge of their unvoiced thoughts and beliefs. Sommers has noted the extreme difficulty of obtaining from the novel a clear picture of Ixca's bodily characteristics: "Never completely real, his physical appearance is always communicated in abstract terms ('Cienfuegos' paralyzed smile was denied by his dense and obscure eyes, narrowed in a gaze of hatred . . .')." [18]

Mythic is one term that comes to mind to describe Ixca's exceptional dimension. Ixca's story does not follow any known myth, and indeed he has no narrative line of his own in the novel, instead intervening in the plots developed around other characters. Still, he is presented as an entity of mythic qualities. Ixca's actions destroy the career of the industrialist—although the latter was already harboring a desire to escape his own success—and provoke the death of the man's ambitious wife. There are strong hints that, by inserting himself into other people's lives, Ixca is seeking out a victim for expiatory sacrifice. His mentor is an indigenous woman, an urban priestess who regularly speaks of her need for sacrifices, and Ixca's destructive actions are those of an officiating sacrificer.

As the novel unfolds, it becomes increasingly evident that, while Ixca may appear to pop up anywhere and everywhere, his interventions follow an underlying program. Ixca's purpose is not so different from the argument about Mexican culture made by the novel in which he appears. In his exchanges with other characters, he is eager to prod them to an awareness of something they might gladly forget, Mexico's indigenous past and the weight that past exerts on life in the present.

In his protean insubstantiality, Ixca typifies a change underway in Spanish American narrative: new concepts of what constitutes a literary character and new practices in characterization. The character who remains within one essentially stable identity and who can be appreciated as resembling real-world individuals is now in decline. This transformation has fascinated many observers and given rise to such phrases as "the disappearing hero." Noé Jitrik has been perhaps the most thorough in tracing this development. Surveying a sample of Spanish American works from the 1920s onwards, Jitrik identifies a number of innovations that have deprived literary characters of their stability and apparent solidity. Among these are the character who must share part or all of his or her identity with another and, inversely, the character who enjoys the use of multiple identities. Many narratives make it unmistakably clear that a character has been created, not to give the effect of coming to life, but strictly to serve a designated function in the workings of the text.[19]

In 1962 Fuentes published a novel of even wider impact than *Where the Air Is Clear* and one that has stayed more current with the passage of time. *La muerte de Artemio Cruz* (*The Death of Artemio Cruz*) was in the long line of novels treating the Mexican Revolution. To keep current, the novel of the Revolution had had to evolve far beyond its original focus on the armed conflict and combatants, tracing a broader and broader sweep of material. From its rough, rustic, action-packed beginnings in *The Under Dogs*, it had come to include a text as urban and sophisticated, and reaching as far into mid-century Mexico, as *Artemio Cruz*. Artemio, encountered on his deathbed, is, like Federico Robles of *Where the Air Is Clear*, a revolutionary grown rich, corrupt, and self-loathing. Following a long literary tradition, placing the protagonist at the very end of his life provides the opportunity to review the way he has lived and reach a judgment.

The likelihood of a favorable assessment of Cruz is small, since both his career and his personal life were marked by betrayals, above all the betrayal of the Mexican Revolution, capitulations, and a persistent attempt to dominate and exploit others. The novel gradually divulges a long history of unethical behavior and attitudes. These begin with Cruz's willingness to reveal the location and plans of revolutionary troops in order to avoid a firing squad. Cruz later marries a wealthy young woman, the sister of a fellow soldier who preserved his personal integrity and accepted death to support his cause at the same time that Cruz was capitulating. Cruz quickly places the enterprises, capital, and connections of his wife's family at his own disposal. Utilizing the rhetoric and legal apparatus of revolutionary land reform, he manages to accumulate large holdings in a short time. (Strengthening the novel's picture of Mexico as caught in hard-to-break cycles is the fact that Cruz's in-laws had amassed their wealth partly by taking advantage of the changes brought by the reform government of a half-century before. Confiscated church holdings slotted for redistribution had passed into the family's hands.)

Cruz's cold treatment of his wife and his indifference toward his daughter, from whom he can perceive no potential advantage, are among the signs of his failure as an ethical human being. His dereliction is as marked in the personal as the public realm. More ambiguous are the decisions Cruz makes concerning his son. Cruz makes it possible for the son to go fight and die in the Spanish Civil War, evidently as a vicarious way of fulfilling the revolutionary mission that he himself had botched during the Mexican Revolution. On the positive side, revelations about Cruz's childhood and early adult life make it possible to understand how he came to be who he was. Joseph Sommers explains the duality readers have typically found in the characterization of Cruz: "The complex, contradictory personality of Artemio Cruz emerges in a portrait which Carlos Fuentes paints with both deep contempt and sensitive understanding, even compassion."[20]

Glimpses of Cruz's childhood in Veracruz province, where he was a poor plantation boy, his early radicalization by a committed rural teacher, and his initially earnest involvement in the Revolution show the struggle he underwent to attain his place. The emphasis is on the possibilities he once had, and then deliberately ruined through unworthy life decisions, of becoming a moral member of the human community. A segment revealing the death of a woman Cruz loved, a fellow combatant, contains the suggestion that the shock of this loss was a factor in Cruz's subsequent moral decline. Although the brief scenes from the protagonist's childhood and early adulthood give his characterization a more human cast, they cannot be said to justify his later actions or turn the mature Cruz into a sympathetic figure. The reader always receives a greater proportion of damaging information about Cruz's character, outweighing the items that would tend to ameliorate the novel's generally harsh judgment of its protagonist.

Artemio Cruz is a much more tightly organized novel than *Where the Air Is Clear*. The earlier novel wandered here and there across the urban scene, creating a collage, including extensive samples of cocktail-party chatter, and making room for essaylike ruminations. *Artemio Cruz* follows strictly a pattern whose design and purpose have been the object of much critical study. The most famous feature of the novel's construction is the rotation between three types of narration, distinguished by the pronouns they employ. Cruz (or his consciousness) is heard in the first person; the dying man's physical pain and his disturbed reaction to his ruined body are reflected in his expression, which is often a stream of consciousness. Visitors exacerbate Cruz's distress; as a skilled manipulator, he easily recognizes their self-seeking behavior toward him and is repelled and irritated by it.

There is also a voice that, generating a mysterious effect, addresses itself directly to Cruz from an unknown vantage point. This narrator is the one who most draws readers' attention to his own way of speaking; although he supplies information about Cruz, he often expresses himself in a lyrical or meditative vein. The use of second-person narration, an option always available to writers but seldom used, has proven extremely attractive to critics concerned with the construction of fiction. Adding to the anomaly is the fact that this narrator uses verbs in the future tense to speak of events located in the past (at least, from the reader's vantage point the events are past ones). Though nothing in the text specifies his identity, the second-person narrator appears to be a second self or extension of the protagonist. His information about Cruz is neither more nor less than what Cruz could be expected to know about himself. His outlook and the range of what he is willing to discuss and reveal differ somewhat from Cruz's. Cruz's expression reveals his deterioration as he approaches death and his unwillingness to think about certain unhappy truths, particularly areas in which he, and the nation he epitomizes, have betrayed their early promise. The second-person narrator is clear-eyed, disinterested, and straightforward in telling and commenting upon the trajectory of Cruz's life and appears to be attempting to prompt or wound Cruz's conscience. Lanin A. Gyurko summarizes: "The self-exalting I-narrative of Cruz the potentate contrasts markedly with the self-evaluating and self-condemning second-person voice of conscience."[21] The striking effect produced by the voice addressing and accusing the very self from which it emanates is recreated in Sam Hileman's English version:

> *You will feel satisfied to have imposed your will upon*
> *them—confess it: you imposed your will so that they*

*would admit that you are their equal: seldom have you
felt happier. For ever since you began to be what you
are, to learn to appreciate the feel of fine cloth, the
taste of good liquor, the scent of rich lotions, all those
things that in recent years have been your only, isolated
pleasures; ever since then you have lived with regret for
the geographical error that prevents you from being one
of them. You admire their efficiency, their comforts,
their hygiene, their power, their strength of will; and
you look around you and find intolerable the incompe-
tence, misery, dirt, the weakness and nakedness of this
impoverished country that has nothing. You ache because you know that no matter how hard you try, you
can never be what they are but can become at most
only a pale copy, a near approximation.[22]*

One way to account for the second-person narrator's participation is to
see him as a Cruz who has already lived his life, but a serenely disembod-
ied Cruz as opposed to the pain-wracked, angry Cruz of the first-person
narration. He may be attempting to chide and warn the young Cruz by
predicting the sorry course the latter's life will take if he does not develop
more of an ethical orientation. Alternately, he may be speaking to the
dying Cruz and reproaching him with the wrong turns he took on those
occasions when he faced a crucial juncture in his life. Richard M. Reeve
has examined Fuentes's use of second-person narration in detail, both in
Artemio Cruz and the very short novel *Aura*, published the same year.
(Also named after its self-splitting heroine in the English version, *Aura*
shows Fuentes's talent for intricately worked gothic narratives.) Reeve
cites variant interpretations, including some suggestions from Fuentes, on
the identity and meaning of the unnamed narrator who addresses Cruz.[23]

A fairly standard third-person omniscient narrator relates what transpired on selected days out of Cruz's life, not presented in chronological
order. This traditional, neutral-sounding narrator becomes a central,
stable presence in the novel. His information sounds as if it may be
trusted, whereas Cruz is obviously viewing and recalling events in a way
that turns them to his own advantage and disguises or downplays his failures. Of the three narrators, the third-person speaker takes the longest
turns narrating, and his information is the most detailed and precise, each
of his segments beginning with a specific date.

The treatment of time in *Artemio Cruz* also follows a complex plan of organization. The novel's third-person passages relate a selection of significant and revealing episodes from the protagonist's life, occurring on the days singled out for scrutiny. These sections appear out of chronological sequence, but it is clear that their order is not a random one that could be replaced by any other. The order of appearance of the chapters determines how readers become more fully acquainted with Artemio Cruz and his story and how they judge him and his nearly completed life. The evocations of Cruz's childhood, which would tend to promote sympathy for him, appear only toward the end of the novel, after the reader already knows the misdeeds Cruz would commit in the course of his life.

Artemio Cruz became one of the works most cited as exemplifying the new Spanish American narrative. It figures on many degree-program reading lists, and its English version is a staple of U.S. university courses in Spanish American literature in translation. Fuentes's novel deviates slightly from being the archetypal boom-era novel in its lack of overtly magical, mythical, or fantastic elements. At the very most, Cruz's ability to split off a second identity that addresses him might be construed as the magical transformation of the self into an entity partially other. In other respects, *Artemio Cruz* exhibits the qualities that attracted an international readership to contemporary Spanish American writing. Its novelistic construction follows a plan that is so complex as to require considerable concentration on the part of the reader; the strikingly original organization of the text virtually invites critics to map it out and interpret the purpose behind its spectacular techniques. New Spanish American writing was often praised for combining social criticism and narrative experimentation, and *Artemio Cruz* is perhaps the most perfect example of this fusion. But fascinating as the exact plan of its construction may be, the novel also owes its ability to attract and hold readers to its strong relation to Mexican social and political history. It is equally a denunciation of the failures and betrayals that followed the Mexican Revolution and a demonstration of untried possibilities in the use of narrative voice and the novelistic treatment of space and time.

Julio Cortázar (1914–1984), after some early publications not very indicative of his eventual contribution, began in the 1950s to publish work in what would become internationally recognized as his original mode. Technically innovative in his writing and articulate in person, Cortázar was the single Argentine writer who most fully benefited from the sales and publicity brought by the boom. Internationally,

Cortázar enjoyed his most intense, if temporary, celebrity when one of his stories became the basis of Michelangelo Antonioni's 1966 film *Blow-Up*. The movie drew enormous contemporary attention, some of which went to Cortázar, even though the filmic version does not follow his short story very closely. (The original, hard-to-translate title of Cortázar's story, "Las babas del diablo," is replaced in the English translation by the title of Antonioni's much-noted film.)

Cortázar lived his intellectual life in the public eye, involved in literary conferences, debates, and polemics. In the transformations he underwent over the course of his career, he exemplified the dilemmas facing Spanish American writers. During his early years, he was identified as part of the country's intellectual and artistic elite. Cortázar was often characterized as the literary heir of the aristocratic Borges. In fact, Borges had published, in a magazine he edited and with illustrations by his sister Norah Borges, the younger writer's first short story, "Casa tomada" ("House Taken Over"). Cortázar's image was that of a detached, artful writer, given to making capricious jokes and best appreciated by a highly cultured readership. The fact that, from 1951 onward, he made his home in Paris further disturbed Cortázar's detractors, who saw him as insufficiently concerned with Latin America's social realities. Over the years, he became politically radicalized; his social commitment affected both his essays and journalism and certain of his later novels, most notably the 1974 *El libro de Manuel* (*A Manual for Manuel*). Yet, characteristically, the earnestness of his political purpose never diminished his fondness for including bits of amusing nonsense and whimsical, at times precious, jokes in his texts.

During the 1950s, Cortázar began to gain distinction for his ability to develop new forms of the fantastic, or at least highly imaginative, short story. He had clearly studied the history of fantastic narrative back to classical antiquity, when tales of fabulous creatures circulated. Above all he was a knowing reader of the "stories of effect," designed to produce sensations of alarm and suspense in readers, cultivated by French- and English-language writers of the nineteenth century. (Born to Argentine parents in Brussels, Cortázar was a French-Spanish bilingual, conversant with the literary cultures of both languages; he was also proficient in English.) Cortázar maintained into adulthood his childhood fascination with Jules Verne, to whom he often alluded, and was responsible for the Spanish version of Poe's prose works. It is clear that he has examined carefully the methods devised by Guy de Maupassant and other adepts of the chilling tale. In addition, he was an astute reader of his more immediate predecessors, such River Plate practitioners of the hair-raising effect-producing story as Lugones and Quiroga. He draws upon the repertory of techniques that had already been built up to intrigue and unsettle readers. In the time-honored spine-tingling tradition, the Cortázar protagonist is liable to encounter an alternate version of him- or herself; doubles abound throughout his work. A disturbing dream may prove to be the dreamer's waking life, or at least invade daylight reality. Hands may carry out deeds of mischief or cruelty, acting of their own autonomous will, and dolls or other pseudohuman artifacts may take on characteristics of their animated models. Vampires hold a special fascination for Cortázar, and many variants of the "undead" crop up in the course of his works, along with a number of characters who are to some degree phantoms.

Yet, while paying homage to the inventive legacy of the great fantastic writers, Cortázar's fiction evolves beyond their achievements. Jaime Alazraki has used the term *neofantastic* for Cortázar's work to indicate that, after assimilating the classical fantastic from French and English models, this recognizably twentieth-century Argentine writer has substantially transformed it in his own writing. Going against the general perception, Alazraki states that "neither [Borges nor Cortázar] has much in common with the nineteenth-century European and American writers who, between 1820 and 1850, produced the masterpieces of the fantastic genre."[24] In Alazraki's analysis, Cortázar practices the fantastic primarily to jolt readers out of their accustomed conceptual categories, particularly concerning time, space, and causality. By moving readers away from the usual order they believe to be running the universe, Cortázar enables them to glimpse a secret, indescribable pattern running through events and phenomena. Following in the steps of twentieth-century avant-gardism, and above all the surrealism to which he acknowledges a debt, Cortázar depends on startling metaphors to produce this disorienting and reorienting effect.[25]

Apart from his renovation of the fantastic, Cortázar's work is marked by many touches typical of him personally. Cortázar was a great enthusiast of the light-hearted, eccentric side of surrealism, such as the cheerfully bizarre literary behavior of the surrealist absurdist Alfred Jarry. An aficionado of all types of nonsense, he drew to his readers' attention prized examples of silliness and clowning in literature and the curiosities of real-world cranks. Consonant with his interest in unusual forms of consciousness, Cortázar relayed to readers stories of art generated by demented, drugged, or otherwise altered imaginations.

Certain of Cortázar's personal enthusiasms surface in his fiction and essays. Individuals who claim Cortázar's admiration, whether celebrities or simply personal friends, have their names appear in his texts, at times rather arbitrarily employed. Jazz, less its performance than the potentially transforming experience of listening to jazz, is an element in many Cortázar texts. Advertising seemed to fascinate Cortázar; brand names and slogans appear in his fiction, and many of his illustrated essays include excerpts from catalogues and flyers.

The ideal of an intergeneric, multimedia text held a great attraction for Cortázar. The author looked with nostalgia to the days when book illustrators regularly added the products of their imaginations to those of writers of fiction. He lamented the current-day virtual disappearance of graphics from all but children's books. In a number of his texts, Cortázar experiments with distinctly twentieth-century replacements for illustrated fiction. The surrealists' fascination with collage is evident in a number of his texts, where improbable juxtapositions are employed to engage the reader's creative powers. He often worked in collaboration with practitioners of other arts, most notably the photographic team of Sara Facio and Alicia d'Amico and the painter and sculptor Julio Silva, a like-minded namesake who Cortázar hinted was his doppelgänger.

Cortázar's most celebrated experiment in interarts format is his 1969 *Ultimo round* (Final round), strikingly notable for its division into two tiers, with each page sliced across the middle and different material running through each level. The 1967 *La vuelta al día en ochenta mundos* (Around the day in eighty worlds) is another ambitious book of juxtaposed fragments. From the title on, an homage to Jules Verne, his illustrators, and his enthralled readers is one of the currents running through the heterogeneous text.

Assiduous students of Cortázar's literary work have combed these kaleidoscopic assemblages in search of clues to his more conventionally composed publications. Yet, beyond the hints they may give to his standard writing, the fragmentary books stand on their own. They show Cortázar engaged in an effort to create a new form of popular culture. In his last years, an increasingly populist vision of culture drove Cortázar to experiment with forms that he hoped would attract a wider public than the usual readers of literature. The 1975 *Fantomas contra los vampiros multinacionales* (*Fantomas versus the Multinational Vampires*) uses a modified comic-book format, supplementing the drawn sequences with written-out narrative and documentary materials, to carry its social critique.

Typical, too, of Cortázar's stories is the appearance of a variety of animals—some members of real-world species, others creatures of fable, and still others undefined beings that have emerged from the imaginations of his protagonists. Cortázar's first collection, the 1951 *Bestiario* (*Bestiary*) takes as its point of departure the books of beasts that circulated among medieval and Renaissance readers. The characters in animal form interact in unexpected ways with the human characters, frequently smudging the line of demarcation between the human species and all others. "Axolotl," one of his most cited stories, exemplifies this softening of boundaries; its hero begins the story as a man, becomes increasingly drawn to visit and gaze upon the exotic salamander of the title, and by the tale's end is looking out at the world from inside the object of his fascination.

As is typical of many contemporary Spanish American writers, Cortázar devised many ways of treating narrative time and space. Linear chronology, generally considered the most standard mode for realist fiction, now is avoided in favor of arrangements requiring more concentration on the reader's part. A central concept in several of Cortázar's stories is that what is in essence a single sequence of events may be unfolding in more than one era.

Cortázar was a critic as well as a creative writer, and his stories often speak to students, as well as simply readers, of literature. The way in which art succeeds in communicating, and the understanding and interpretation of literature and other art forms, are recurring issues in Cortázar's fiction. The famous story "El perseguidor" ("The Pursuer"), from the 1958 collection *Las armas secretas* (Secret weapons), contains implicit warnings and advice to students of the arts. Its positive character is a saxophone player whose genius is for improvisation and who sums up the element in art that cannot be rationalized away. This spontaneous talent has the misfortune to attract a dogged exegete. The musician has no need of an interpreter to communicate with his audience, but the critic is dependent on his subject to provide raw material for explication. The story may seem to characterize critical analysis as a job for parasites. Still it implicitly projects, in opposition to this negative portrait, a positive image of the task of understanding esthetic expression. The author of the story and its insightful and sympathetic readers are presumed to be well attuned to the freedom and fluidity of art represented by the saxophone player. Such a comprehension of art, and of the need to accept it on its own premises, is the starting place for a more productive study in which the critic must respect the creative work for what it is, then go beyond it to construct a new work. As Jitrik summarized the story's warning, the "satellite" activity of the perennially explicating, after-the-fact interpreter must give way to "critical work." In the latter undertaking, the critic moves beyond the accumulation of bits of information and conjecture about artists and artworks to make an original contribution to the organization of human knowledge.[26]

The international literary reputation of Cortázar rests principally on his 1963 novel *Rayuela* (*Hopscotch*). *Hopscotch* is second only to García Márquez's *One Hundred Years of Solitude* among works that sum up the qualities readers found fascinating in Spanish American fiction of the boom era. The former novel, with its erudite references and elaborate construction, spoke more to a critically trained audience, while the latter brought the Spanish American new narrative to a broad public. Both novels benefited from English-language editions that stood on their own as memorable narrative texts. Both these outstanding versions were the work of a single translator, the prolific Gregory Rabassa, whose successful translations did much to spread contemporary Spanish American and Brazilian prose fiction through the English-speaking world. The English *Hopscotch* (1966) is considered a model of apt translation; it was the first book to be awarded a National Book Award in honor of the translator's work.

Hopscotch is the lengthy, wide-ranging novel of exceedingly intricate pattern much cultivated in the 1960s and early 1970s and at the time often referred to as the "totalizing novel." Like many contemporary novels, it follows its protagonist through a quest whose outcome is at best a very incomplete and ambiguous success. Its lackluster hero is an aging, unproductive Bohemian named Oliveira, as he drifts through events first in Paris and then in Buenos Aires. A summary of the plot certainly would not convey why *Hopscotch* is regarded as such an important text. In its scant reliance on story line, *Hopscotch* resembles much experimental fiction of the 1960s. (Of the Spanish American writers who gained prominence during the 1960s, only García Márquez stood out for his skill in plotting.) It also presents a clear contrast with Spanish American narrative of the late 1970s and onward, when the laying of an intricate and memorable plot again became a valued skill among writers of fiction.

At the center of activity in *Hopscotch*, though not directing it, is Oliveira, afflicted with an inability to stop his obsessive intellectualizing, even when confronted by life situations that call for a more immediate type of engagement. He allows events to happen to him because his exhaustive analysis leaves little room for direct action. In the first half of the novel, set in Paris, Oliveira appears coldly cerebral in contrast to his lover. The latter, an uneducated woman who has difficulty coping with ordinary life, nonetheless is the novel's most engaging character, its representative of spontaneity and intuition. The second half, whose location is Buenos Aires, shows him attaining some degree of freewheeling high spirits.

Shortly after he loosens his rationalizing hold on matters, Oliveira goes beyond light-hearted and childlike play to become outright demented, suggesting that he lacks the flexibility needed for self-transformation. He falls considerably short of his goal, to reach the transcendentally "other" state metaphorically represented by the top square in hopscotch.

The novelistic construction of *Hopscotch* is a famous case of the narrative experimentation much admired in the 1960s and early 1970s. At the outset, Cortázar asserts, "In its own way, this book consists of many books, but two books above all."[27] One of these books is simply a reading of all the chapters that set out the plot in the linear, chronological order in which they appear. There is a strong suggestion that only the most despicably idle readers will be satisfied with such an approach. The alternative is to supplement the straightforward reading with an expanded and variegated one. Cortázar offers a special "Table of Instructions" for the broadened reading. Yet his elaborate directions are offered in a somewhat joking spirit, rather like the Rube Goldberg contraptions that amused Cortázar. The suggestion is that readers would do best to create for themselves the reading that suits them. This second reading alters the order of chapters and splices into the narrative a set of additional chapters found at the back of the book. The choice between modes of reading separates the "accomplice reader," able to share responsibility for bringing the text fully into being, from the type of reader that Cortázar unfortunately refers to as "female."

Only a few of the supplementary chapters serve to supply the plot with new details. Instead, freed from the need to move the story along, these chapters allow Cortázar to expand on the issues *Hopscotch* raises, such topics as the processes of reading and writing, the nature of esthetic expression and response, and the search for a transcendental vision. Some of the chapters are citations from real-world writers whose concerns overlap with Cortázar's, while others offer the formulations of a fictitious literary theorist, Morelli, who greatly resembles the historical Macedonio Fernández. Like Macedonio, Morelli envisions a literary utopia in which readers will carry no less of the responsibility for elaborating a novel than will the author. The ideal would be for the author's function to stop at generating the idea or premise for the work; short of this goal, authors must gradually ease the work of writing onto the shoulders of their formerly idle readers. The passive reader's vision of literature, inherited from positivism, is of a given set of authors and works. Morelli would replace this static view with a constantly evolving landscape of reading and writing, reciprocal activities that should move toward becoming one and the same.

One of Cortázar's preoccupations was the search for a way of writing about erotic experience that would sound at home in literary Spanish and in a twentieth-century literary work. *Hopscotch* contains several different experiments in this vein, including one passage composed in a curiously altered language Cortázar invented for the occasion. The following, linguistically more usual, passage is from number 144 of the extra chapters:

> *On some days the smell of seaweed would become mixed up with a thicker cadence, then I would have to have recourse to perversion—but it was a Palatine perversion, you understand, a Bulgaroctonous luxury, that of a seneschal surrounded by nocturnal obedience—, to bring my lips to hers, touch with my tongue that light pink flame that fluttered surrounded by shadow, and then, as I now do with you, I would slowly separate her thighs, hold her a little to one side and breathe into her interminably, feeling how her hand, without my asking, would begin to break me up the way a flame begins to pick its topazes out of a wrinkled newspaper. Then the perfumes would stop miraculously and everything was taste, biting, essential juices running about the mouth, the fall into that shadow, the primeval darkness, the hub of the wheel of origins. Yes, in that instant of the most crouching animality, closest to excretion and its unspeakable apparatus, there the initial and final figures are sketched, there in the viscous cavern of your daily relaxation stands the trembling Aldebaran, genes and constellations jump, everything becomes alpha and omega . . .*[28]

García Márquez, Fuentes, and Cortázar were the most important writers to attain prominence with the boom. The two other authors most associated with the phenomenon were the Peruvian Mario Vargas Llosa (b. 1936) and José Donoso (b. 1924) of Chile. While both these writers have continued to publish new work, Donoso has never quite regained the prominence he enjoyed during the upsurge of interest in Spanish American fiction in the 1960s and early 1970s. In contrast, Vargas Llosa, a dramatic figure, has never ceased to occupy a place in the public eye. His conception and practice of fiction have undergone extraordinary transformations over the years, intriguing his readership with unexpected evolutions. During the late 1970s, he left behind the new narrative to become a major practitioner and exponent of the presumably more straightforward "return to storytelling" in Spanish American narrative. He has further increased his visibility through his secondary career as a journalist, specializing in semidocumentary recreations of highly charged news events. His involvement in public life has included a polemical break with the intellectual left and culminated in a lengthy and fascinating, if unsuccessful, campaign for the presidency of Peru.

After publishing well-received short fiction, Vargas Llosa was able to achieve a fast breakthrough into international recognition with his 1963 novel *La ciudad y los perros*. (The English translation carries the title *The Time of the Hero*, an adaptation of a Spanish-language working title the author eventually discarded.) As do a number of well-known works of fiction, *The Time of the Hero* has as its setting a military academy, which becomes a microcosm of the society around it. In this case, the context is Lima; the military school brings together representatives of the city's diverse social strata from the lower middle class upward. A summary of the plot of the work would give little idea of why it was greeted as an innovative twentieth-century novel. The story centers on moral problems, with the emphasis turned away from a personal, individualistic concept of morality and toward the ethics necessary to the well-being of an entire community or society. In some cases, the novel projects a moral judgment that is easy to identify, particularly in its treatment of the military's habit of obscuring information that might tarnish its image. In other instances, though, *The Time of the Hero* generates ambiguity around the moral weight to be assigned to the decisions and actions taken by the various characters.

A chemistry examination is stolen at the outset, setting off the events of the plot. An inquiry into the theft begins to reveal all types of misconduct among the cadets, shielded by a hierarchy of domination through violence and intimidation. The initial impulse to discover the source of the problem is quickly overridden by the urge to prevent scandal from touching the school and the institution of the military. One cadet, an informer, is killed in retaliation and to discourage any further revelations. His murder, which poses the central problem in the novel, becomes the source of ethical ambiguity. The victim was known in life for his exceptional cowardice, weakness, and subservience. In addition, his motive in informing was not to restore justice, but simply to reap personal benefit from his revelations.

The murderer is a cadet known as the Jaguar, a rough young man who imposes his will through aggression toward his fellow students, nearly all

of whom are of a higher social class than he. Yet it would not be entirely
ironic to identify this violent adolescent as, in some sense, the hero alluded
to in the English-language title. Certainly he is the character who raises
the most complex moral questions. Although he is an aggressor and at
times a bully, his strength, resolution, and relative simplicity cast him in
a progressively more positive light throughout the novel, especially as he
is set in contrast to soft, accommodating, and devious figures. He appears
even more favorably in the epilogue, where he spontaneously offers a long-
delayed admission of his crime. (Characteristically for this novel, his con-
fession, which at first seems refreshingly straightforward, later becomes
the source of new ambiguities.) In his moment of self-inculpation, he not
only exhibits a conscience but also an unexpected—for a character who
seems so hardened—degree of insight into the complex implications of
recent events. At the time he comes forward as the murderer, the cadet
admits having made a moral mistake and discusses with surprising intelligence and powers of analysis his own and others' actions. At this point
it seems obvious that he has undergone an experiential process of learning
to arrive at his realization. But it is dubious whether this education will
have any value in his subsequent life, which appears to be headed toward
stagnation in a clerk-level job.

Another student, the only friend of the slain cadet, has already identified the murderer. His motivation for assuming the risky role of informer
is murky. His action could be construed as a quest to reestablish justice,
but it is also, less disinterestedly, a move to obtain revenge for the death
of a friend. In either case, his willingness to come forward has no effect
on the outcome of events. Perceived as a troublesome whistle-blower, he
is forced by school officials to recant his accusations.

The novel is unambiguously harsh in the judgment it passes on the
characters who represent the military; of the officers portrayed, only one
strong-minded lieutenant has a positive role to play. After hearing the
murderer's identity, this lone figure tries to insist on getting to the bottom
of the trouble at the academy. By the novel's end, though, he finds himself
posted away to a remote station. Though incorruptible to the end, he
becomes exhausted, and by the novel's close he is overheard counseling a
cadet to despair of bringing about justice in the military environment.

The cadets most clearly in focus during the novel are a group of gradu-
ating seniors who long ago formed into a self-protective pack. They represent a variety of social classes and formative experiences. The construction of the novel links the story they play out in the academy to their lives
outside, both before and after their military schooling and during the ca-

dets' forays into the city. Their lives before entering the academy are connected to the main narrative by means of periodic flashbacks, while the closing pages of the novel, presented as an epilogue, offer glimpses of the former cadets after graduation. At the end, it becomes evident that, far from learning from the ethical drama in which they have been involved, most of the young characters are entering adulthood having perfected a hardened indifference to moral considerations. The character who had appeared on the verge of a breakthrough into moral concern, the student who took it upon himself to denounce the most aggressive and powerful of the cadets, proves a disappointment to the reader. In the epilogue, he is overheard fantasizing avidly about the soft, easy, and hypocritical life to which he will have access as a member of the professional class.

The novelistic design of *The Time of the Hero*, much more than its themes or story line, marks it as a typically twentieth-century innovative novel. Throughout the text, there are swift and unannounced changes in the voice that is heard speaking. Frequently, passages must be read with extreme care for evidence that would enable one to identify which of the characters is the speaker. Extremely typical of Vargas Llosa is the strategy of temporarily obscuring from the reader an item of information, only to disclose it later on in the narrative. This technique of delayed revelation affects the reader's ability to recognize the speaker, so that clues appearing farther on in the text may point to the source of a voice that, when it first began to speak, seemed impossible to specify. In *The Time of the Hero* an unspecified voice appears from time to time, reminiscing about his childhood in a reflective, sincere manner. Only at the novel's close does it become evident that this thoughtful and very likable autobiographer is the Jaguar. As Dick Gerdes observes, the postponed recognition of the speaker drives up the reader's appraisal of the rough cadet, since the passages display an innocent honesty and clarity of insight that his outward actions would tend to disguise.[29]

At the same time, though, the novel does have a central, general narrator whose voice is consistent and stable, providing a point of reference. The events narrated in the course of the novel can eventually be fitted into a linear, unidirectional sequence. However, they appear in a complexly patterned alternate order that makes their chronological sequence quite a puzzle to reassemble. The revelation of certain key pieces of information is delayed; only toward its end does the novel provide all the narrative data required to establish a clear chronology of events.

The Time of the Hero is experimental in composition in that it frequently throws readers off with its rapid changes in speaking voice, time, and place. On the other hand, a dedicated reader can reconstruct from its intricate form something that could well have been a fairly straightforward realist novel. Sara Castro-Klarén summarizes: "In *The Time of the Hero*, unlike in the surrealist project, the novelist mixes up, changes around, puts together, takes apart, at will and without giving the reader warning, the ancient unities of time, character, narrator, but he also leaves open the possibility of reconstructing the object into an object that can take its place in the world of daily reality, that is, the essential referent of literary realism." [30]

The novel shares many features with the realist narratives cultivated in the nineteenth century. Not least of these is the care taken to create characters who give the effect of resembling real-world human beings, who pass through turmoil with which readers can identify, and who undergo transformations as they are affected by the events of the story.

The Time of the Hero exemplifies one of the strengths of the Spanish American new novel that proved particularly satisfying to readers left doubtful about the worth of novelistic experimentation. Spanish American fiction of the 1960s and 1970s was often constructed according to innovative designs, especially as regarded the treatment of time and space. Yet it is rare to find a case in which the handling of formal aspects of narrative draws attention to itself so notably as to upstage the work's ability to comment on real-world matters. Only an extremely skewed and partial reading of *The Time of the Hero* could manage to omit the judgments generated by the novel on the society shown and on such institutions as the military, the church, and the bourgeois family. Spanish American works in the vein of *The Time of the Hero* are apt to be the subject of favorable comparisons with the French *nouveau roman*, in which the author's choices in the treatment of novelistic form may take center stage.

José Donoso came to international fame after the boom was well underway. During the early part of his career, he was known principally to Chilean readers, who identified him as a member of that country's Generation of 1950. He began to build his reputation with subtle, acute short stories reminiscent of Henry James. Donoso, who learned English early in life, has strong links to English-language literary culture and has spent time as a student at Princeton, as a lecturer in the University of Iowa's creative writing program, and as visiting faculty elsewhere in the United States. His very first two published stories (1951) were written in English and appeared in *MSS*, a Princeton-based literary review.

At the same time he had admired many English-language writers, Donoso was greatly struck by the novels of Spanish American writers who had achieved fame slightly before him. Carpentier's *The Lost Steps* and Fuentes's *Where the Air Is Clear* are two such works that Donoso has singled out as having been revelations for him, showing how a novel may be technically innovative, yet distinctively Spanish American. In his sometimes acid and mocking 1972 memoir, *Historia personal del "boom"* (English version *The Boom in Spanish American Literature*), he characterizes himself as a late-blooming, almost second-generation boom author who had to learn from the success of envied predecessors.

In their construction, his early stories do not give much of a hint of the lengthy "totalizing novel," breaking sharply with realist convention, with which Donoso would later win his world fame. Yet the early publications show one preoccupation that would be a constant throughout this author's career: a critical examination of the rigidly hierarchical class system, illustrated by Chilean society, and, above all, a knowledgeable and mocking treatment of the upper-middle and upper classes. They also reveal Donoso's fascination with devices that distort and confuse identity, such as the peculiar mirror that gives a disturbing new coloration to the heroine of one of his very early stories in English from *MSS*, "The Blue Woman." Donoso's narratives contain a proliferation of objects and processes that destabilize identity. Masks, disguises, and costumes abound in Donoso's writing, along with such identity-confusing phenomena as namesakes, characters with multiple names, and even organ transplants.

In Donoso's fictional outlook, both the bourgeoisie and the aristocracy are ridiculous for their self-centered preoccupation with their own holdings and belongings, prestige, ancestry, and power. The meaningless repetition of conventions believed to confer respectability comes in for satirical treatment in several Donoso pieces. Still, the rigidity of inherited customs is never sufficient to prevent an occasional creative individual from escaping from the pattern through force of imagination.

A much-admired story that pursues this idea is "Paseo" ("The Walk"). Its narrator is a motherless child raised by three middle-aged siblings, two respected male lawyers and a sister devoted to them. Now adult, he is attempting to reconstruct the curious story of his aunt, a task made difficult by his family's polite silence on the matter.

In the narrator's reminiscences, the family occupies one of the many oppressive, even threatening, old houses that appear in Donoso's fiction. These dwellings often play as much of a role as any character, dominating and overwhelming their human inhabitants. The archetypal Donoso house muffles or confuses sounds and lets in only a limited amount of light. In decor, it features heavy, enveloping draperies and furniture built to impress rather than for comfort. The sound-quenching, curtained, and veiled environment corresponds to the owners' effort to evade any disagreeable or threatening thought. A typical Donoso touch is baffling passageways, courtyards, and outcroppings whose function has long since been forgotten. In "The Walk," an obsessive, ritualized perfectionism keeps the family home well maintained. Yet more often the houses that appear in Donoso's fiction are in advanced stages of decay. The ruined houses in this author's work are, on the one hand, metaphors of an upper social stratum that has lost its vitality and coherence. Beyond their figurative significance, these deteriorating structures give Donoso the opportunity to display one of his distinguishing gifts and obsessions as a writer, the literary treatment of objects, beings, and personalities in the process of disintegrating and destroying themselves.

The household in "The Walk" is regulated by a fanatically detailed routine in accordance with long-standing family tradition, although the rationale for the rituals has become lost. The narrator's starchy maiden aunt at first appears to be a grim priestess of tradition, devoutly holding the household to its exacting timetable. Yet she begins to show an unexpected deviance by allowing into her perfectly regulated house a stray dog, a foraging street creature whose mongrel ancestry would normally be disdained by the lineage-proud family. The more disruptive the anarchic pet proves to the family's calcified routine, the more the aunt's loyalty is transferred toward it. Walking the dog becomes an event charged with special excitement: "Later, her outings inexplicably took more time. She was no longer a woman who walked her dog for reasons of hygiene; out there in the streets, in the city, there was something powerful attracting her" (Andree Conrad's translation).[31] Finally, she appears to have chosen to become a fellow stray rather than remain in the constraining house of which she was once obsessively proud. The aunt typifies a number of Donoso characters who, feeling the need to break free of the inanely strict conventions of their bourgeois environments, turn longingly to members of lower social classes, whom they see as possessing a vitality and vigor long since sacrificed by the powerful classes. In these relations, the upper class partner can offer material comforts—the aunt heals and feeds the stray—while the lower class counterpart provides vigor and élan.

Donoso's critical reputation took another leap forward with his 1957 novel *Coronación* (*Coronation*), but his international renown was secured with the 1970 *El obsceno pájaro de la noche* (*The Obscene Bird of Night*), probably the last of the great boom novels. *Obscene Bird* carries over thematic strains from Donoso's previous texts. Yet it makes all his earlier writing look conventionally straightforward, for it displays an extreme indeterminacy of time, place, and person. The plot of this lengthy narrative, filled with bizarre phantasmagoria, could not be summarized in plain language without reducing it to virtual incoherence. Yet the unclear events possess a unifying meaning as they are held in the mind of the narrator-protagonist. While several personae speak in the novel, they all turn out to be extensions or disguises of a single narrator. Lacking any defined identity, he must continually be cobbling one together, frequently borrowing selves or portions of selves from those with whom he comes into contact. *Schizophrenia* is a term frequently invoked to account for the exceptional qualities of this narrative, and indeed its narrator and his language do appear to display the signs of the disorder. Using this common observation as a point of departure, George R. McMurray has specified the points of convergence between psychoanalytical concepts of schizophrenia and the literary version of the phenomenon found in Donoso's famous novel. McMurray accurately notes that schizophrenic thinking has a ready point of entry into Donoso's literary discourse. The disordered thought and expression of the schizophrenic resemble the highly irrational discourse cultivated by the surrealists, who in an extended sense are Donoso's predecessors.[32]

Humberto Peñaloza, the narrator of *Obscene Bird*, is a struggling writer, the son of a grade-school teacher of working-class origin. In one of the complex trans-class, interdependent bonds that fascinate Donoso, Humberto has installed himself as personal secretary to a powerful aristocrat, politician, and property owner, Don Jerónimo Azcoitía. Humberto is assigned the most diverse activities in the service of the Azcoitía family, from managing its estate to composing its official history. Don Jerónimo is the degenerating product of a depleted family line and has grown to rely on his secretary to bring a fresh impetus to his life. Humberto's supplementary vigor is somehow needed even for Don Jerónimo to father a child, whose conception is narrated in the most ambiguous terms. Humberto is able to assume some portion of his employer's identity and to speak and narrate in the latter's voice.

Don Jerónimo's wife and distant cousin Inés offers a feminine version of her husband's situation. While the husband gains power through political posts and property, Doña Inés campaigns for importance through a self-seeking respectability and piety. She lobbies the Vatican to canonize an eighteenth-century ancestor who is also her exact namesake. The

family whose glory she is eager to display, though presumed to have enjoyed former splendor, is now in decline in every sense. The inbred Azcoitía line is in danger of dying out when the present generation long
remains without issue. Doña Inés's poor record as a childbearer places her
prestige in jeopardy, and, as age starts to encroach on her, she resorts to
bizarre stratagems to produce a single wretchedly deformed son.

Doña Inés, too, is in an intimate relation of mutual exploitation and
dependency with a person of lower social class, in her case, a shrewd,
witchcraft-practicing servant. The maid's identity has so overlapped that
of her mistress that, in the narrator's account, the latter not only is coming
to resemble the former but has been implanted with a number of her
organs. Seeking to affirm her high status through her relations with social
inferiors, Doña Inés plays the part of Lady Bountiful toward the elderly
women housed in one of the family's properties, but, never able to pass
up an opportunity, she gambles with them and wins away their meager,
ratty belongings.

Don Jerónimo is the proprietor of two vast, sinister, labyrinthine constructions that figure importantly in the plot. One is La Rinconada, a
family estate in the country. Among other purposes, it comes to house
monsters who surround the owner's deformed son and prevent him from
discovering his abnormality. The other is an urban property, the Casa, a
vast, crumbling building from the Spanish colonial era. The Azcoitías
built the Casa and dedicated it as a religious retreat, but its function was
widely recognized as that of providing a refuge for the now-legendary Inés
de Azcoitía. This young woman, who is at the center of two centuries of
controversy, had to be kept safeguarded behind thick walls. Some say that
her father caught her practicing some ungodly black-arts ritual; others,
that she was inconveniently pregnant; the Azcoitías maintain that her
saintly purity made her unsuited for life out in the world. Since her death,
she has haunted the imagination of the rich and poor alike and is the object
not only of myths and rumors but also reported sightings.

Since the days of its colonial splendor, the Casa has declined from its
origins as a religious retreat to serve as a warehouse for elderly women
servants discarded by elite families. Its mazelike halls and rooms are filled
with castoff objects and persons, at times indistinguishable from one another in the undifferentiated chaos of gloom and disorder. Perenially
threatened with demolition, it epitomizes the decay and deterioration that
are a preoccupation throughout the novel. The relation between the Azcoitía family and their houses is ambivalent and tense; Don Jerónimo at

times wishes he could destroy both structures. The retreat house represents the family's hope of achieving supreme respectability; they offer it as proof of their prominence and wealth going back to colonial times and of their record of piety. At the same time, it sullies the Azcoitía name, for it has always given rise to lurid local gossip, and in the present day is filled with sorcery and corruption.

The interrelations between the two metaphorically charged houses constitute a subplot in themselves, undergoing delicate, meaningful permutations and transformations throughout the novel. Hugo Achugar has observed that the narrator and characters often describe these two significant houses as if they were the same: "*The Obscene Bird of Night* develops two basic spaces: the Casa de Ejercicios Espirituales de la Chimba and La Rinconada: Two spaces that are described in several passages in an almost identical fashion."[33] The two houses share an identity even though one is a wealthy family's private country house and the other an urban asylum, neglected and turned over to the poor. The resemblance is fraught with paradoxes: "The descriptions resemble one another and the labyrinthine character of both is accentuated. . . . But still the reader and also the characters clearly differentiate one place from another, even though they feel that they are indissolubly connected. Of course, they are through the story. Both places belong to the Azcoitía family and their interrelatedness goes back centuries, since the fact . . . that linked La Rinconada with the Casa de la Chimba has as its protagonist Inés de Azcoitía (saintly woman and witch) who goes from one space to another, establishing a causal connection."[34] Humberto, too, is impelled back and forth between the houses until his final deterioration drives him to the Casa.

Obscene Bird is exceptionally difficult to follow. A basic rule in the text is that the narrator always proves to be Humberto; nonetheless, it may be difficult to determine who Humberto is at any moment and where he is in time and space. Cedomil Goic sums up the difficulty of specifying the narrative voice and point of view in the novel: "In his disintegration, the narrator goes into a formless fluctuation between multiple identities, replacing and sharing varied personae and, at the same time, entering into a reductive mode associated with his diminution, with a shrinking to a miniscule, unworthy size."[35] Together with the fluidity resulting from the narrator's magical vision of the universe, the instability of Humberto's identity produces an especially demanding text: "With the fluctuations of the narrator—of the narrator's identity—the reader must constantly readjust the perspective so it will correspond with the 'origin of the speaking voice.' The disintegration of the narrator, in this way, becomes part of a general indeterminacy. The narrator's identity, personality, speaking voice, the temporo-spatial position, are fluctuating and contradictory."[36]

Difficult as *Obscene Bird* is, it has proved absorbing to readers and critics. Among its most impressive literary accomplishments are its vivid, nightmarish renderings of delusional thinking and hallucinations. The most memorable of these surround Humberto's surgery for an ulcer he has developed while attempting to manage the Azcoitía estate, with its population of monsters. (Donoso was eager to tell interviewers that these passages had their origin in his own hallucinatory experiences when undergoing ulcer surgery.) Humberto's isolation among the freaks of La Rinconada has already made him paranoid, and, his instability exacerbated by anesthesia and painkillers, he experiences fantastic visions. Subsequently, Humberto harbors the conviction that the surgeon has removed 80 percent of his internal organs, with a corresponding reduction of his self, now headed toward disappearance. His tendency to let his identity wander into other beings grows stronger; he becomes, among other things, a deaf servant in the Casa (his strongest secondary identity), a dog, a bird, an old woman, a splotch of grease on the wall, two different babies, a fetus, a giant with a huge papier-mâché head, an undifferentiated being wrapped in layers of burlap, and a child whose orifices have been sewn shut by witches. At the end, he has been reduced to some vague, insubstantial matter and is ingloriously discarded like a bundle of trash.

As readers can anticipate, the fragile, decadent Azcoitías have met wretched fates by the time the novel ends. The wife has been taken away to a mental asylum. The husband's ruin is more intricate and more in tune with the novel's obsession with disturbances of identity. It occurs at a costume party where Don Jerónimo, misled, fails to wear the right type of disguise. He is forced to view his reflection in a pond, distorted by ripples, and drowns while attempting to tear off his face, which he believes to be a disfiguring mask. At the same time the Azcoitías and their middle-class hanger-on Humberto disappear from the scene, the less clearly differentiated lower-class characters seem to succeed in surviving and persisting. The novel itself, and not just the upper-class characters, seems to be attributing to the lower classes a vitality and endurance missing in the more rarified regions of society.

It is typical of *Obscene Bird*, as of the Spanish American novel generally, that even in the passages where hallucinatory images abound, the social background is not lost from sight. No matter how impressed a reader may be by the fluctuations in time, space, and personal identity, it would be difficult to ignore the importance that the class system and interclass relations have in the novel. At the same time that Humberto is undergoing mutations and finally disintegration in his sense of self, the novel reminds readers of the events that are transpiring in contemporary social history, from the Vietnam war to the cultural radicalism of late-1960s youth movements.

Gabriel García Márquez (Colombia, b. 1928) was the boom writer whose writing, along with that of Borges from an earlier generation, represented new Spanish American narrative and, especially, magical realism to the largest and most popular international readership. While all the major authors of the boom have been rumored to be under serious consideration for the Nobel Prize in Literature, García Márquez, the 1982 winner, has been the first of this group to be awarded the honor. He is known first and foremost for his 1967 novel *Cien años de soledad* (*One Hundred Years of Solitude*). Probably the most easily read of the great novels produced during the boom era, *One Hundred Years* draws its readers along with an ingeniously worked-out plot and memorable characters and episodes. It is the novel that consolidated García Márquez's image as the great teller of tales among the writers of his generation. *One Hundred Years* demonstrates to the full García Márquez's ability to utilize the repertory of stratagems a skilled plot-weaver employs to captivate an audience. Yet, for all its enthralling and charming qualities, it is at the same time an elaborately patterned fictional construction that has provided abundant material for critical analysis. *One Hundred Years* expertly interconnects itself to many other texts. The resonances it absorbs and develops from these allusive bonds to existing texts may or may not be recognized by readers, yet the comprehension of the work does not depend on their recognition. The Hebrew Bible, novels of chivalry, the chronicles composed by New World discoverers, and the work of several modern novelists, particularly Faulkner, all appear to have provided antecedents for García Márquez to incorporate, transforming them thoroughly, into his own writing.

Many of García Márquez's stories and novels, including *One Hundred Years*, have a typical setting that is abundantly familiar to his longtime readers. This fictional locale is an isolated, backward town near the Caribbean coast of Colombia. Readers who view fiction as autobiography have been quick to identify the town with Aracataca, Colombia, where the author spent much of his childhood; when García Márquez attained his great fame, journalists and photographers made their way to Aracataca in hopes that the real-world pilgrimage might somehow shed light on the fiction. García Márquez has stated that as early as 1944—that is, in his adolescence—he had begun to write a novel, to be entitled *La casa* (The house), in which he began to develop the setting and characters that became famous in *One Hundred Years*. By 1950, he had published a short story in which a town and family appear with many of the same features as the ones familiar to readers of *One Hundred Years*. This story, "La casa de los Buendía" (The house of the Buendías), was reprinted after the enormous success of the 1967 novel and is readily recognizable as a prototype version of *One Hundred Years*.[37]

In García Márquez's invented town, it is perennially humid, and when the rains come, they are torrential. In *One Hundred Years* it rains for four years, eleven months, and two days. (It is a hallmark of García Márquez's fiction that larger-than-life occurrences are at times made to seem more convincing by narrating them with the use of exact sums and quantities; at other times, he leaves duration and amount extremely vague.) All of nature often appears to be the agent of divine or cosmic wrath in the harsh treatment it metes out to the characters, along the lines of the plagues and chastisements visited on the Hebrews in biblical narrative. The event-filled plot of *One Hundred Years* includes, as well as the monumental rain and infestations of pests, such unusual collective afflictions as a plague of insomnia followed by massive outbreaks of amnesia.

In *One Hundred Years* and certain other fictions, the archetypal small, humid town bears the name Macondo; in other of the author's texts, a nameless town exhibits the same characteristics. The first clearly recalled member of the Buendía family is the mythic founder of Macondo, José Arcadio Buendía. He is the charismatic patriarch after whom many subsequent José Arcadio Buendías will be named; all his proliferating namesakes share his strong and impulsive personality. (The other name given to male Buendías, Aureliano, is bestowed upon children of a more thoughtful, less mercurial temperament.) In a pattern loosely adapted from biblical narrative, the tremendously vigorous, if overexcitable, José Arcadio has spent about two years wandering in the wilderness. Exiled for killing a man who had cast aspersions on his virility, he leads several families in search of an existence less complicated with difficulties. Their trek ends at a site where their leader experiences a visionary dream of a town of mirrored walls. Here he orders his followers to establish a settlement and confers upon it the name, Macondo, by which a voice in his dream had called the envisioned town.

In succeeding generations, the fortunes of the Buendías are always intertwined with those of the town, and both decline together and meet the same cataclysmic end. Macondo is always affected by the collective character of its leading family, especially the Buendías' growing eccentricity and propensity to fritter away their time and energy in whimsical pursuits. Since the novel popularized the word *Macondo*, it has been applied jokingly to any confused situation in which the official mechanisms for maintaining order only increase the reigning chaos. García Márquez's characters live far from the nation's center, and their attempted contacts with the national government are irregular, frustrating, and perplexing.

Yet their location in a neglected backwater offers them no protection from the impact of the nation's turmoil. In their earliest years, the town and family are remembered as enjoying a golden age in which history had no power over them and their society was exempt from the need to change and evolve. Supposedly their concerns never strayed beyond the immediacies of family and community, all interaction was face to face, and no governing organization was needed. But this paradise of timelessness cannot be preserved. When the first agent from the central government appears, bearing the title of *corregidor* (literally, corrector), the townspeople tell him that there is nothing to correct in Macondo. Government involvement, though, proves inevitable, along with the intrusions of commerce and trade, science and technology, the church, and, generally, modern styles of social organization. The inhabitants of Macondo, as would the members of any real-world community, have no choice but to live within history and experience the effects of social change. As several years of political violence sweep the country, the townspeople are vulnerable to its ravages. One of the Buendía sons, Colonel Aureliano Buendía, fights in thirty-two successive civil wars and survives seventy-three ambushes, fourteen assassination attempts, a firing squad, and the revenge killing, all in one night, of the seventeen sons he has fathered during his prodigious campaigns. Yet, after all these events have come to pass, the exact motive for this massive and chronic violence remains opaque even to the colonel who was its protagonist. The exploitation of foreign firms is another of the scourges that afflict the town. A banana importer moves in and begins to work its transformations, building a second Macondo exclusively for the foreign company's employees. Before it leaves, it suppresses a strike with a great massacre and succeeds in denying that the killings ever took place.

Because communication is unreliable, information about new developments in the world reaches Macondo at an unpredictable, sporadic rate. For a time a band of gypsies, in its periodic visits, brings modern concepts, information, and technology to the town in an out-of-sequence, pell-mell order. Thus the inhabitants may be expertly sophisticated in certain areas, yet uninformed and provincial in other ways, or may combine the culture and outlook of diverse historical periods. For example, when photography becomes available, José Arcadio seeks to use the new technology to obtain a photograph of God, which would be the best proof yet of the divinity's existence. In Macondo's irregular time, there is not necessarily any gap between the effort to prove the existence of God, normally associated with the twelfth-century heyday of scholastic philosophy, and the popularization of photography. Courtly love, its manners and rhetoric, comes in for a new flourishing in Macondo. The solitude in which the characters live is not only personal and individual but collective and social, for Macondo is isolated from the mainstream of the nation's life.

The title of *One Hundred Years* has several meanings, but its primary reference is to a prophetic curse which the Buendías, and the town whose fortunes are fused with those of the family, are unwittingly living out. Judging from the number of generations the Buendías produce and the references to historical and fictional events, the action of the novel would probably take somewhat over a century to play itself out. So far as one can tell from allusions to real-world developments, the latest occurrences narrated must take place in the 1920s. However, the narrator of *One Hundred Years* treats chronology with the casual inexactitude of a peasant storyteller for whom "one hundred years" might also be used to designate simply "a long time." The novel contains few specific time markers; the passage of time is often signaled, folk style, simply by saying that "many" or "several" years, or "a lot" of time, transpired. The narrator feels quite free to embellish his tale with anecdotes that cannot be fitted into the hundred-year time frame, as when he includes an episode involving Sir Francis Drake.

The Buendías' allotted hundred years in Macondo are the time the family line needs to deteriorate and extinguish itself. The energetic, creative vision of José Arcadio Buendía and the sturdy good sense of his stalwart wife Ursula at first make the Buendías appear a vigorous tribe, but the family character easily declines into pointless eccentricity. Even the original José Arcadio lives out a personal history of decadence, as the heated, inventive imagination that once spurred him to found a new community degenerates into insanity. Though he haunts the house and continues to exercise an influence, his powerful personality is never again the impelling force it once was. Ursula lives a long and stable life, at least 115 years, but when she dies, the family loses its solid grounding. While Ursula is a firmly established matriarchal figure, later Buendía women are unable to recapture her motherly strength. Though the Buendía men engender quantities of offspring, barrenness seems to be the common destiny of their sisters. The novel's overall story proves to be one of a community in demographic, moral, and material decline. As well as the overarching curse that determines the family's existence from the settlement of Macondo to the extinction of the line, the novel is full of minor prophecies, threatening curses, and ominous glimpses of things to come. Throughout their history, the frequently inbred Buendías are apprehensive that their too-close unions will result in the birth of a child with a tail, and indeed such a monster appears as the family line is about to die out.

One Hundred Years presents a fascinatingly complicated variant of the time-honored strategy whereby an author pretends to have wandered across an abandoned manuscript and to be offering the reader a transcription of that stray document as the text of his or her story or novel. At the end of *One Hundred Years*, the sole surviving Buendía, the last of a dying breed, discovers, written out in exact detail, the entire story that his family has been living. The document the character finds and deciphers was composed on parchment in Sanskrit. It is the work of a gypsy, a sort of mentor to the Buendías, whose spirit had taken over a room of the family house. But its contents are, presumably, the same story that is told in the text of the novel *One Hundred Years of Solitude*.

To say that the gypsy is the narrator of *One Hundred Years* is too simple and destroys the mysterious effect generated by the paradoxical relations between the parchments and the novel. The words of *One Hundred Years* are modern Spanish, not the gypsy's Sanskrit, a difference which implies the mediation of a transcriber-translator. It is not clear who carried out this textual work or how the reader has access to the resulting document; the Buendía who discovered the parchments was swept away into nothingness by a devastating wind while reading them. Melquíades, the magic prophet, must have used quite a different tone from that of the highly expert teller of tales who narrates *One Hundred Years of Solitude*. Moreover, the two accounts differ in their temporal aspects. The gypsy's parchments contain prophecies, while the novel tells of events already transpired. The narration of *One Hundred Years* proceeds from episode to episode, although the order of the episodes is not necessarily a chronological one. But the gypsy's manuscript has a magic ability to hold a lengthy sequence of narrated events in simultaneity, so that the story of the Buendías in Macondo can be absorbed in one intense moment of reading and thought. According to the parchments, not only will the Buendía family die out, but its history will be consigned to oblivion. Yet the Buendía story is recorded and proliferates through the writing and reproduction of *One Hundred Years*.

The curious discrepancies and disjunctures between the gypsy's prophetic history and the text of García Márquez's novel have tantalized critics seeking to account for them. Ricardo Gullón puzzles over the relation of the two accounts and, sensibly, ends with an open question:

> *The narration of the events was written twice: in a language unintelligible to the inhabitants of Macondo (in Sanskrit) by Melquíades, before they happened: a prophet-chronicler, he has seen the future . . . and he anticipates it in his history; in Spanish, by the narrator, after the fact: he tells the past, and on the first page he skips ahead to the execution of Colonel Aureliano Buendía, which will not be carried out, and will be frustrated until years (or centuries) later. Is the narrator a reflection of Melquíades, or, stated in the terms of the work, is he a reincarnation of Melquíades?* [38]

Probably more important than any single hypothesis that one might formulate about the fictional status of *One Hundred Years* is the special quality conferred upon the novel by its seemingly impossible origin. It is as if the reader were only by force of magic enjoying access to a story that should by all rights be not only unreadable but also completely annihilated and obliterated from the memory of humankind. García Márquez, here as elsewhere, assumes the role of a professional storyteller whose success depends on being able to amaze his audience with elaborate hocuspocus.

Time and its nature are abiding preoccupations in *One Hundred Years*. Not only have García Márquez and his critics shown a concern with the temporal structure of the novel, but the characters themselves are heard within the novel expressing various degrees of puzzlement and disturbance over the phenomenon of time. The principal focus of their concern is the issue of whether time is progressing forward, presumably toward some goal or to some purpose. The idea of a forward march that gives a purpose to temporality would be reassuring. But it is constantly under threat from two competing notions: that time is cyclical and that under certain circumstances it reverses its progress and flows back toward what has already transpired.

Although Ursula is usually immersed in her practical duties and seldom expresses herself at a high level of abstraction, she occasionally stands back to observe apprehensively that time is following a circular course. The notion of temporal cycles receives reinforcement from such oddities as the assignment of the same names over and over to the family's children, who then exhibit the same traits as their like-named predecessors, and the recurring threat of incest and deformed offspring. José Arcadio is tormented by the discovery that time may be leading nowhere. The family's gypsy mentor, who was initiating José Arcadio into the mysteries of alchemy and philosophy, first mentioned to him the concept of regressions in time. Subsequently the idea took over his pupil's imagination. His decline into madness is attributed to the horror of contemplating a time that wavers and zigzags in its path to nowhere.

However cyclical or reversible time may appear in certain respects, by the novel's end it is clear that time is running out for the Buendías. They have used the stretch of time allotted them to head unidirectionally toward degeneration and self-extinction. The prophecy is unambiguous in stating that they will receive no second chance to reestablish their depleted line.

Magical realism may never have been so unmistakably exemplified as in *One Hundred Years*. At the most obvious level, readers cannot miss the co-occurrence of such realistic elements as the story of the banana company with such magical and mythical features as the bizarre disturbances in nature that accompany Ursula's death. Yet the fact that such disparate components have been placed in the same novel is not in itself the achievement for which García Márquez was celebrated. What has impressed readers more is the uniformity that the narrative maintains as it presents both lifelike occurrences and fantastic ones. The latter are introduced with no fanfare, and there is no indication that the reader should find them more noteworthy or stimulating to read about than the more verisimilar portions of the plot.

This unexcitable, matter-of-fact manner of retelling amazing events offers a vivid contrast with the tradition of fantastic literature. Lugones and other adepts of the "tale of effect" dedicated their narrative skills to heightening the exceptional quality of fantastic events. In a typical convention, the narrator of such a story would emphasize the shocking impact that the unusual occurrences produced on him, saying that he or she turned cold all over, went pale, or was on the brink of madness. In contrast is the stolid narrator of *One Hundred Years*, as Gullón characterizes him:

> *The tone corresponds, as it must, to the voice of the narrator, and the narrator is the Narrator: someone uninvolved in what is narrated, who knows what there is to be known about the events and tells of them as a chronicler, without editorializing, imperturbable and unperturbed, without making moral or any other type of judgments on what has happened. He doesn't question the facts; for him, there is no difference between what's realistically probable and what's not; he sticks to his mission—or function—of telling everything and speaks of the living just as he does of the dead, associating without blinking a ghost with tangible reality. His imperturbability is manifested in his unchanging tone; from the first page to the last, the same level is maintained, without fluctuations, without variations.*[39]

The following passage, taken from Rabassa's much-praised English version, shows the impassive quality Gullón describes as well as García Márquez's admixture of the amazing with the banal and everyday. Here the rain that cosmic wrath visits upon Macondo is treated jointly with the disruption of an extramarital affair and the issue of household maintenance:

> *It rained for four years, eleven months, and two days. There were periods of drizzle during which everyone put on his full dress and a convalescent look to celebrate the clearing, but the people soon grew accustomed to interpret the pauses as a sign of redoubled rain. The sky crumbled into a set of destructive storms and out of the north came hurricanes that scattered roofs about and knocked down walls and uprooted every last plant of the banana groves. Just as during the insomnia plague, as Ursula came to remember during those days, the calamity itself inspired defenses against boredom. Aureliano Segundo was one of those who worked hardest not to be conquered by idleness. He had gone home for some minor matter on the night that*

> *Mr. Brown unleashed the storm, and Fernanda tried*
> *to help him with a half-blown-out umbrella that she*
> *found in a closet. "I don't need it," he said. "I'll stay*
> *until it clears." That was not, of course, an ironclad*
> *promise, but he would accomplish it literally. Since his*
> *clothes were at Petra Cotes's, every three days he would*
> *take off what he had on and wait in his shorts until*
> *they were washed. In order not to become bored, he*
> *dedicated himself to the task of repairing things that*
> *needed fixing in the house. He adjusted hinges, oiled*
> *locks, screwed knockers tight, and planed doorjambs.*[40]

Readers of *One Hundred Years* were so enthralled with the novel that they produced a demand for writing that seemed somehow to offer them more of the novel's delights. The publishing industry quickly supplied not only further editions of *One Hundred Years*, which brought a great bonanza to the Sudamericana house of Buenos Aires, but also speedily produced reissues of all García Márquez writings that had the same appealing qualities as the 1967 novel. The 1955 *La hojarasca* (*Leafstorm*) and the 1961 *El coronel no tiene quien le escriba* (*No One Writes to the Colonel*) are two worthy examples of his early fiction that became available in English translation.

During the same period—the mid- to late 1960s—a subgroup of Spanish American writers obtained a fame somewhat less widespread than that of the giants of the boom. These writers were practitioners of an elaborately mannered writing that has sometimes been categorized as Caribbean baroque. (It should be remembered that Carpentier had long been identifying the baroque as the style best suited to the region's distinctive reality.) The three major writers of this neobaroque fiction were all Cuban: José Lezama Lima (1912–1976), Guillermo Cabrera Infante (b. 1929), and Severo Sarduy (1937–1993).

Lezama Lima was first and foremost a poet, and before his debut as a novelist he had won a critical reputation with his elaborate, hermetic verse. He spent many years—by some accounts, up to twenty—conceiving, thinking through, and writing his immensely complex novel *Paradiso*, which bears the same title in Gregory Rabassa's English version. Before it appeared in 1966, the novel was the subject of rumor and legend in the literary world. Julio Cortázar, who had read it in manuscript, was concerned lest this unique literary monument, initially daunting to readers, never see the light of print. He helped Lezama bring his text into its final form and place it. *Paradiso* was launched with the help of enthusiastic recommendations from Cortázar, Vargas Llosa, and the critic Emir Rodríguez Monegal.

As its Dante-derived title suggests, *Paradiso* depends a great deal on allegory and symbolism. Imagistic description predominates over plot, although at least the first part of the work is organized along a biographical story line. *Paradiso* is linguistically dense, composed in a highly compact, intricate poet's prose that communicates more through allusion and metaphor than statement. The system of cultural references in *Paradiso* is not only wide but also at times arcane, reflecting Lezama's general erudition and his special preoccupation with such subjects as alchemy, divination, and African Cuban religious syncretism. At the time of its publication, some readers considered *Paradiso* daring for its treatment of male homosexuality, although it should be noted that the novel deals with this theme in the poetic, diffuse manner that prevails throughout; it would be an exaggeration to call it a novel of gay life. While offering inexhaustible opportunities for critical analysis, *Paradiso* makes such demands on its readers that it has never reached as wide a readership as the fiction of the major boom authors.

Cabrera Infante is a film critic, cultural journalist, and screenwriter as well as an author of fiction. Earlier Cuban literary intellectuals, the great example being Carpentier, had been knowledgeable about the nation's folklore. Cabrera Infante stood out by his expertise in the popular culture that mass communications had spread throughout Cuba: a culture that was undergoing rapid change and that showed the signs of commercial pressures and U.S. influence. Together with his ability to draw on mass culture, this author's great strength has been his linguistic invention and playfulness. He exhibits a fondness for bizarre, sometimes troubling puns, such as his oddly guilt-wracked pseudonym G. Cain. Cabrera has a facility for devising anagrams, palindromes, ambiguous phrases, and other playful linguistic anomalies.

Tres tristes tigres (*Three Trapped Tigers*), his novel named for a tongue-twister, is an ambivalent homage to the culture of pre-Castro Havana, which the novel turns into a lurid dream and a showcase for the author's unusual linguistic constructions. *Three Trapped Tigers* offers up a spectacle of decadence, yet in the version of the novel that was finally published in 1967, the vision of Havana by night is not a straightforwardly censorious one. The text was already completed and had won the Seix Barral Prize for a new novel in 1964, but its publication was postponed. During the delay, Cabrera Infante grew more disenchanted with the Cuban Revolution and reworked the novel accordingly. Seymour Menton states that in the earlier version late-1950s Havana figured as the antithesis of revolutionary health: "The dissolute, antisocial lives of the protagonists were contrasted with the exemplary behavior of the urban and rural guerrillas."[41] The published *Three Trapped Tigers* shows a decaying state of affairs, but also glories in the luxuriant world of diversion that the revolution swept away.

While it was fashionable during the 1960s to assert that the true protagonist of a given novel was language, in the case of *Three Trapped Tigers* the statement is a fair one. Indeed, one character, who is well remembered by his friends, lived out his last days in the grips of an all-consuming linguistic obsession; his monomania drove him in a seemingly fatal quest for palindromes, boustrophedons, and other rare constructions. In the last third of the text, an actor and a newspaper man drive aimlessly through Havana, spurring one another on in a delirious paroxysm of spontaneous punning. The characters' linguistic games supplement those of the author, who creates bizarre effects through typographical anomalies and, displaying his talent for mimicry, imitates poor spellers, speakers of dialects, and writers tagged by their affectations.

Cabrera Infante, who took up residence in London after leaving Cuba, is an expert in English-language popular culture and as able to pun in English as in Spanish. He has been a cotranslator of the English editions of his works; for instance, for *Three Trapped Tigers* Cabrera Infante assisted Donald Gardner and Suzanne Jill Levine, the latter his frequent and close collaborator. While he never had a second success to match that of *Tigers*, he has produced an unusually diverse set of writings, including such works of undefinable genre as the 1985 *Holy Smoke* (original in English), meditations on the cigar and its cultural implications.

Sarduy, who originally set out to be an art historian and critic, came to France to study at the École du Louvre and settled in Paris. He became associated with the Tel Quel group of literary and cultural theorists and was a companion of the celebrated literary critic Roland Barthes. His bicultural background, wide reading, and eye for new tendencies established him as an influential editorial consultant and arbiter of tastes.

Sarduy's own fiction is known for an identifiable nucleus of recurring concerns. Experimentation with concepts of narrative form is a constant in his writing. A Sarduy work can appear repetitive and disorganized until one discovers the internal logic of the text. Cross-dressing and other violations of the usual gender boundaries are both themes and structuring elements in Sarduy's writing. Specific Sarduy characters literally cross-dress; for example, the eponymous protagonist of the 1972 novel *Cobra* is a transvestite. But more broadly, dressing across genders becomes a metaphor for many types of transformations, including the changes through which a literary text would ideally pass as it undergoes the processes of reading and writing.

Like many Cuban intellectuals, Sarduy knows a good deal about popular music and turns his expertise in this area to literary advantage. Sexual subcultures, such as the demimonde of pre-Castro Havana, constitute another of his special preoccupations. The baroque, both as a critical concept and a practice in creative writing, is a long-standing concern of Sarduy's. While many of his contemporaries are expansive writers, Sarduy prizes and cultivates a lapidary brevity in his fiction and essays.

This author continues to be best known for the 1967 novel *De dónde son los cantantes*, whose title is an excerpt from a famous song lyric (English version *From Cuba with a Song*). *From Cuba with a Song* is constructed as a theme and variations; it elaborates essentially the same minimal plot line three times over. Through its tripartite structure, it pays homage to three ethnic strains in Cuban culture: the African, the Asian, and the Hispanic. In a characteristic Sarduy touch, at first the characters appear simply to be engaged in cross-dressing, but as the narrative develops, they reveal themselves to be caught up in much more thoroughgoing metamorphoses than can be effected through clothing.

After the boom had subsided, it became evident in retrospect that no woman writer had fully reaped the benefits of the excitement over Spanish American fiction. Yet there were women whose work exhibited the same qualities that had attracted large readerships to the boom authors. An exemplary case is that of the Mexican dramatist and fiction writer Elena Garro (b. 1920), practitioner of a subtle form of magical realism with a strong subcurrent of social commentary. Though Garro was producing her lyrical, mythlike writing during the boom, critical studies of her work date for the most part from the late 1970s forward, when a number of previously overlooked women writers came in for sudden discovery. Garro, who had too often been identified principally as the former wife of Octavio Paz, now stood on her own as the author of narratives centered on powerful metaphors.

In prose fiction Garro is best known for her lyrical novel of 1963, *Los recuerdos del porvenir*. Winner of the 1964 Xavier Villaurrutia Prize, the novel was translated by Ruth L. C. Simms as *Recollections of Things to Come*. The narrator of *Recollections* is a small town in the south of Mexico, which offers a collective first-person-singular account of itself. Government troops have occupied the community in an attempt to subdue the ultra-religious counterrevolution sweeping the region.

Although the novel speaks of history, making an acid comment on the outcome of the Mexican Revolution, it presents many concepts of and metaphors for atemporality. The town believes, collectively, in concepts of time opposed to unidimensional, linear chronology; these include a mythical time-outside-of-time and a reversible temporal flow. As the title hints, the future lies within the grasp of memory, since it contains fundamentally the same material as the past. The town speaks matter-of-factly of standardly occurring violations of linear temporality. Among these are the practice of stopping clocks in order to halt time and that of searching recall for prophecies.

The two halves of *Recollections* focus in turn on the two successive mistresses of the commanding officer of the occupying troops. Each of these women, endowed with almost mythical qualities of beauty and capacity for love, dominates one of the two major divisions of the novel. Each woman's story ends the way a myth should end; the officer's first mistress vanishes with a magical foreigner, while the second becomes a stone image of herself. The axial importance of women characters is typical of Garro's work. In her plays as well as her narrative fiction, women are often in the foreground. Garro's heroines occupy difficult and uncomfortable roles in the social order; the woman in *Recollections* petrifies after separating from her family and loving an outsider. When the 1970s resurgence of feminism directed fresh attention to women authors, Garro's work naturally came in for reissues and new critical readings.

Fascinating as the intricate novels of the boom years were, the excitement could not be prolonged indefinitely by writing in the same vein. The search for the totalizing novel, able to create its own complex and detailed world, seemed to be losing its impetus by the beginning of the 1970s. During the height of the boom, readers had tended to demand of Spanish American novels an extreme intricacy in their novelistic construction. The practice of narrating a strong plot straightforwardly, in an order that was fundamentally sequential and chronological, had become devalued during the late 1960s and was often referred to, with no small exaggeration, as the "traditional nineteenth-century novel" that the new narrative had left in the dust. But now, after so many experiments in nonlinear narrative design, the old *modo standard* no longer seemed so reprehensibly convention-bound. Novelists and readers now spoke of a renewed appreciation for the time-honored skills of plot and character development; the term "return to storytelling" became fashionable. During the boom, it had become almost too easy to identify Spanish America's major contemporary writers, works of fiction, and tendencies in narrative innovation. Subsequently, more competing trends coexisted and claimed equal attention; the region's fiction grew difficult to characterize in generalities.

Needless to say, it was impossible for the concept and practice of fiction to revert to what they had been before the narrative innovations of the twentieth century. The writers and readers who claimed to be turning back to the old-fashioned virtues in fiction were like the neoorthodox turning back to the faith of their forebears. That is to say, they could not divest themselves of the experience of having passed through modernity. The result, in Spanish American fiction, was a generation of novels and stories less ambitious in sweep and in construction than the great novels of the boom, yet representing a distinct departure from the realism that had been practiced in Spanish American writing of the first part of the century.

Six

THE POSTBOOM: NEW VOICES AND BELATED DISCOVERIES, 1968–1990

E/ven before the international heyday of the new Spanish American narrative was over, as early as the late 1960s, varieties of writing clearly distinctive from the typical boom fiction had begun appearing all over Spanish America. The type of work most likely to score a success during the boom era was a large, ambitious novel of notably complex construction, mixing realism and social commentary with myth and magic. These works could seem weighty and imposing, not only by virtue of their often monumental length, but also because of the missions they set themselves. The text characteristically confronted inexhaustible issues, such as the relation between language and the phenomena to which it alludes. A number of contemporary works sought to create a complete, autonomous world within the fiction.

Such a totalizing grand sweep stands in contrast to the postboom tendency to allow fiction to be frankly insubstantial and incomplete. On the whole, the later era is characterized by works that, if not actually briefer, at least appear more straightforward. Dauntingly lengthy and complex works continued to appear; an outstanding example is Fuentes's 1975 *Terra nostra* (*Terra Nostra* in Margaret Sayers Peden's English version). But younger writers often viewed the quest for the totalizing novel as pretentious, and Spanish American fiction was no longer so strongly identified with vast, demanding texts. Popular culture had by no means been absent from the novels of the boom, but postboom fiction exhibited a particularly strong preoccupation with this material. Many of the newer writers were skilled mimics of the artifacts of advertising and mass media and made their novels and short stories resemble such popular forms as the hard-boiled crime novel or espionage thriller.

Regionalism, above all regional realism, had fallen into low esteem during the boom, when Spanish American narrative won praise for its universality. But now a renewed concern with specific cultures, including the cultures of isolated or vanishing populations, created a demand for literature rich in ethnographic information and insights. Especially prized was writing that spoke of little-known groups, such as displaced peasants living in cities and African-Hispanic populations. During the 1960s Spanish American narrative won the greatest appreciation when it commented subtly and obliquely on social realities. From the 1970s forward, fiction with an undisguised political message made a pronounced comeback.

The postboom, as it came to be known, involved a number of new writers usually younger than the giants of the boom. At the same time, the very writers who had created the boom produced new writing in a different mode, changing with the literary times. Fuentes, for example, followed *Terra Nostra* with briefer, more accessible fiction patterned on such popular forms as the spy novel and the gothic tale. While this chapter is devoted principally to writers who emerged into the spotlight of international attention as representatives of the postboom, it should be kept in mind that the earlier-established boom authors were still enjoying enviable publicity and sales. Still, among the writers associated with the boom, the great successes that had established their names proved hard to reduplicate. For example, García Márquez enjoyed the recognition of the Nobel Prize in 1982 and continued to publish new novels. Yet he never again created such an original and widely acclaimed work as his 1967 *One Hundred Years of Solitude*, perhaps the quintessential boom novel.

The word *boom* offended some by seeming to reduce the flowering of Spanish American fiction to a question of good sales and strong publicity. Nonetheless, the success enjoyed by some Spanish American authors from the late 1950s until the end of the 1960s was, in fact, dependent on prosperity and a certain glamor that had become attached to authors from the region. As the 1970s advanced, both Spanish American and general world economies grew less and less reliable. There was a shift in what was considered culturally "hot," and Spanish American writers lost some of their chic. It became more difficult for a writer from this part of the world to launch a stellar career or attract widespread notice in the United States and Europe.

The boom had represented a new flowering of an innovative impulse that first manifested itself in the avant-garde movements of the 1920s. *Avant-garde* and *boom* both correlate fairly well to *modernism*, not in its Spanish American sense, but in the way the term is used in the discussion of international literature and culture. Many aspects of the postboom may also be seen as traits of *postmodernism*, the term and concept that, introduced by Jean-François Lyotard, Jean Baudrillard, and others, has spread quickly through the discussion of late twentieth-century culture.

Postboom texts are postmodern in assuming a less authoritative and definitive presence than those of the boom. In comparison with boom novels, which sought to establish a firm place as milestones in the history of narrative innovation, postboom fiction appears provisional and irresolute, not governed by any strong program. In many instances, the text's authority is weakened by the lack of any central, organizing narrator or other equivalent means of orienting the reader. Raymond Leslie Williams, the critic who has been foremost in identifying the Spanish American postboom with postmodernism, has characterized a number of younger authors and their writing as postmodern. He finds the absence of a directing narrative voice or other guiding information source typical of postmodern, postboom texts. Williams's concept of the postboom as postmodernism is summed up in his comments on a younger Colombian writer: "[Marco Tulio] Aguilera Garramuño has postmodern texts in the sense that they present no privileged narrator upon whom the reader can rely, nor is there an authoritative discourse or figure to whom the reader can turn for something like an objective, final truth regarding its fiction."[1] Such works are so constructed as to frustrate the reader's efforts to determine what is considered "reality" within the fiction. In Williams's analysis, the difficulty of establishing narrative data arises from a diminished concern with "truth" in and of itself: "Selected Latin American postmodern novels question the truth industry of modernism. What is at stake for the Latin American postmoderns who have emerged since the late 1960s . . . is not truth."[2]

Williams has made a correct and important observation in noting how many recent Spanish American narratives deny readers basic orienting information about either their own internal truth or real-world truths. Still, it should be remembered that the same characteristic appears occasionally in earlier experiments, such as Arlt's 1929 *The Seven Madmen*, and that formal features alone cannot define postmodernism.

A postmodern outlook or attitude appears more diffusely in many postboom works. The confidence that twentieth-century Spanish American literature is opening new frontiers has diminished. The decline of belief in art's historical progress is the aspect of postmodernism that most interests Fredric Jameson in his often-cited study of the phenomenon: "In art, at least, the notion of progress and telos remained alive and well up to very recent times indeed."[3] There has been an attenuation of the belief that art, with its lasting significance, can distinguish itself sharply from more insubstantial and ephemeral human endeavors. Many texts of the postboom present themselves as indistinct from the general run of popular culture and discussion of issues, without much claim to the status of art. Others appear to be documents about real-world conditions as much as they are imaginative writing. The erosion of confidence in twentieth-century art's ability to perform dramatically special, unique feats, and particularly feats of novelty and originality, seems to typify the postmodern era.

Many other features proposed as traits of the much-disputed postmodernism can be recognized in Spanish American postboom narrative. Among these are a self-conscious attitude typical of writers who are aware of current tendencies in literary theory and analysis. Postmodernism is often associated with a return to esthetic pleasures that modernism had inhibited in its austere drive to reduce the decorative element. The "return to storytelling" often postulated as one postboom current could be viewed as a reclaiming of neglected sources of reading enjoyment, even though the most famous boom novel, *One Hundred Years of Solitude*, is full of the embellishments of a skilled tale-teller. However, any more extensive reflection on postmodernism in the postboom would quickly lead to a lengthy study, and the current survey must stop at noting the parallelisms between the two *post-* phenomena.

One of the characteristics of the postboom era is that attention went to a greater number of different writers rather than a relatively few giants. An effort to include all the postboom writers who have established themselves since the end of the 1960s decade would preclude the consideration of individual texts. To allow for readings of specific narratives, this survey covers only a selective sample of postboom writers. The deliberate restriction of coverage to a few representative writers by no means implies any lack of equally deserving and significant contemporaries, some of whom are excluded with regret.

Among the writers who exemplified the postboom era, the one to attain the widest recognition was Manuel Puig (Argentina, 1929–1990). Chronologically a contemporary of the boom writers, he was unlike them in his literary outlook and practices. Despite the author's fondness for devising technical innovations, especially in narrative voice and point of view, Puig's works were organized around easily summarized plots and characters with well-marked, if at times shallow, personalities.

When Puig began to publish his novels, beginning in 1967 with *La traición de Rita Hayworth* (*Betrayed by Rita Hayworth*), there was a tendency to apply the term *pop* to both him and his novel. Puig, who had set out to become a scriptwriter, was an expert not only on film but on mass media and culture in their diverse forms. Beyond any doubt, the novel abounded in allusions to the pop culture spread through mass media. The characters, the inhabitants of a listless small town, go through life with their imaginations in thrall to the movies.

Nonetheless, *Rita Hayworth* does not itself constitute a part of pop culture. Its construction makes demands on the reader's concentration well beyond those acceptable in popular narrative. For example, in the opening chapter several voices speak of diverse and often trivial matters. Only with effort and patience can the reader recognize them as family and townspeople surrounding the protagonist, who is still a newborn. The last chapter, a reproachful letter that was never mailed, explains a number of circumstances that were hitherto difficult to account for. Though it cannot be counted itself as popular culture, the novel stands in an intimate relation to this culture and generates an ambivalent, half-mocking, and half-affectionate commentary upon it.

Rita Hayworth gained a certain reputation as an amusing and clever, and even somewhat frivolous, literary incursion into pop culture. Yet the novel communicates an often biting critique of the small-town society it portrays. In the many problems suffered by the characters, the strongest common factor is their entrapment in unworkable, inflexible sex roles. The men feel pressure to live up to the standards of *machismo*, while the women are obsessed with making a display of their attractiveness and achieving the highest prestige possible through their marriage, family, and place of residence. The chief complaint about popular culture is that it further rigidifies the already constricting expectations for male and female behavior. The public for the mass media faces a steady erosion of its imagination for what men, women, and sexuality might be, and other possibilities are cut off. After the glamorous image presented in the media, the characters are left with a feeling that their real-world personae and lives fail to measure up.

At the same time, it would be too simple to call *Rita Hayworth* a satire of mass media and the culture they transmit. While critical of the values popular culture encourages, the novel lovingly recreates the enchantment of moviegoing, particularly strong for the excitable young protagonist. Besides, the alternatives to mass culture do not necessarily present an improvement. Two characters, the protagonist and the town piano teacher, consider themselves superior to their neighbors because of their appreciation for European art music and their shared discussions, in which they attempt to maintain an intellectual culture. Yet their approach to cultural matters is as wrongheaded as that of their fellow townspeople who are content with moviegoing. The problem seems to lie in the passivity and lack of creativity with which they replicate high-status forms of cultural behavior, expecting a magic glamor, inherent in prestigious music or intellectual topics, to irradiate them.

Puig's *Boquitas pintadas* (English version *Heartbreak Tango*), the novel he published in 1969, came closer to actually entering the category of popular culture. He designed it to look like a serialized, heart-wringing romance, gave it the subtitle *folletín* (*A Serial* in the English version), and even set out to publish it in installments. Unlike *Rita Hayworth*, *Heartbreak Tango* does not require its readers to puzzle out the identity of speakers or to reconstruct a plot presented out of chronological order. Although it is always difficult to know who actually reads a given work, *Heartbreak Tango* is believed to have reached a more popular audience than any other of Puig's pop-influenced fictions. It was the success of the accessible *Heartbreak Tango* that led to the 1970 reissue of *Rita Hayworth;* newly launched by the large Sudamericana house, the earlier novel now sold much more briskly.

Many features link *Heartbreak Tango* to different popular forms. As epigraphs, the novel uses lines from tango lyrics, and many other borrowings are worked into the text. Puig has been interested in the problems of translating pop culture, not only from the mass media to literature but from language to language. Working on the English edition with his translator Suzanne Jill Levine, Puig developed such modifications as the substitution of a different set of tango lyrics by a different lyricist, since the original selection lost its poignancy in English.

Puig's last major success was *El beso de la mujer araña* (*Kiss of the Spider Woman*). The 1976 novel was the basis for a film so successful that the international public now identifies Puig primarily with this one work. The most celebrated structural feature of *Spider Woman* is the highly selective and embellished retelling, by one of the two chief characters to the other, of the plots of six films. *Spider Woman* may be, of all Puig's novels, the one that best sums up the preoccupations that characterized this author. The character who is a gay man provides the occasion to consider issues of sexuality and its expression or repression. The political activist with whom he shares a jail cell brings to the novel a concern with the overall shape future society will take, but the radical's vision must be widened to include cultural and affective factors.

Puig was one of the very few postboom authors to win international fame in the way that the boom writers had done. In general, Spanish American writers would have greater difficulty establishing their names in the 1970s, 1980s, and 1990s than they had during the period from the late 1950s to 1970.

While Puig represented an alternative to the established figures of Argentine literature, these giants were themselves seeking alternatives to what they had done hitherto. Borges had not published any new stories for some twelve years when, in the latter 1960s, he shocked his public with his renewed work in this genre. Borges's late stories, unlike anything he had written before, appear in the 1970 collection *El informe de Brodie* (*Doctor Brodie's Report*) and the 1975 *El libro de arena* (*The Book of Sand*). In his celebrated stories of 1936–1954, Borges had dazzled readers with his baroque style and plots laden with detailed information and convoluted in their development. During his long absence from the short story genre, he had been cultivating an artless, plain-spoken narration, which at times resembles the fireside telling of ghost stories. Borges now exhibited a fascination with the pagan British Isles and Scandinavia, especially with their ritual writing systems and cultivation of unusual metaphors. He was not only telling stories about magic but also exploring the idea of storytelling itself as an ancient form of magic. The new fiction required critics to learn all over again how to read Borges. The complexities were no longer so visible, but could be teased out through close examination of the narratives' symbolism and analogies.

Cortázar, too, was changing, although with less of a plan or identifiable direction than Borges. Increasingly identified with the left, Cortázar experimented with different ways of infusing social commentary into his fiction. His best-known effort in this vein, the 1974 *El libro de Manuel* (*A Manual for Manuel*), attracted some negative criticism for showing a band of revolutionaries as winsome and imaginative but inefficacious. Cortázar experimented with forms derived from the mass media and appeared to be seeking, in a spirit of cultural populism, some middle ground between literature and popular culture during the last years of his career, ending with his death in 1984. Though he was an important figure in Spanish American culture to the end, he never again composed a work that stood out as had the 1963 *Hopscotch*.

The restlessness exhibited by young people in the 1960s—the counterculture, student movements, the cult of rock music—was the point of departure for the Mexican writing known as *literatura de la onda* ("with-it," or "hip," literature). As the designation suggests, *onda* writers were attuned to the youth scene, attentively following trends in rock music, dress, drug use, slang, the expression of sexuality, and general attitudes among young people. At the same time, though, there was a persistent strain of mockery of the youthful hip culture, whose participants often appear vacuous and self-indulgent. The protagonists belong to the youth subculture; when the voice is that of a central narrator, the language still incorporates features of young people's speech. The characters are not knowing, hardened hipsters but rather insecure adolescents and postadolescents. Even their participation in the sexual revolution, a feature of the *onda* that disturbed some readers, is limited by their youth and inexperience. Not only are the theme of youth and the speech and attitudes of the young pervasive in this fiction, but the two writers who most clearly made their names as *onderos*, Gustavo Sainz (b. 1940) and José Agustín (b. 1944; real name José Agustín Ramírez Gómez), were chronologically part of the rebellious 1960s generation. Both had begun to publish books at an early age, an achievement characteristic of relatively prosperous decades when the publishing industry is on an upswing. (Though Agustín and Sainz were by far the most publicized, the *onda* included such lesser-known figures as Parménides García Saldaña.) An outstandingly clever and up-to-date literary critic, Margo Glantz, became the most sympathetic discussant of the *onda* writers. Herself an enthusiast of rock music and the examination of popular culture, Glantz was able to demonstrate that Sainz, Agustín, and others represented an evolution in Mexican narrative and not simply one more of the crazes that proliferated in the 1960s. Her enthusiastic critical anthology of writing from this generation, the 1971 *Onda y escritura en México* (*Onda* and writing in Mexico) is still the most useful orienting work on the literary phenomenon.[4]

Though it had its defenders, such as Glantz and the writers Juan José Arreola and José Revueltas, the literary *onda* came in for a good deal of adverse criticism for its irreverent, flippant, even disrespectful attitude. Agustín in particular appeared as a figure of scandal. At moments he attracted less attention for his writing than for his complicated amorous life, association with the rock music scene, detention on suspicion of drug possession, and taunting remarks about Mexico's best-esteemed authors.

Of the works considered to express the hip, resentful outlook of the *onda*, Sainz's much-translated novel of 1965, *Gazapo*, which retains the same title in English, is the one to achieve the widest international success. The nucleus of *onda* fiction consists of *Gazapo* together with Agustín's 1964 *La tumba* (The grave) and 1966 *De perfil* (In profile); the latter is the bestseller that put Agustín on the literary map. Agustín's very short story "Cuál es la onda," collected in his 1968 *Inventando que sueño* (Pretending I'm dreaming), provides perhaps the most condensed sample of the prime characteristics of *onda* writing. Its title is the Spanish-language version of the ubiquitous hip tagline of the 1960s, "What's happening." The characters talk and talk in a jargon utterly specific to their moment and subculture while arbitrarily careening from one disreputable hotel to another.

The countercultural side of the *onda* is epitomized by Agustín's novel of 1974, *Se está haciendo tarde (final en laguna)*. While the main title translates straightforwardly as "It's getting late," the subtitle ambiguously alludes either to the fact that the finale involves a trip into a lake (*laguna*) or to the open ending of the novel (*laguna* also means "lacuna" or "blank space"). The novel is set in Acapulco, a city Agustín knew well and of which he made knowing literary use. Dedicated in great part to entertaining foreign tourists, featuring an uneasy coexistence of English and Spanish, Acapulco figures in Agustín's fiction as a sleazy, but dreamlike, setting. *Se está haciendo tarde*, full of the special language and humor of the drug subculture, was Agustín's last salute to the *onda* before moving on to other types of writing.

Onda fiction began to appear while the boom was still in full swing, but the younger writers differentiated themselves from such established giants as Fuentes. (One might note, though, that Fuentes, Cortázar, and Donoso had already begun utilizing mass-culture allusions and of-the-moment catch phrases before the *onderos* became controversial for these innovations.) The writing of the *onda* did not have a monumental or totalizing scope. At times, the relatively brief texts appeared wispy and insubstantial, so unpretentious as to verge on playful doodling. A good deal of page space was devoted to the characters' conversations, at times vacuous and at times capriciously arbitrary, and to hip, highly verbal humor on the part of the narrator. Part of what made *onda* writing appear daring and nose-thumbing was the *onderos'* willingness to make space in the literary text for such seemingly frivolous word play or citations from the most ephemeral forms of mass culture; their texts did not display a need to appear weighty with significance.

Clearly not designed to have a classical, timeless ring to it, *onda* fiction incorporates many allusions indelibly marked as belonging to the moment in cultural history, such as brand names, scraps of advertising, and, most famously, excerpts from rock lyrics. The linguistic mix included slang that was extremely specific to a given time, place, generation, and milieu. During the late 1960s, disapproving critics made the dire prediction that *onda* literature would become unreadable in a short time and would never be appreciated outside Mexico. It is true that the *onda* was a bigger phenomenon in Mexico than elsewhere. However, the fiction generated under its impetus did not go out of date as drastically as foretold. The 1980s and 1990s saw the continued reading, discussion, and analysis of the early fiction of Sainz and Agustín. Rather than decay into incomprehensibility, the original *onda* texts stand as testimony to a bygone era, recorded in the very words of that era. While texts of the late 1960s and early 1970s may have lost some of the up-to-the-minute vitality they once possessed, the *onda* authors have continued to evolve with the times. Both writers have faced the uncomfortable circumstance of being permanently identified with their early fame as hippie novelists, despite their diverse later successes, though there have been critical efforts to recognize their post-*onda* evolution.[5]

A contemporary of Sainz and Agustín, though not directly related literarily, is José Emilio Pacheco (Mexico, b.1939). Pacheco made his name as a poet and a literary historian and critic, but has also authored novels. He is constantly trying new directions, and his novels are unusually different each from the other. His writing brings home to readers the evidence of living in a world of massive, global communications and rapid technological change. In Pacheco's vision, it is no longer possible to maintain a classical, high culture; society's awareness becomes cluttered with the ephemera of pop culture. The writer, like everyone else in society, is inundated daily with an unassimilable mass of information, the trivial and ephemeral commingled with the significant, history and fiction jumbled together. This overload in turn shows up in a variegated text, often bearing many allusions to mass culture.

Both Pacheco's poetry and his fiction reveal anxiety over the rapid pace of change, especially such threatening developments as the proliferation of nuclear arms. His characters are sometimes seized with a sensation that everything around them is condemned to imminent transformation. They are disconcerted not simply by the timeless issue of the flux and mutability of existence, but by the modern acceleration of change. The narrator of the very short 1981 novel *Las batallas en el desierto* (Desert battles) sees Mexico City being demolished and rebuilt all around him and the nation's culture and language becoming unrecognizable.

A great deal of sometimes heated contemporary discussion was devoted to the topic of documentary and semidocumentary writing that exhibits literary qualities. Many variants exist within documentary or, as it is often called in Spanish America, testimonial literature. Yet there is a common feature: the use of techniques borrowed from fiction to present narrative data taken from real-world events. As is immediately apparent, it is almost impossible to construct a definition that will include all texts that might reasonably be called *documentary* without including certain texts that are obviously meant, written, and read as fiction. For instance, many narrative works were conceived when their authors read or heard accounts of some happening, yet their elaboration is primarily fictional. The difficulty of pinning down the term and concept, together with a sudden proliferation of texts belonging to the category, produced an inexhaustible theme for examination.

The upsurge of interest in both the production and the critical discussion of documentary literature occurred in the late 1960s. Of course, there were many previous cases of Spanish American writers employing literary techniques to make factual accounts more exciting or, as the case may be, utilizing their fiction as an opportunity to present facts the public ought to know. Perhaps the most obvious case is that of writers eager to be ethnologically correct in describing indigenous or partly indigenous rural populations. Hoping to avoid embellishing the facts, to persuade readers that their accounts were reliable, and to decrease the general ignorance about native peoples, these authors had at times adopted a mode closer to reportage than to imaginative literature, in some cases working with Indian informants. It should be recalled that the anthropologist Oscar Lewis (1914–1970), noted for his first-person accounts of life in poverty, had often worked in Spanish American countries. His 1961 *The Children of Sanchez: The Autobiography of a Mexican Family* had aroused a great polemic when it appeared in Mexico, although the focus of the debate was not the nature of documentary literature but whether Lewis had maligned the Mexicans.

The Cuban Miguel Barnet (b. 1941) started out working as both a poet and an anthropologist before combining his literary and ethnological interests. An admirer of the highly original Cuban anthropologist Fernando Ortiz (1881–1969), Barnet has made creative use of his mentor's thought. He has been a practitioner and a theorist of what he terms the *novela testimonio*, in which the editor-transcriber draws upon the novelist's resources to help bear witness to social history. While many Cuban intellectuals encountered difficulties with the Castro government's involvement in the nation's cultural life, Barnet was able to thrive on the new network of institutes, programs, and sponsored writing projects. He produced his famous works in collaboration with informants who had lived through significant aspects of Cuban history and could give experiential accounts of them. He interviewed them at length and, making unembarrassed use of narrative artistry, developed from their responses texts similar to memoir-novels. The first of his famous informants was Esteban Montejo, an ex-slave he located in a nursing home. The observant, loquacious, reflective Montejo, with his sly rural wit, was the ideal oral historian's subject. Supposedly over one hundred years old, Montejo had been born into slavery, had escaped to live in the wilderness, and had been a sharp-eyed witness to a variety of now-vanished social phenomena. *Biografía de un cimarrón* (*Biography of a Runaway Slave*), published in 1966 from Barnet's conversations with Montejo, is one of the most successful of the many contemporary documentary narratives. According to Barnet's concept of the *novela testimonio*, it is because of his artistic intervention that the text convincingly seems to present the escaped slave speaking for himself. Barnet's heavy intervention in editing Montejo's account has been the topic of a long controversy; he was rumored to have completely reinvented the ex-slave's speech rather than rely on the transcripts of interviews.

Barnet's 1969 *La canción de Rachel* (*Rachel's Song*) is based on the life of a demimondaine who flourished when Havana was one of the world's great after-dark cities. This second text was not as well received as its predecessor, in part because it is less able to create the impression that a witness to history is speaking to the reader. There was no single real-world Rachel; she is a composite figure, a well-researched fiction. Rachel's words are supplemented by documents on Havana's era of decadent splendor. The ex-courtesan appears a less insightful and informative subject than the witty ex-slave. The contrast suggests that, however adept documentary writers might be in the artful editing and juxtaposition of transcripts, the success of their works was often attributable to an informant with interesting and significant experiences. The contribution made by the typically lower-class, uneducated interview subject should not be underestimated, even though it is the more literate author who determines the final form of a documentary narrative.

The hybrid texts of the Paris-born Mexican journalist Elena Poniatowska (b. 1933) have been influential in the development of documentary literature. Poniatowska's documentary writing stands out for its intimacy; she spends long periods learning to know her subjects. She had become known as a skilled interviewer who, in part because of the angelically naive presence she projected, was able to elicit the most unguarded remarks even from hardened interview subjects. In line with her interest in more extensive and profound interviewing, she worked briefly as a research assistant for Oscar Lewis when he was obtaining accounts of life in lower-class Mexico City households. However, she left Lewis's employ, and her own work shows more divergences from than similarities to Lewis's documentary narratives. Poniatowska's 1969 *Hasta no verte, Jesús mío* aroused a great deal of commentary at the time. (The title, a breezy toast addressed to Jesus, became *Until We Meet Again* in Magda Bogin's English version.) The well-bred Poniatowska had managed to make friends with a Mexico City woman of distinctly lower class, despite the latter's understandable suspicion at being the object of a society girl's curiosity and attention. Poniatowska had been simply getting to know Jesusa Palancares (as she is known in the text) as a friend as well as interviewing her for many years before formulating the text in which the woman appears to narrate her own life story. Poniatowska's friend and informant was, like Montejo, an ideal subject. She could speak first-hand of women's participation in the Mexican Revolution, among other topics of sure interest. Moreover, she was no average representative of the oral narrative tradition but an individual gifted with exceptional narrative prowess. Readers of *Until We Meet Again* came away convinced that they had experienced the speech of a woman of the Mexican people by means of a book. The work had the ability to make them forget the intervention of Poniatowska.

Poniatowska had another much-discussed best-seller in the 1971 *La noche de Tlatelolco* (English version *Massacre in Mexico*). Here she dealt with a national trauma, the massacre of protesters in the Plaza de las Tres Culturas on October 2, 1968. To approach the hard-to-think-about topic, Poniatowska gathered statements from a variety of participants who might have a telling comment to make. Some were leaders of the student movement; Poniatowska conducted some of her interviews in the prison where activists were detained. But at other times she cites more peripherally involved persons, some of whom exhibit attitudes toward, more than knowledge of, the student movement and massacre. Slogans and excerpts from contemporary documents also enter into the collagelike text. The result is a set of outlooks on the event, edited so as to convey, without tendentious statement, how wrong the government's action was.

Barnet's and Poniatowska's work helped legitimate documentary writers' artistic freedom to rework the material they had gathered, resulting in a text that was the writer's own. The other possible strategy, to intervene as little as possible and let the interview subject's words stand, also had its exponents and practitioners. An international success emerged from the widespread effort to elicit autobiographies from members of minority groups. Rigoberta Menchú (b. 1959), who produced her life story together with Elizabeth Burgos, in 1983 won sudden fame for *Yo soy Rigoberta Menchú y así me nació la conciencia* (*I, Rigoberta Menchu: An Indian Woman in Guatemala*); in 1992, she was the recipient of the Nobel Peace Prize. Menchú comes from a Quiché-speaking village in Guatemala which, as she describes it, maintained intact much of its traditional social structure and folkways; at the same time, she is a modern radicalized intellectual. Her family became involved in political protest after experiencing the exploitation to which Menchú would later testify in memorable detail. As a result of their activism, both Menchú's parents and her brother were killed and she had to flee the country. The interviewee gained far more celebrity from the book than the non-Indian woman who had helped develop her narrative, a reversal of the usual outcome.

Dissident Cuban writers younger than Cabrera Infante gained attention during the period from the end of the 1960s onward. Around 1980 a number of highly esteemed Cuban writers chose exile. In some cases, they became part of U.S. literary culture, lectured or held positions at U.S. universities, and attracted English-language translators. The publishing house Ediciones del Norte, headed by Frank Janney, which issues Spanish American literature in both English and Spanish, played an important role in disseminating the writing of first-class Cuban writers in exile, and the most prominent of these authors were able to place their work with large commercial houses.

Reinaldo Arenas (Cuba, 1943–1990) had his first major success with the 1969 Spanish-language publication of *El mundo alucinante* (*Hallucinations*), a novel which had appeared in French the year before and had won the *Le Monde* prize for international novels. Here Arenas empathetically re-creates the experience of Fray Servando Teresa de Mier (1763–1827), a

Mexican friar best known for a 1794 sermon promoting the belief that Christianity had been promulgated in the New World prior to the Spanish Conquest. This notion had implications that were political as much as they were religious, since it meant that Spanish America, far from having been saved from paganism by Spanish friars, owed nothing spiritually to Spain. In the elaboration of this novel, Arenas often drew quite directly on Fray Servando's memoirs, with emphasis on the persecutions the friar endured because of his divergent views. At the same time, the novelist supplemented these borrowings with highly inventive embellishments of his own.

Fray Servando here appears as an admirably Quixotic misfit, a dissident from the establishment beliefs he had originally set out to defend. He is also gifted with a hyperexcitable consciousness that, when stimulated, rapidly transforms his world into a delirious, lurid dream. Arenas creates for *Hallucinations* a type of imagery that changes with feverish swiftness and reflects the polymorphous, anarchic sexuality that the novel attributes to Fray Servando.

The novel opens with a narrator from a later era sending Fray Servando a letter, professing a fascination with him and seeking to establish a bond. Fray Servando speaks as a memoirist, telling of the complicated, event-filled life he led after airing his heretical beliefs. The plot of *Hallucinations* integrates the story of the letter-writer's successful struggle to reach out across time to Fray Servando with that of the friar's frenetic existence. By the end of the novel, Fray Servando and the modern narrator have achieved a fusion that defies continuous, unidirectional chronology.

Arenas was himself a figure of dissidence who had a string of difficulties in Cuba, both as a result of the government's antihomosexual campaign and as a writer out of line with the officially sponsored vision of literature. During the 1970s Arenas was jailed and released on parole only with special conditions. In 1980 followers of Hispanic literature, reading news of the new wave of emigrants from the port of Mariel, were struck by a detail. Among the over 100,000 refugees who had turned up on U.S. shores was the writer of fiction Reinaldo Arenas. Arenas's U.S. stay was troubled with poverty and illness and ended in suicide. Still he succeeded in organizing and publishing several works that he had not been able to bring to fruition in Cuba. He came into contact with English-language translators and readers, and several of his works had appeared in that language by the early 1990s. He was the founder of the magazine *Mariel*, a focal point for new Cuban American writing. Arenas worked well with the translator Andrew Hurley, who has often rendered Cuban exile writing. Hurley was responsible for the English version of the 1982 *Otra vez el mar* (*Farewell to the Sea*), the most important of Arenas's late narratives.

Antonio Benítez Rojo (b. 1931) is a writer whose training was in accounting, finance, and statistics. During the first part of his career, he held posts concerned with public services, planning, and development before a period of forced immobility drove him to creative writing. He is one of the most original and conceptually wide-ranging of the Cuban exile writers. While still in Castro's Cuba, he made his name as a skillful short story writer, winning both major state-sponsored prizes, the Casa de las Américas and the Cuban National Writers' and Artists' Union awards. Of his work written while in Cuba, the outstanding piece is probably "Estatuas sepultadas" ("Buried Statues"). In this story a wealthy Cuban family has been living inside its estate since the 1959 revolution. During almost a decade of retreat, these aristocrats have let the gate rust shut and rely on only one outside contact to bring provisions. They have no news of current Cuba, living as they do without electricity, a working radio, or newspapers. The three young cousins of the family, of whom the narrator is one, live in a secluded intimacy that encourages incest and voyeurism. Magical symbolism in this text typifies Benítez Rojo's approach. The three young people chase butterflies for amusement, but the heroine is convinced that one golden butterfly is an outside agent who has attacked her. An unknown woman gains admittance to the family's home, and she also turns out to be threatening and peculiarly golden. At the end the narrator learns that the self-transforming creature has lured the most promising of the three cousins—the family's "golden boy"—outside into the living Cuba.

Benítez Rojo's 1980 move into exile surprised many observers. While he had his ups and downs with the Cuban government, he had held very important posts in state-sponsored cultural organizations and was traveling with a government delegation when he defected. He has since become part of the U.S. academic scene, holding a post at Amherst College and visiting at other universities. His 1985 novel *El mar de las lentejas* (*The Lentil Sea*) and long essay *La isla que se repite: el Caribe y la perspectiva posmodernista* (*The Repeating Island: The Caribbean and the Postmodernist Perspective*) are both cerebral works that have fascinated an educated readership. *The Lentil Sea* is a closely researched historical novel of the Spanish colonization. The colonial New World appears, ingloriously, as a lawless frontier society. In *The Repeating Island* Benítez Rojo borrows from his readings in the quantitative sciences. It is famous for its application of chaos theory, derived from modern physics, to the analysis of Cuban and Caribbean culture.

Benítez Rojo hypothesizes that the Caribbean and its social and cultural history present many characteristics of a chaotic phenomenon; yet, if the chaos is subjected to careful observation, it reveals significant symmetries that yield up meaning and thus a certain coherence. An English-language anthology of Benítez Rojo's fiction, edited by Frank Janney, bears the title *The Magic Dog and Other Stories.*

The postboom brought several newer Puerto Rican writers to prominence. Rosario Ferré (b. 1942) published her *Papeles de Pandora* (English version *The Youngest Doll*), a collection of stories and poetry, in 1976. The volume appealed especially to the growing readership interested in the literary treatment of issues of gender and class. Ferré is a subtle writer with a strong bent for fantastic symbolism and the ironic reworking of familiar stories. She is an erudite author who holds a doctoral degree in Spanish literature and draws on her extensive readings. Many of her female characters are known to readers from earlier appearances in biblical narrative, Greco-Roman myth, folktales, or masterworks of Western literature, but Ferré gives these heroines and their stories sardonically eloquent new turnabouts. Her work often illustrates how standardized patterns of masculinity and femininity support the social hierarchy.

While many Spanish American writers are reluctant to be called feminists, even while their work shows clearly the influence of feminist thought, Ferré frankly identifies herself with the feminist tradition and cites Simone de Beauvoir and Virginia Woolf as her original models. As a founding editor of the 1972–1976 journal *Zona de Carga y Descarga*, she early published an article unambiguously advocating a movement for women's liberation. She has participated in conferences on feminist literary criticism. One of her most reprinted essays is "El coloquio de las perras" (The colloquy of the bitches; the Spanish *perras*, however, does not imply that the female dogs who debate are snidely malicious). This debate, modeled on a famous Cervantes piece in which canine discussants bring an unbiased perspective to human issues, wittily sums up the central dilemmas of feminist criticism and the effort to identify a mode of writing distinctive to women.

Ferré's characteristic heroines are upper-class women required to cultivate markedly feminine social graces, beauty, and charm. In their younger years they serve as prestigious adornments to their fathers' estates; they then win high-status mates and use their graces to bolster their husbands' importance. In unguarded moments the male characters refer to their wives and daughters as if they were luxury merchandise, whose possession and display promotes their purchasers' careers. Several of Ferré's narratives dissolve the distinction between these women, resembling consumer items, and life-size dolls. The protagonist of "Marina y el león" ("Marina and the Lion"), from *The Youngest Doll*, makes a grand entrance at her costume ball not only dressed as a doll, but packaged like deluxe goods in a silk-lined box and wrapped in cellophane.

Ferré's heroines are outwardly demure and submissive women whose sheltered lives give them a limited range of action. The women inevitably belong to the domain of some powerful male. Yet, fueled by hidden rage and rebellion, these imaginative women can resort to fantasy and even magic to escape from or sabotage the patriarchal order. The heroine of "Marina and the Lion" maintains her doll-like passivity to the other guests at the ball. Yet she is inwardly unreeling strings of bizarre verbal associations and fantastic imagery that the narrator reveals to the reader. Marina must live in the household of her ostentatious brother-in-law, who acquires a lion to emblemize his ambition and power. Yet she also exercises symbolic power by purchasing a parrot, exceptionally beautiful even though its feathers are damaged by captivity. While her brother-in-law keeps his totemic animal confined in his great house, Marina frees hers from its too-small cage. Subsequently the parrot kills the lion and Marina is able to destroy the house, although her revenge and escape require her own death. "La muñeca menor" ("The Youngest Doll"), from the same collection, is Ferré's best-known story. It features a protagonist who, sharply aware of her exploitation, devises an elaborate, magical retaliation that takes years to unfold. This often-reprinted narrative succeeds as a fantastic tale and a satisfying story of revenge as well as feminist fiction.

Ferré is one of three postboom women writers discussed in this chapter to draw upon the resources of fantastic narrative in order to deliver a feminist critique. Isabel Allende of Chile and the Argentine Luisa Valenzuela also vary the tradition of magical realism to bring in an implicit analysis of gender issues.

Luis Rafael Sánchez (b. 1936) made his reputation with the 1976 *La guaracha del Macho Camacho* (*Macho Camacho's Beat*). The novel comments on Puerto Rican culture through the story of a hit song, a dance number so irresistibly catchy that it seizes the collective imagination of everyone on the island. Even the elite, who would like to believe themselves above the appeal of its African Caribbean rhythms, find the infectious tune and its lyrics inexpugnably present in their consciousness. While the novel celebrates popular Caribbean music for its contagious beat and ability to cut across class and racial barriers, it also projects a critical vision of Puerto Rican culture. Even if a song can momentarily unite the island, Puerto Rico is seen as made up of competing classes, ethnicities, and subcultures. *Beat* also critiques commercial mass culture; to examine this media phenomenon, Sánchez makes freewheeling use of modern information theory.

Ana Lydia Vega (b. 1946) stands out among the newer Puerto Rican authors for her ability to amuse and entertain while developing her sardonic vision of Caribbean culture. Vega is a professor of French, having written her doctoral dissertation on French Caribbean literature. She writes with a wide scope on the Caribbean, taking in the Spanish-, the French-, and at times the English-speaking islands. The perennial Utopian dream of a Caribbean federation fascinates Vega, as do other efforts to think of the Caribbean as one entity. The popularity of Vega and her work owes much to the contemporary surge of interest in Caribbean cultural studies. Many of her stories draw on the islands' oral traditions of jokes and scary tales, with suspense-creating hooks and punch lines that throw the previous narrative into a new perspective.

Vega's stories in the 1988 *Pasión de historia y otras historias de pasión* (A passion for history and other histories of passion) are most remarkable for their women narrators. The female characters who speak in *Pasión* are from diverse social classes and ethnicities, but her typical heroine is tough, slangy in an almost exaggeratedly Puerto Rican way, ironically witty, and a sharp observer of the social order. Vega exhibits a special fascination with women who make an aggressive sexual display, yet are intelligently aware of what they are doing and derive humor from thinking about human sexuality. One story in *Pasión*, seemingly a deviation from Vega's wryly feminist norm, has a male narrator determined to conquer a divorcée. This narrator, though, is a clear-eyed adolescent who has not yet assimilated the conventions of *machismo*. He takes the same mocking and self-mocking view of sexuality as the women who narrate most of the volume. Whether female, male, or unmarked, Vega's narrators share an extreme verbal facility, deriving humorous and eloquent effects from sudden shifts into English and other characteristics of Puerto Rican Spanish.

Isabel Allende (Chile, b. 1942) was the first Spanish American woman to make a world reputation, including massive sales, with her fiction. Many foreign readers, who associated Spanish American fiction with Borges and the boom writers, exaggeratedly hailed her as the first important woman writer from the region.

To note an often-observed connection, Allende is first cousin, once re-moved, and goddaughter of the late Chilean president Salvador Allende, known for his strong program of social reform. Isabel Allende has a his-tory of involvement in agencies and projects concerned with hunger, hu-man rights, and other social problems. After the 1973 military coup that toppled Salvador Allende, Isabel Allende at first remained in Chile, en-gaged in grassroots efforts aimed at alleviating hunger and human rights abuses. During this time, she collected firsthand accounts from victims of political repression and their families; this testimonial material became a source for the fiction she would write after going into exile in 1975.

Her fame as a creative writer rests on the 1982 novel *La casa de los espíritus* (*The House of the Spirits*). This international best-seller displays strong parallels to *One Hundred Years of Solitude;* like García Márquez's fa-mous novel, *House* follows a dynasty over approximately a century and exhibits features of magical realism. Critics have been quick to observe the evident similarities and have often faulted Allende's novel on this point. *House* tells the story of four generations of an upper-class family, inter-twined with Chilean political history from the turn of the century to the 1973 military takeover and its aftermath. The text of the novel is presented as the reconstructive project of the gentle but resilient Alba. She has un-dertaken a chronicle of her family's and her country's history in an effort to recover from recent traumas. While held by the military regime, she has been raped, as vengeance, by a representative of the underclass of her own family, an unrecognized branch originated by one of the many rapes committed by Esteban Trueba, the family's patriarch. Her restorative writing project is a collective enterprise, with the family patriarch contrib-uting to telling the dynastic story and Alba's dead grandmother having left valuable source material.

Although the fictional family maintains the appearance of a patriarchy governed by the tyrannical macho Trueba, the novel is dominated by women characters, whose vigor and endurance have often been singled out for praise by commentators. The women exercise a gentle strength that stands in contrast to the men's attempts to prevail by force, although the domineering Trueba also displays moments of tenderness and is far from a hated tyrant. Indeed, the feature that most clearly sets *House* apart from *One Hundred Years of Solitude* is the marked focus upon women char-acters and personality traits considered "feminine," such as compassion and the sharing of intimacies. Allende's novel has often been singled out for its affectionate, understanding, and compassionate attitude toward even its morally deficient characters; while some readers have found *House* excessively sweet, others praise it for its warmth.

Luisa Valenzuela (Argentina, b. 1938) is known for her work in human rights and anticensorship organizations as well as her fiction, which consists primarily of short stories with some short novels. In 1979 she left Argentina; since then New York has been her primary residence, and she has developed an English-language career, seeing nearly all her work published in English as well as Spanish. She has held writer-in-residence posts in U.S. universities and lectured widely. As a lecturer, her chief issues have been women's writing and censorship and political repression. The central preoccupation in her work is hierarchical patterns of domination and subjugation. She is concerned with such vast, rigidly constructed systems as the Catholic church and military governments, but also with such small-group hierarchies as male-female couples. In her writing she establishes parallels between the domination exercised through complex organizations and the unjust mechanisms of control in intimate relations between men and women.

Valenzuela's writing conveys a warning against the repressive potential of certain types of rhetoric; even single words hold the potential for domination. Her work highlights the catch phrases, slogans, and figures of speech that encourage compliance with the existing order of society. In the tradition of George Orwell, she shows politically designed metaphors taking on the power to remake perception. A vision of society promoted through manipulative language contradicts and overrides the conclusions citizens would otherwise draw from their own experiences of repression and exploitation. In Valenzuela's outlook, women are especially affected by language that encourages them to accept a disadvantageous role. Yet they can grasp and reverse the situation by boldly and ironically reprising their oppressors' rhetoric and showing themselves unintimidated by its powers. Sharon Magnarelli, the critic who has most closely examined Valenzuela's work, has often analyzed this author's concepts of repression and rebellion through language.[6]

Mid-1970s Argentina, with its right- and left-wing guerrilla and vigilante violence and economic chaos, is the backdrop for the short stories of Valenzuela's 1975 *Aquí pasan cosas raras* (*Strange Things Happen Here*). These stories communicate vividly the shock with which Argentines saw their society lose its stability and Buenos Aires deteriorate from its fabled splendor. It marks a shift from Valenzuela's earlier concern with the church to her later interest in political repression.

Valenzuela has become absorbed in the difficult problem of identifying a difference in women's writing. In her lectures and essays she has been aggressive in promoting the idea that women writers can, at best, exercise distinctive virtues and powers not available to their male colleagues. Her 1983 *Cambio de armas* (*Other Weapons*) tests out the concept of a writing marked by woman's difference. In each of its short stories, the speaking voice is that of a woman, and the experience of female protagonists is invariably in the foreground.

The postboom made an opening for the emergence of authors who had been overshadowed by the great figures of the new novel. For example, Gustavo Alvarez Gardeazábal (Colombia, b. 1945), though prolific and controversial, had been obscured by García Márquez, already established as Colombia's great contemporary novelist. Toward the end of the 1970s, Gardeazábal became known internationally as well as at home, particularly after his work was presented and analyzed by the well-known specialist in Colombian literature, the earlier-cited Raymond L. Williams.[7]

Gardeazábal was known early on as a regional writer, one who treated backwoods realities with an iconoclastic, unsentimental outlook. His hometown of Tuluá in the scenically famed Cauca Valley figures importantly in his fiction. In the early 1970s he published a "Tuluá cycle," consisting first of short stories and then of a rapid succession of novels set in that provincial ambience, where ancient feuds and bizarre folk beliefs hold sway. Power in the region is the prerogative of an entrenched, interrelated few families, whom Gardeazábal subjects to inventively raucous contempt. Gardeazábal has also been noted as a novelist of La Violencia, the upheaval in 1940s–1950s Colombia whose literary treatment had been the theme of Gardeazábal's thesis. As environmentalism gained strength, Gardeazábal stood out as a "green" and a writer concerned with the biosphere. In his newspaper columns, he exposed cases of environmental negligence and criticized the human tendency to disregard the welfare of other species. His fiction drew on the natural sciences, teeming with an abundance of life forms.

Same-sex liaisons have long appeared in Gardeazábal's texts; the author treats them with the same casual, ingenious ribaldry he accords to heterosexual trysts and entanglements. But it was the publication of the 1986 *El Divino* (The divine one) that identified him as a novelist of gay life. *The Divine One* continues as well Gardeazábal's long-standing preoccupation with the difficult relations between human beings and other species, since its characters are not only homosexual or sexually polymorphous but zoomorphic. In the fluid reality of the novel, these protean beings assume a multiplicity of animate forms.

Gardeazábal's readers have come to expect this author to display several of his distinctive talents in each new work. Merrily scabrous humor at the expense of the church, in the manner of the picaresque, is among his most appreciated specialties. The 1974 novel *El bazar de los idiotas* (*Bazaar of the Idiots*) ridicules miracle cults with the story of a healing craze set off when an ex–beauty queen claims to have been cured of an inexplicable paralysis by two idiot brothers masturbating in her presence. All manner of dissolute or demented clergy and self-seeking exemplars of piety appear in the pages of Gardeazábal's fiction. Gardeazábal takes special delight in showing how, under cover of Catholicism, Colombia is swarming with folk magicians, wonder-workers, diviners, and local messiahs. An exuberantly amoral neopaganism flourishes in *The Divine One*, borrowing eclectically from Catholic convention.

Williams has observed how Gardeazábal's storytelling often makes a self-conscious use of the markers of oral narrative, such as the tag phrase "they say." Even when the narrator is not playing the part of a tale-teller, Gardeazábal's fiction exhibits a sharp awareness of the complex relations between oral and written culture in a region where the two coexist. Gardeazábal's narrator tempts the reader by promising disclosures from his endless supply of local rumors and secrets, which include aspects of local history that others have forgotten or suppressed. Like García Márquez, Gardeazábal treats the passage of time with the imprecision typical of folk expression.

The literary public and critics enjoy certain advantages in reading works of their own historical moment. Yet contemporaries have a poor record in judging which texts and writers will be important to subsequent generations. The provisional quality of the term *postboom* is an indication that neither the general audience nor specialists really know where Spanish American narrative is headed or which of the several tendencies at work in it will emerge as most significant.

In this chapter the goal has been not to predict long-term winners in literary history but to impress upon the reader the many varieties of fiction that have gained prominence since the late 1960s as alternatives to the characteristic boom novel. One shift has clearly been away from the effort to create a complex narrative masterwork. The idea of the enduring masterpiece now seems almost old-fashioned. Spanish American writers have been less wary of ephemeral or apparently lightweight material that, in some cases, not only imitates the mass media but verges on turning the text into a pop artifact. A certain fear of simplicity haunted the literary scene earlier, bringing an anxiety that a tale told in a straightforward manner might not be valued. Now writers speak of a return to storytelling, although their supposedly plain style of narration still reveals the traces of the just-past era of extreme narrative complexity.

If it were necessary to risk predictions about what on the current scene will most last, individual authors' names would probably not be the best choices. At this point, Puig may be the only postboom author who can be said to have left his mark. His innovations have not only fascinated a large public but also provided material for much critical and theoretical discussion. More than particular writers, certain trends and tendencies have established their importance.

Formal novelty has been less in demand since the end of the boom, with its masterpieces of unusual novelistic design. Since approximately 1970, there has been less of a belief that a narrative must exhibit notable technical innovations to be considered important. Some of the writers who have gained greatest celebrity since the 1970s, such as Isabel Allende, have not been engaged in the development of new variants of narrative technique. The demand for continual new breakthroughs in form seems to have receded, and there is a greater willingness to value writers who are more outstanding for their thematic material than for their approach to narration. Writers who are frankly preoccupied with describing and criticizing society, like Elena Poniatowska, have been more valued than when experiments in form were often seen as the hallmark of serious literature.

There will be a continuing interest in developing new types of narrative that bring to culturally mainstream readers the verbatim words of members of native groups or of ethnicities of mixed ancestry. In earlier years such individuals could in most cases express themselves in Spanish American narrative only at second hand, as native informants to ethnologist-writers. Greater access to education has produced, for example, Rigoberta Menchú, an intellectual as well as a woman who grew up in a native community and is more able to tell her own story in terms attractive to a non-Indian public. Globalization seems likely to bring native American authors able to compose Spanish-language narratives of broad appeal without assistance from non-Indians.

Readers of Spanish American literature may expect more narratives whose purpose is in great part to convey, with as little mediation as possible, the experiences and *ipsissima verba* of slum dwellers and representatives of other groups seldom audible to the educated public. The postboom has stimulated a widespread eagerness to have the category of literature include the verbatim, or nearly verbatim, words of all socially disadvantaged groups, including members of sexual undergrounds, youth movements, prison populations, street-dwelling society, and isolated ethnic niches.

The last years of the boom coincided with a general recognition that Spanish American women writers had not been receiving a fair proportion of attention. Many efforts were made to bring women's writing to a public that in many cases was now eager to read texts capable of communicating women's particular experience, or simply to discover women writers. This trend can be expected to continue, although as more women's texts are published, it will come as less of a revelation to the public that Spanish American fiction includes so many female-authored narratives. It is difficult to imagine a return to the situation of twenty years ago, when many students of Spanish American writing knew the work of only a few women who had contributed to this literature.

If one overall statement can be made of the postboom era, in contrast with the boom, it is that more varied types of prose texts from Spanish America are able to capture the attention of the reading public. Now nobody can describe one variety of fiction typical of the region. Spanish American literature has become more fragmented, but also more diverse.

CONCLUSION

Spanish American narrative reached the final decade of the twentieth century much altered from what it had been at the century's outset. Not only the type of texts being produced but also the way literature was conceptualized had been through many changes. At the same time, many of the dilemmas that confronted Spanish American prose writers of 1900 are still difficult issues today, even if they are stated in different terms.

A prime example of a perennial yet continually changing problem for Spanish American authors is the search for a worthy literary treatment of the varied ethnicities and cultures that play a prominent role in many Spanish American countries. This category includes native peoples, African Hispanics, populations of mixed ancestry and culture, and the element of indigenous or African culture in the general society.

Here the region's writers enjoy a special advantage in that they can draw on a reservoir of material largely unavailable to European writers. Yet the search for the best way to benefit from this rich source has posed a long series of dilemmas for Spanish American authors. A fundamental problem is that the writers of literature have not come from the regional and ethnic cultures they seek to represent, with a few quite recent exceptions such as the Guatemalan Quiché Indian Rigoberta Menchú, and there has always been some awkwardness in outsiders' efforts to speak about or on behalf of these groups.

The twentieth century saw a number of approaches to the issue. As the century opened, literature about ethnic minorities was associated with social protest; with the rise of anthropology, ethnographic detail was often prominent. In the second half of the century, new Indian- and African-

theme writers brought to their fiction a more experiential, insider's knowledge of native culture than their predecessors. A Spanish-language writer
with native competence in an indigenous language, such as José María
Arguedas possessed, could add new complexities to Indian-theme fiction.
In addition, the statements of members of indigenous and African Hispanic cultures were either reproduced verbatim or recreated in documentary texts. The idea that indigenous or African culture permeates the life
of a given Spanish American country, affecting the outlook even of the
most outwardly European citizens, was still capable of causing shock
when writers like Asturias took it up. By mid-century it was starting to
be a commonplace of Spanish American intellectual life. As more representatives of previously isolated populations gain access to the means of
publishing their stories, there will be future permutations in the line of
narrative designed to speak of these groups' experience.

Another perennial issue is the degree to which a writer who experiments with form or utilizes myth and fantasy is taking time and thought
away from the critical analysis of social realities. At the century's outset,
this point was the topic of heated debate. Opinion was divided as to the
writer's first priority: to perfect an artistic creation or to sharpen social
awareness. Though there were two sides to the debate, the discussants
shared a consensus that these two missions were in competition with each
other. This view, though powerfully influential, never corresponded very
exactly to the actual practice of literature. Many writers identified as
cultivators of esthetic novelties, such as the modernists and many avant-
gardists, in their creative writing gave some of the most eloquent testimony to contemporary social thought. Certain defenders of a social realism in which art must be subordinate, such as the Argentine Roberto
Mariani, at the same time were innovative and imaginative in their narrative technique.

Succeeding decades produced no weakening of the belief, strong in
Spanish American countries, that the words and attitudes of literary authors were important in guiding a society toward an understanding of its
problems. However, there were constant changes in the range of what
constituted socially committed writing. By the 1940s, two major writers,
Miguel Angel Asturias and Alejo Carpentier, had established that an inventive treatment of narrative form, with nonrealistic elements, could be
the vehicle of social commentary. The phrases used to support the earlier
dichotomy, such as "art for art's sake" and "social literature," now seem to
belong to a bygone era. The abandonment of these rallying cries may be
part of a larger tendency away from literary factions, movements, and

group statements. Whereas many isms were formed in the early twentieth century, from mid-century onward the only major new one is magical realism; this is a term applied by critics and not by adherents to a movement.

Though the category of social literature is not kept distinct from writing generally, there is still a strong belief that writers are important in determining the political culture. This concept has been strengthened by such phenomena as the involvement of writers in Nicaragua's Sandinista revolution (1979) and the presidential campaign of Mario Vargas Llosa (1990–1991).

A pronounced change is the greater involvement of women in literary life and the success of a number of women writers. No woman was an important modernist, and there were very few women avant-gardists. But starting with Teresa de la Parra and her 1924 *Iphigenia*, a line of women writers may be traced. Many of these stand out for their fictional analyses of women's experience in society; De la Parra is an expert in this task, as is the next woman writer to achieve general acclaim, María Luisa Bombal. Others compose original and intelligent fiction that gives little, if any, clue to its author's experience as a member of a particular sex.

In the nineteenth century a Spanish American novelist explicitly identified herself as a supporter of the emancipation of women—the Cuban Gertrudis Gómez de Avellaneda (1814–1873). Yet it was some time into the twentieth century before prominent women literary intellectuals were willing to be viewed as feminists. (The term *feminism*, which in the United States can refer to a general outlook or set of beliefs, in the Spanish American context is often taken to imply militancy in a movement.) Rosario Castellanos is the first important twentieth-century woman writer to accept *feminist* as a definition of herself and her work. While women authors were reluctant to be publicly identified as feminists, in many cases their narratives exhibited an unmistakable concern with women's role, status, and ability to participate in the general society.

The feminist literary criticism developed during the 1970s proved useful in bringing out the element of gender analysis in works written by authors of both sexes earlier in the century. As the women's movement brought fresh attention to bear on women's accomplishments, even readers who were not concerned with carrying out a feminist analysis became eager to encounter the work of Spanish American women writers. Novels and short stories by Spanish American women were reissued and included in anthologies at an increased rate, leading to a number of rediscoveries and upgraded literary reputations. Women writers who began publishing their fiction in the 1970s, 1980s, and 1990s faced fewer obstacles in their literary careers than had their predecessors, and many of the postboom authors are women. It is only in the postboom era that Spanish American women writers gain international, commercial success, as do Isabel Allende and Luisa Valenzuela.

During the twentieth century, Spanish American nations became more interrelated with Europe and the United States. The closer ties are nowhere more obvious than in patterns of foreign trade and foreign investment; the economies of Spanish American countries became so connected with European and U.S. business that depressions in those foreign economies quickly pulled down the region. In cultural matters, connections were both more intense and more reciprocal. While publics in Spanish American countries have long read French- and English-language literatures in translation, it is only in this century that Spanish American writers have captured international readerships in translation. Access to these new, large, and often lucrative publics is a dizzying prospect, and even more so when it brings Spanish American writers international prizes and declarations of influence from European and U.S. writers.

The sudden upsurge of interest produced both new recognition and respect for Spanish American writing and some less desirable side effects. The book-reading public in an author's home country was apt to be familiar with the many types of writing being practiced in that literary culture. Foreign readers depended on selections made for them by translators and editors and could not get a look at the full range of texts from which translated works had been chosen. The result was often a vision of Spanish American writing as consisting of a few stunningly original works, usually innovative prose fiction such as that of Borges and García Márquez. This distortion was especially common during the boom, when the world public became fascinated with the narrative inventions of a small number of writers. In the years since the boom, there has been an increase in the different types of Spanish American writing available in translation, giving foreign readers a broader perspective on this literature. One of the goals this overview has meant to achieve is to show the most celebrated works of Spanish American fiction in the context of an evolving literature not always visible to international readers.

At the same time that the Spanish American literary scene became more intertwined with those of Europe and the United States, especially through the foreign marketing of Spanish American literature, there was an increased awareness of the properties that made Spanish American writing distinctive. Observers had often noticed that Spanish American literary history was developing according to a timetable not that of Europe.

For example, romanticism not only occurred later in Spanish America than in Europe and lasted longer, but also frequently co-occurred in the same work with realistic, naturalistic, or modernist features. The appearance of modernism, a literary movement originating in Spanish American nations, made it clear that these countries were not simply following Europe's lead.

In the twentieth century, literary intellectuals devoted much thought to trying to specify the difference that made Spanish America's literature develop along distinctive lines. It is very notable that many attempts to define magical realism cited an otherness attributable to Spanish American realities as well as literary expression. The search for the unique qualities of Spanish American writing seems most fruitful when its basis is an examination of the growth of this literature in the context of social history. While the properties that make Spanish American literature other than U.S. and European writing may never be fully accounted for, the century brought an increased acceptance of the concept that Spanish American letters were different and that their study would require continual adjustment of critical concepts originally designed to characterize those literatures whose dominance was long established.

Notes

1. TWENTIETH-CENTURY
MODERNIST PROSE, 1900 – 1920

1. Martí had been killed in an invasion of Cuba. Manuel Gutiérrez Nájera (Mexico, 1859–1895), known especially for the pleasing and evocative rhythmic patterns of his prose and its ability to evoke scenes with sensuous vividness, died the same year. José Asunción Silva (Colombia, 1865–1896), poet and author of one of the few novels to emerge from early modernism, and Julián del Casal (Cuba, 1863–1893), known for his poetry and experimental prose, also died within the same three-year period.

2. Aníbal González, *La novela modernista hispanoamericana* (Madrid: Gredos, 1987), pp. 54–55, notes that Martí "repudiated" his novel at first, then "found merit in it," but even while planning its reissue, he exhibited ambivalence toward the work, based in part on his doubts about the worth of the novel as a genre.

3. Ibid., p. 116. A major premise of González's study is that "modernist novels are all . . . fictions of the intellectual, narratives about the role of the intellectual in the modern world" (p. 12), with special reference to the intellectual's difficult relations with Latin American society.

4. José Enrique Rodó, *Ariel* (Buenos Aires: Kapelusz, 1962), p. 109.

5. Roberto Fernández Retamar, *Calibán* (Montevideo: Aquí Testimonio, 1973); appears in English in *Calibán and Other Essays*, trans. Edward Baker (Minneapolis: University of Minnesota Press, 1989).

6. Angel Rama inaugurated this vein of investigation with his 1967 *Los poetas modernistas en el mercado económico* (Montevideo: Facultad de Humanidades y Ciencias), issued in working-papers format. This study is incorporated into his 1970 book *Rubén Darío y el modernismo (Circunstancias socioeconómicas de un arte americano)* (Caracas: Universidad Central de Venezuela). Rama's further development of this

research topic can be seen in his posthumous collection of essays *Las máscaras democráticas del modernismo* (Montevideo: Arca, 1985).

7. Jean Franco, "Dependency Theory and Literary History: The Case of Latin America," *Minnesota Review* 5 (1975): 66.

8. Octavio Paz, "The Siren and the Seashell," *The Siren and the Seashell and Other Essays on Poets and Poetry*, trans. Lysander Kemp and Margaret Sayers Peden (Austin: University of Texas Press, 1976), p. 23.

9. Pedro Luis Barcia, "Introducción biográfica y crítica," in *Cuentos fantásticos*, by Leopoldo Lugones (Madrid: Clásicos Castalia, 1987), pp. 9–54.

10. Lugones, *Cuentos fantásticos*, p. 102.

11. Hernán Vidal, "*Sangre patricia* y la conjunción naturalista-simbolista," *Hispania* 52, no. 2 (May 1969): 183–192.

12. John S. Brushwood, *The Spanish American Novel: A Twentieth-Century Survey* (Austin: University of Texas Press, 1975), pp. 5–7.

13. Manuel Díaz Rodríguez, *Sangre patricia* (Madrid: Sociedad Española de Librería, n.d.), p. 152.

14. Ibid., p. 88.

15. Amado Nervo, "La serpiente que se muerde la cola," *Obras completas* (Madrid: Aguilar, 1955), 2:394–395.

16. Enrique Larreta, *La gloria de don Ramiro* (Paris: Garnier, n.d.), p. 291.

17. Pedro Prado, *La reina de Rapa Nui* (Santiago: Editorial Nascimento, 1962), p. 32.

18. Ibid., p. 168.

19. Ibid., p. 169.

20. John R. Kelly, *Pedro Prado* (New York: Twayne, 1974), p. 80.

21. Arturo Torres-Rioseco, *Novelistas contemporáneos de América* (Santiago: Nascimento, 1939), p. 393.

22. Prado, *Alsino* (Santiago: Nascimento, 1920), p. 59.

23. Julio Arriagada A. and Hugo Goldsack, "Pedro Prado, un clásico de América," *Atenea* 106 (May 1952): 323; their complete argument is presented on pp. 305–334.

24. Ibid., pp. 328–334.

25. González, *La novela modernista*, pp. 47–48.

26. Brushwood, *The Spanish American Novel*, pp. 9–18.

2. REALISM AND NATURALISM, 1900–1930

1. Federico Gamboa, *Santa* (Mexico City: Ediciones Botas, 1960), p. 210.

2. Ibid., p. 119.

3. Ibid., p. 134.

4. Ibid., p. 32.

5. Margo Glantz, "Santa y la carne," *La lengua en la mano* (Tlahuapan, Puebla: Premiá, 1983), p. 47.

6. Baldomero Lillo, *Sub terra* (Santiago: Nascimento, 1948), p. 8.

7. Jean Franco, *Introduction to Spanish-American Literature* (Cambridge: Cambridge University Press, 1969), p. 181.

8. Carmelo Virgillo, "Symbolic Imagery in Baldomero Lillo's 'La compuerta número 12'," *Revista Canadiense de Estudios Hispánicos* 2, no. 2 (1978): 142–153.

9. Myron I. Lichtblau, *Manuel Gálvez* (New York: Twayne, 1972), p. 77.

10. Noé Jitrik, "Los desplazamientos de la culpa en las obras 'sociales' de Manuel Gálvez," *Ensayos y estudios de literatura argentina* (Buenos Aires: Galerna, 1970), p. 71.

11. Lichtblau, *Manuel Gálvez*, pp. 43–44.

12. David William Foster, "Ideological Ruptures in Manuel Gálvez's *Historia de arrabal*," *Hispanic Journal* 4, no. 2 (1983): 21–27.

13. Noé Jitrik, "Propuesta para una descripción del escritor reaccionario," *El escritor argentino: dependencia o libertad* (Buenos Aires: Ediciones del Candil, 1967), pp. 59–82.

14. John S. Brushwood, *Mexico in Its Novel: A Nation's Search for Identity* (Austin: University of Texas Press, 1966), pp. 180–181.

15. Mariano Azuela, *Los de abajo* (Mexico City: Fondo de Cultura Económica, 1969), p. 140.

16. Torres-Rioseco, *Novelistas contemporáneos*, pp. 219–220.

17. Alcides Arguedas, *Raza de bronce* (1919; reprint La Paz: Editores Gisbert, 1976, p. 192.

18. Franco, *Introduction*, p. 186.

19. Ariel Dorfman, *Imaginación y violencia en América* (Santiago: Editorial Universitaria, 1970), p. 19.

20. Horacio Quiroga, *The Decapitated Chicken and Other Stories*, trans. Margaret Sayers Peden (Austin: University of Texas Press, 1976), pp. 124–125.

21. The source of this information is Louis Antoine Lemaître's biography *Between Flight and Longing: The Journey of Teresa de la Parra* (New York: Vantage Press, 1986), p. 60.

22. Ibid., p. 65.

23. Laura M. Febres, *Cinco perspectivas críticas sobre la obra de Teresa de la Parra* (Caracas: Editorial Arte, 1984), p. 14.

3. AVANT-GARDE, IMAGINATIVE,
AND FANTASTIC MODES,
1920–1950

1. Marta Scrimaglio, *Literatura argentina de vanguardia* (Rosario, Argentina: Editorial Biblioteca, 1974).

2. Oliverio Girondo, "Manifiesto de MARTIN FIERRO" (1924), reprinted in *Recopilación de documentos sobre los vanguardismos en la América Latina*, ed. Oscar Collazos (Havana: Casa de las Américas, 1970), pp. 203–204.

3. Oliverio Girondo, *Veinte poemas para ser leídos en el tranvía* (Buenos Aires: Editorial Martín Fierro, 1925), n.p.

4. The often counterproductive isolation of the *estridentistas* is one of the features most noted by commentators. See, for example, Luis Leal, "El movimiento estridentista," and Carlos Monsiváis, "Los estridentistas y los agoristas," pp. 157–166 and pp. 169–173 respectively of Collazos's compilation, cited in note 2. Stephen M. Bell remarks: "The Estridentistas tried to unite the two electrified poles of socialism and futurism, and in the end they mostly got burned: they were too hermetic for the social realists and too naively proletarianist for the cosmopolitans." See his "Mexico," in *Handbook of Latin American Literature*, ed. David William Foster, rev. (New York: Garland, 1987), p. 372.

5. Sonja Karsen, "Introducción," in *Versos y prosas*, by Jaime Torres Bodet (Madrid: Ediciones Iberoamericanas, 1966), p. 42.

6. Ibid., pp. 42–53.

7. Jaime Torres Bodet, *Margarita de nieblá*, in ibid., p. 134.

8. Carlos J. Alonso, *The Spanish American Regional Novel: Modernity and Autochthony* (Cambridge: Cambridge University Press, 1990), p. 94.

9. Ibid., p. 95.

10. Noé Jitrik, *"Don Segundo Sombra*: Ricardo Güiraldes," *Escritores argentinos: dependencia o libertad* (Buenos Aires: Ediciones del Candil, 1967), pp. 95–101.

11. Macedonio Fernández, *Papeles de recienvenido, poemas, relatos, cuentos, miscelánea* (Buenos Aires: Centro Editor de América Latina, 1966), p. 153.

12. Ibid.

13. Ibid.

14. Macedonio Fernández, *Museo de la novela de la Eterna* (Buenos Aires: Centro Editor de América Latina, 1967), p. 21.

15. Roberto Arlt, *The Seven Madmen*, trans. Naomi Lindstrom (Boston: David R. Godine, 1984), pp. 63–64.

16. José Eustasio Rivera, *La vorágine* (Santiago: Editora Zig Zag, 1953), p. 318.

17. Ibid., p. 321.

18. See, for example, Seymour Menton's archetypal analysis in *"La vorágine*: el triángulo y el círculo," in *La vorágine: textos críticos*, ed. Monserrat Ordónez Vila (Bogotá: Alianza Editorial Colombiana, 1987), pp. 199–228, and Richard J. Callan's work using a similar approach in "The Archetype of Psychic Renewal in *La vorágine*," in *Woman as Myth and Metaphor in Latin American Literature*, ed. Carmelo Virgillo and Naomi Lindstrom (Columbia: University of Missouri Press, 1985), pp. 15–26.

19. Raymond L. Williams, *The Colombian Novel 1844–1987* (Austin: University of Texas Press, 1991), p. 70. On pp. 70–75 Williams presents a valid argument that *La vorágine* is a self-conscious text, a "novel about writing" (p. 75).

20. Rómulo Gallegos, *Doña Bárbara* (México: Orión, 1967), p. 143.

21. Ibid., p. 128.

22. Enrique Anderson Imbert, *Spanish-American Literature*, trans. John V. Falconieri (Detroit: Wayne State University Press, 1963), p. 379.

23. Roberto González Echevarría, *Myth and Archive: A Theory of Latin American Narrative* (New York: Cambridge University Press, 1990), p. 158.

24. Ibid., pp. 158–159.

25. John Beverly, "Venezuela," in Foster, ed., *Handbook*, p. 570.

26. Alonso, *Spanish American Regional Novel*, p. 111.

27. Alejo Carpentier, cited in ibid., p. 112.

28. Arturo Uslar Pietri, *Letras y hombres de Venezuela* (Mexico City: Fondo de Cultura Económica, 1948), p. 161.

29. See, for example, Inés Dölz-Blackburn, "Elementos narrativos tradicionales en la obra de María Luisa Bombal y su relación con motivos folklóricos universales," in *María Luisa Bombal: apreciaciones críticas*, ed. Marjorie Agosín et al. (Tempe, Ariz.: Bilingual Press, 1987), pp. 51–71.

30. Gabriela Mora, "El ala que socava arquetipos," in ibid., p. 167.

31. Martin S. Stabb, *Jorge Luis Borges* (New York: Twayne Publishers, 1970), p. 46.

32. Jorge Luis Borges, "Funes the Memorious," trans. Anthony Kerrigan, *Fictions* (New York: Grove Press, 1962), p. 101.

33. Ibid., p. 102.

34. Nancy Gray Díaz, "Metamorphosis as Integration: *Hombres de maíz*," *The Radical Self: Metamorphosis to Animal Form in Modern Latin American Narrative* (Columbia: University of Missouri Press, 1988), pp. 34–50.

35. Alejo Carpentier, "Prólogo," *El reino de este mundo* (1949; reprint Havana: Ediciones Unión, 1964), pp. viv–xc.

36. González Echevarría, *Alejo Carpentier: The Pilgrim at Home* (Ithaca: Cornell University Press, 1977), pp. 132–134.

37. Ibid., p. 129.

4. REALISM AND BEYOND,
1930–1960

1. Ariel Dorfman, *Violencia e imaginación en América* (Santiago: Editorial Universitaria, 1970), pp. 9–10.

2. Jorge Icaza, *Huasipungo* (Buenos Aires: Losada, 1965), p. 45.

3. Ibid., p. 47.

4. Humberto E. Robles, *Testimonio y tendencia mítica en la obra de José de la Cuadra* (Quito: Editorial Casa de la Cultura Ecuatoriana, 1976).

5. Demetrio Aguilera Malta, *Don Goyo* (Quito: Ediciones Antorcha, 1938), p. 63.

6. Ciro Alegría, *The Golden Serpent*, trans. Harriet de Onís (New York: Signet/New American Library, 1963), p. 91.

7. Ibid., p. 92.

8. James Higgins, *A History of Peruvian Literature* (Liverpool: Francis Cairns, 1987), p. 131.

9. Joseph Sommers, "Changing View of the Indian in Mexican Literature," *Hispania* 47 (1964): 47–55, and "The Indian-Oriented Novel in Latin America: New Spirit, New Forms, New Scope," *Journal of Inter-American Studies*, no. 6 (1964): 249–265, sketch out for Latin Americanist literary criticism the principal lines of transition from *indigenista* writing to a new type of literature featuring Indian issues and characters.

10. Mauricio Magdaleno, *El resplandor* (Mexico: Ediciones Botas, 1937), p. 171.

11. Agustín Yáñez, *The Edge of the Storm*, trans. Ethel Brinton (Austin: University of Texas Press, 1963), p. 6.

12. Ibid., pp. 3–4.

13. Joseph Sommers, *After the Storm: Landmarks of the Modern Mexican Novel* (Albuquerque: University of New Mexico Press, 1968), p. 47.

14. Alberto Escobar, *Arguedas, o, la utopía de la lengua* (Lima: Instituto de Estudios Peruanos, 1984).

5. THE BOOM AND ITS ANTECEDENTS, 1950 – 1970

1. Raymond L. Williams, "Truth Claims, Postmodernism, and the Latin American Novel," in *Profession 92*, ed. Phyllis Franklin (New York: Modern Language Association, 1992), p. 7. Williams associates the writing of the boom years with modernism, and the era following the boom with postmodernism, even when the same authors are involved. In his "Colombia," in Foster, ed., *Handbook*, he notes that García Márquez "used [modernist techniques] in what is an identifiable modernist project—the seeking of order and the expression of the ineffable in a world lacking order and waiting to be named. García Márquez, like certain other Latin American writers (e.g., Vargas Llosa and Fuentes), is rooted in the moderns, but not consistently so. He has also read the postmoderns and in his later work participates in some of their subversive and self-conscious exercises" (p. 212).

2. Josefina Ludmer, "Homenaje a 'La vida breve'," *Onetti: los procesos de construcción del relato* (Buenos Aires: Sudamericana, 1977).

3. Roberto Ferro, *Juan Carlos Onetti: La vida breve* (Buenos Aires: Hachette, 1986).

4. Ludmer, "Homenaje," pp. 30–31.

5. Gustavo Pérez Firmat, *The Cuban Condition: Translation and Identity in Modern Cuban Culture* (Cambridge: Cambridge University Press, 1989), p. 157.

6. Ibid., p. 156.

7. Roberto González Echevarría, *Alejo Carpentier: The Pilgrim at Home* (Ithaca: Cornell University Press, 1977), p. 164.

8. Ibid., p. 183.

9. Ibid., p. 166.

10. Alejo Carpentier examines baroque qualities in Latin American expression in his influential collection of essays, *Tientos y diferencias* (Mexico City: Universidad Nacional Autónoma, 1964; also Montevideo: Arca, 1967); see particularly the direct discussion of the topic in the essays "Problemática de la actual novela latinoamericana," on literature, and "La ciudad de las columnas," on architecture.

11. Carpentier, *The Lost Steps*, trans. Harriet de Onís (New York: Knopf, 1956), pp. 43–44.

12. Joseph Sommers, "A través de la ventana de la sepultura: *Pedro Páramo*," in *La narrativa de Juan Rulfo: Interpretaciones críticas*, ed. Joseph Sommers (Mexico City: Secretaría de Educación Pública, 1974), p. 161.

13. Ibid., p. 157.

14. Juan Rulfo, *Pedro Páramo*, trans. Lysander Kemp (New York: Grove Press, 1969), p. 4.

15. Ibid., p. 123.

16. John S. Brushwood, *Mexico in Its Novel: A Nation's Search for Identity* (Austin: University of Texas Press, 1966), p. 31.

17. Rulfo, *Pedro Páramo*, p. 123.

18. Joseph Sommers, *After the Storm: Landmarks of the Modern Mexican Novel* (Albuquerque: University of New Mexico Press, 1968), p. 102.

19. Noé Jitrik, *El no existente caballero, la idea de personaje y su evolución en la narrativa latinoamericana* (Buenos Aires: Megápolis, 1975).

20. Sommers, *After the Storm*, p. 154.

21. Lanin A. Gyurko, "*La muerte de Artemio Cruz* and *Citizen Kane*: A Comparative Analysis," in *Carlos Fuentes: A Critical View*, ed. Robert Brody and Charles Rossman (Austin: University of Texas Press, 1982), p. 67.

22. Carlos Fuentes, *The Death of Artemio Cruz*, trans. Sam Hileman (New York: Farrar, Straus and Giroux, 1964), p. 28.

23. Richard M. Reeve, "Carlos Fuentes y el desarrollo del narrador en segunda persona: Un ensayo exploratorio," in *Homenaje a Carlos Fuentes: variaciones interpretativas en torno a su obra*, ed. Helmy F. Giacoman (New York: Las Américas, 1971), p. 85.

24. Jaime Alazraki, "Introduction: Toward the Last Square of the Hopscotch," in *The Final Island: The Fiction of Julio Cortázar*, ed. Jaime Alazraki and Ivar Ivask (Norman: University of Oklahoma Press, 1976), p. 7.

25. Alazraki presents these ideas in "The Fantastic as Surrealist Metaphors in Cortázar's Short Fiction," *Dada/Surrealism* (New York), no. 5 (1975): 28–33, and develops them further in *La busca del unicornio: los cuentos de Julio Cortázar; elementos para una poética de lo neofantástico* (Madrid: Gredos, 1983).

26. Noé Jitrik, "Crítica satélite y trabajo crítico en 'El perseguidor' de Julio

Cortázar," *Producción literaria y producción social* (Buenos Aires: Sudamericana, 1975), pp. 82–129.

27. Julio Cortázar, "Table of Instructions," *Hopscotch*, trans. Gregory Rabassa (New York: Avon, 1975), n.p.

28. Cortázar, *Hopscotch*, p. 552.

29. Dick Gerdes, *Mario Vargas Llosa* (Boston: Twayne, 1985), p. 43.

30. Sara Castro-Klarén, *Mario Vargas Llosa: análisis introductorio* (Lima: Latinoamericana Editores, 1988), pp. 32–33.

31. José Donoso, "The Walk," *Charleston and Other Stories*, trans. Andree Conrad (New York: David R. Godine, 1977), p. 92.

32. George R. McMurray, *José Donoso* (Boston: Twayne, 1979), pp. 110–113.

33. Hugo Achugar, *Ideología y estructuras narrativas en José Donoso* (Caracas: Centro de Estudios Latinoamericanos Rómulo Gallegos, 1979), p. 240.

34. Ibid., p. 241.

35. Cedomil Goic, "El narrador en el laberinto," in *José Donoso: la destrucción de un mundo*, ed. José Promis Ojeda et al. (Buenos Aires: Fernando García Cambeiro, 1975), p. 115.

36. Ibid., p. 117.

37. Jacques Joset, "Introducción," in *Cien años de soledad*, by Gabriel García Márquez (Madrid: Cátedra, 1984), p. 27.

38. Ricardo Gullón, "García Márquez o el olvidado arte de contar," in *Homenaje a Gabriel García Márquez: variaciones interpretativas en torno a su obra*, ed. Helmy F. Giacoman (New York: Las Américas, 1972), p. 149.

39. Ibid., p. 148.

40. Gabriel García Márquez, *One Hundred Years of Solitude*, trans. Gregory Rabassa (New York: Avon, 1971).

41. Seymour Menton, *Prose Fiction of the Cuban Revolution* (Austin: University of Texas Press, 1975), p. 67.

6. THE POSTBOOM: NEW VOICES AND BELATED DISCOVERIES, 1968–1990

1. Williams, "Colombia," in Foster, ed., *Handbook*, p. 213.

2. Williams, "Truth Claims," p. 8. In this article (pp. 6–9), Williams sets forth his arguments for identifying the fiction of the boom, by and large, with modernism in the international sense and that of the postboom with postmodernism.

3. Fredric Jameson, *Postmodernism, or, The Cultural Logic of Late Capitalism* (Durham: Duke University Press, 1991), p. xi.

4. Margo Glantz, *Onda y escritura en México: jóvenes de 20 a 30* (Mexico City: Siglo XXI, 1971).

5. See, for example, June C. D. Carter and Donald L. Schmidt, eds., *José Agustín: Onda and Beyond* (Columbia: University of Missouri Press, 1986).

6. Sharon Magnarelli's interpretation of Valenzuela is exemplified in "Women, Language, and Cats in Luisa Valenzuela's *El gato eficaz*: Looking-Glass Games of Fire," *The Lost Rib: Female Characters in the Spanish-American Novel* (Lewisburg, Penn.: Bucknell University Press, 1985), pp. 169–185.

7. Williams, *The Colombian Novel*, pp. 172–181.

Selected Bibliography

The following is a brief listing of works chosen for their coverage of a panoramic range of works and issues in Spanish American fiction. While some are reference works and others are critical discussions, they share the ability to present to the reader broad sectors of Spanish American fiction and its study. English-language editions have received preference in the selection, but some outstandingly useful studies available only in Spanish have been included with the hope that they will appear in English.

Alonso, Carlos J. *The Spanish American Regional Novel: Modernity and Autochthony*. Cambridge: Cambridge University Press, 1990.

Anderson Imbert, Enrique. *Spanish-American Literature*. Translated by John V. Falconieri. Detroit: Wayne State University Press, 1963.

Brotherston, Gordon. *The Emergence of the Latin American Novel*. Cambridge: Cambridge University Press, 1977.

Brushwood, John S. *Mexico in Its Novel: A Nation's Search for Identity*. Austin: University of Texas Press, 1966.

———. *La novela mexicana, 1967–1982*. Mexico City: Grijalbo, 1985.

———. *The Spanish American Novel: A Twentieth-Century Survey*. Austin: University of Texas Press, 1975.

Díaz, Nancy Gray. *The Radical Self: Metamorphosis to Animal Form in Modern Latin American Literature*. Columbia: University of Missouri Press, 1988.

Donoso, José. *The Boom in Spanish American Literature*. Translated by Gregory Kolovakos. New York: Columbia University Press/Center for Inter-American Relations, 1977.

Dorfman, Ariel. *Imaginación y violencia en América*. Santiago: Editorial Universitaria, 1970.

Fitz, Earl E. *Rediscovering the New World: Inter-American Literature in a Comparative Context*. Iowa City: University of Iowa Press, 1991.

Flores, Angel, ed. *Historia y antología del cuento y la novela en Hispanoamérica.* New York: Las Américas, 1959.

————, ed. *Spanish American Authors: The Twentieth Century.* New York: H. W. Wilson, 1992.

Foster, David William. *Studies in the Contemporary Spanish American Short Story.* Columbia: University of Missouri Press, 1979.

————, ed. *A Dictionary of Contemporary Latin American Authors.* Tempe, Arizona: Center for Latin American Studies, 1975.

————, ed. *Handbook of Latin American Literature.* Rev. ed. New York: Garland, 1992.

Franco, Jean. *Introduction to Spanish-American Literature.* Cambridge: Cambridge University Press, 1969.

————. *The Modern Culture of Latin America: Society and the Artist.* Rev. ed. Harmondsworth, Eng.: Penguin, 1970.

————. *Plotting Women: Gender and Representation in Mexico.* New York: Columbia University Press, 1989.

Fuentes, Carlos. *La nueva novela hispanoamericana.* Mexico City: Joaquín Mortiz, 1969.

Gallagher, D. P. *Modern Latin American Literature.* London: Oxford University Press, 1973.

Goic, Cedomil. *Historia de la novela hispanoamericana.* Valparaíso: Universidad de Valparaíso, 1972.

————. *La novela chilena: los mitos degradados.* Santiago: Editorial Universitaria, 1968.

González Echevarría, Roberto. *Myth and Archive: A Theory of Latin American Narrative.* New York: Cambridge University Press, 1990.

————. *The Voice of the Masters: Writing and Authority in Modern Latin American Literature.* Austin: University of Texas Press, 1985.

Harss, Luis, and Barbara Dohmann. *Into the Mainstream: Conversations with Latin American Writers.* New York: Harper and Row, 1967.

Jitrik, Noé. *Ensayos y estudios de literatura argentina.* Buenos Aires: Galerna, 1970.

————. *El no existente caballero, la idea de personaje y su evolución en la narrativa latinoamericana.* Buenos Aires: Megápolis, 1975.

Kadir, Djelal. *Questing Fictions: Latin America's Family Romance.* Minneapolis: University of Minnesota Press, 1986.

Mac Adam, Alfred J. *Modern Latin American Narratives: The Dreams of Reason.* Chicago: University of Chicago Press, 1977.

McMurray, George R. *Spanish American Writing Since 1941: A Critical Survey.* New York: Ungar, 1987.

Martin, Gerald. *Journeys through the Labyrinth: Latin American Fiction in the Twentieth Century.* London: Verso, 1989.

Marting, Diane, ed. *Spanish American Women Writers: A Bio-Bibliographic Source Book.* New York: Greenwood, 1990.

Menton, Seymour. *La novela colombiana: planetas y satélites*. Bogota: Plaza y Janés, 1977.

————. *Prose Fiction of the Cuban Revolution*. Austin: University of Texas Press, 1975.

Orgambide, Pedro, and Roberto Yahni, eds. *Enciclopedia de la literatura argentina*. Buenos Aires: Sudamericana, 1970.

Peden, Margaret Sayers, ed. *The Latin American Short Story: A Critical History*. Boston: Twayne, 1983.

Rama, Angel. *Transculturación narrativa en América Latina*. Mexico City: Siglo XX, 1982.

Sánchez, Luis Alberto. *Proceso y contenido de la novela hispano-americana*. Madrid: Gredos, 1968.

Schwartz, Ronald. *Nomads, Exiles, and Emigres: The Rebirth of the Latin American Narrative 1960–1980*. Metuchen, N.J.: Scarecrow, 1980.

Shaw, Donald L. *Nueva narrativa hispanoamericana*. Madrid: Cátedra, 1981.

Solé, Carlos A., and Maria Isabel Abreu, eds. *Latin American Writers*. New York: Scribner, 1989.

Sommer, Doris. *One Master for Another: Populism as Patriarchal Rhetoric in Dominican Novels*. Lanham, Maryland: University Press of America, 1983.

Sommers, Joseph. *After the Storm: Landmarks of the Modern Mexican Novel*. Albuquerque: University of New Mexico Press, 1968.

Souza, Raymond. *Major Cuban Novelists: Innovation and Tradition*. Columbia: University of Missouri Press, 1976.

Steele, Cynthia. *Politics, Gender, and the Mexican Novel, 1968–1988*. Austin: University of Texas Press, 1992.

Tittler, Jonathan. *Narrative Irony in the Contemporary Spanish American Novel*. Ithaca: Cornell University Press, 1984.

Vidal, Hernán, ed. *Literary and Cultural Grounding for Hispanic and Luso-Brazilian Feminist Literary Criticism*. Minneapolis: Institute for the Study of Ideologies and Literature, 1989.

Williams, Raymond Leslie. *The Colombian Novel 1844–1987*. Austin: University of Texas Press, 1991.

————. *Una década de la novela colombiana: la experiencia de los setenta*. Bogotá: Plaza y Janés, 1981.

Index

Achugar, Hugo, 181
Adán, Martín. *See* Benavides, Rafael de la Fuente
African-Hispanic populations and cultures, 3, 16, 70, 84, 102, 104–105, 115, 192, 198, 207–208, 214, 222–223
Aguilera Garramuño, Marco Tulio, 199
Aguilera Malta, Demetrio, 116, 117–119
Agustín, José. *See* Ramírez Gómez, José Agustín
Agustini, Delmira, 57
Ahern, Maureen, 136
Alazraki, Jaime, 167
Alegría, Ciro, 119–125, 140
Allende, Isabel, 3, 6, 214, 215–217, 220, 225
Allende, Salvador, 216
Allgood, Myralyn, 136
Alone. *See* Arrieta, Hernán Díaz
Alonso, Amado, 27
Alonso, Carlos J., 75, 86
Anderson Imbert, Enrique, 84
Anthropological novel. *See* Ethnographic narratives
Antonioni, Michelangelo, 166

APRA, 111, 119
Arenas, Reinaldo, 210–212
Arguedas, Alcides, 49–52
Arguedas, José María, 125–127, 136–138, 223
Arlt, Roberto, 78–80, 142, 146, 199
Arreola, Juan José, 151–152, 204
Arriagada A., Julio, 32, 33
Arrieta, Hernán Díaz (pseud. Alone), 53
Asturias, Miguel Angel, 2, 11, 98–102, 108–109, 134, 140, 142, 223
Avant garde: organized movements, 62–70, 71–73; general esthetic tendency, 62–109, 142–143, 167, 198–199, 223, 224. *See also* Cubism, Expressionism, Futurism, Surrealism, *Ultraísmo*
Avellaneda, Gertrudis Gómez de, 224
Azuela, Mariano, 44–45, 46

Barcia, Pedro Luis, 20, 22
Barnet, Miguel, 207–209, 210
Baroque, 4, 97, 103, 147, 150–151, 191
Barrios, Eduardo, 47–48
Barthes, Roland, 193

Baudrillard, Jean, 199
Beauvoir, Simone de. *See* De Beauvoir
Benavides, Rafael de la Fuente (pseud.
    Martín Adán), 70–71
Benedetti, Mario, 139
Benítez Rojo, Antonio, 212–213
Beverly, John, 85
Bible, 106, 183, 184, 213
Bioy Casares, Adolfo, 91–92
Blanco Fombona, Rufino, 36
Boedo, 60–61
Bogin, Magda, 209
Bolívar, Simón, 87
Bombal, María Luisa, 11, 52, 88–90,
    109, 224
Boom, 2, 12, 77–78, 79, 140–196,
    205, 221, 225; contrasted with
    postboom, 197–200
Borges, Jorge Luis, 3, 4, 54, 64–68,
    76, 77, 92–95, 97, 109, 140, 142,
    157–158, 166, 203, 215, 225
Borges, Norah, 166
Brinton, Ethel, 130, 132
Brunet, Marta, 52, 53, 130
Brushwood, John S., 24, 45, 156
Burgos, Elizabeth, 210

Cabrera Infante, Guillermo, 191,
    192–193, 210
Calles, Plutarco Elías, 46
Cambaceres, Eugenio, 35
Cansinos-Assens, Rafael, 65
Carpentier, Alejo, 2, 11, 86, 102–106,
    109, 140, 142, 147–151, 177, 191,
    223
Carrasquilla, Tomás, 37
Castellanos, Rosario, 135–136, 224
Castelnuovo, Elías, 60, 61
Castro, Fidel, 192, 212
Castro-Klarén, Sara, 176
Cervantes, Miguel de, 213
Chamula. *See* Tzotzil

Chaos theory, 212–213
Chicano narrative, 6–7
Christophe, Henri. *See* Henri
    Christophe
Collazos, Oscar, 12
Conrad, Andree, 178
Contemporáneos, 71–73
Cortázar, Julio, 2, 12, 77–78,
    165–172, 191, 192, 203–204, 205
Criollismo, 29, 52–53, 127–130, 148
Cuban American fiction, 6–7
Cubism, 67–68

D'Amico, Alicia, 168
Dante Alighieri, 106, 107, 192
Darío, Rubén, 13–14, 17, 19, 20
De Beauvoir, Simone, 213
De la Cuadra, José, 116–117
De la Parra, Teresa. *See* Parra Sanojo,
    Ana Teresa
De Maupassant, Guy, 20, 166
Denevi, Marco, 5–6, 156–157
Detective fiction, 5–6, 156–158
D'Halmar, Augusto. *See* Thompson,
    Augusto Geomine
Díaz, Nancy Gray, 102
Díaz Rodríguez, Manuel, 23–25, 35
Documentary literature, 5, 207–210
Donoso, José, 4, 130, 176–183, 205
Dorfman, Ariel, 52, 114
Dos Passos, John, 63, 129, 159
Drake, Sir Francis, 186

Ediciones del Norte publishing house,
    210
Eliot, T. S., 7, 63
Escobar, Alberto, 138
Estridentismo, 68–70
Ethnographic narratives, 127–129,
    134–135, 198, 207–208, 220, 222
Expressionism, German, 62, 64–65,
    68

Facio, Sara, 168
Fallas, Carlos Luis, 138
Faulkner, William, 63, 129, 143, 183
Fernández, Macedonio, 66, 73, 76–78, 142, 171
Fernández Retamar, Roberto, 16
Ferré, Rosario, 213–214
Ferro, Roberto, 147
Filloy, Juan, 90–91, 142
Fondo de Cultura Económica, 134
Foster, David William, 43
Francis of Assisi, St., 48
Franco, Jean, 18–19, 41, 51
Fray Servando. *See* Mier, Fray Servando Teresa de
Fuentes, Carlos, 158–165, 172, 177, 197, 198, 205
Futurism, Italian, 62, 67

Gallegos, Rómulo, 80–81, 83–86
Gallegos Lara, Joaquín, 116
Gálvez, Manuel, 42–44, 60
Gamboa, Federico, 38–40, 43–44
Gandolfi Herrero, Arístides (pseud. Alvaro Yunque), 60
García Calderón, Ventura, 49
García Márquez, Gabriel, 2, 4, 170, 172, 183–191, 198, 200, 216, 219, 225
García Saldaña, Parménides, 204
Gardeazábal, Gustavo Alvarez, 218–219
Gardner, Donald, 193
Garro, Elena, 194–195
Gerchunoff, Alberto, 28–29
Gerdes, Dick, 175
Gilbert, Enrique Gil, 116
Girondo, Oliverio, 66–67
Glantz, Margo, 40, 204
Godoy de Alcayaga, Lucila (pseud. Gabriela Mistral), 57
Goethe, Johann Wolfgang von, 73

Goic, Cedomil, 181–182
Goldsack, Hugo, 32, 33
Gómez de Avellaneda, Gertrudis. *See* Avellaneda, Gertrudis Gómez de
Gómez de la Serna, Ramón, 68
Gonzaga Urbina, Luis. *See* Urbina, Luis Gonzaga
González, Aníbal, 15, 33
González Echevarría, Roberto, 84–85, 105, 148, 149, 150
Gorostiza, José, 72
Guayaquil group, 115–116
Güiraldes, Ricardo, 66, 73–75, 80–81, 83, 85, 86
Gullón, Ricardo, 188, 190
Guzmán, Martín Luis, 46–47
Gyurko, Lanin A., 163

Haya de la Torre, Raúl, 111–112, 119; and APRA, 111, 119
Henri Christophe, 104
Hernández, Felisberto, 80, 142
Herrera y Reissig, Julio, 14
Higgins, James, 121
Hileman, Sam, 163
Hinojosa, Rolando, 7
Hiperión group, 158
Homer, 106
Huidobro, Vicente, 62
Hurley, Andrew, 5, 211

Ibarbourou, Juana de, 57
Icaza, Jorge, 112–115
Icaza, Xavier, 70
Indians, as authors, 3, 5, 210, 220, 222–223
Indian-theme fiction. See *Indigenismo*, Nahuatl, Otomí, *Popol-Vuh*, Quechua, Quiché Maya, Tzotzil
Indigenismo: earliest manifestations of in fiction, 48–52; as organized in-

tellectual and social movement,
111–112; as novelistic movement,
11, 100–102, 111–129, 134–135,
207, 220, 222–223; new *indigenismo*
in fiction, 135–138, 222–223

Jaimes Freyre, Ricardo, 14
James, Henry, 176
Jameson, Fredric, 199–200
Janney, Frank, 210, 213
Jarry, Alfred, 167
Jitrik, Noé, 43, 75, 161, 169–170
Joyce, James, 7, 63, 128
Jung, C. G., 82

Karsen, Sonja, 72
Kelly, John R., 30
Kemp, Lysander, 34
Knopf, Alfred A., 95, 140

Lane, Helen R., 5
Larreta, Enrique, 14, 26–28
Lectura Semanal, 58
Lemaître, Louis Antoine, 58
Levine, Suzanne Jill, 5, 193, 202
Lewis, Oscar, 207, 209
Lezama Lima, José, 191–192
Lichtblau, Myron I., 43
Lillo, Baldomero, 40–42
López Albújar, Enrique, 49
López y Fuentes, Gregorio, 127–128
Ludmer, Josefina, 147
Lugones, Leopoldo, 14, 20–22, 28,
42, 53–54, 66, 75, 167
Lynch, Marta, 139
Lyotard, Jean-François, 143, 199

Macedonio. *See* Fernández, Macedonio
McMurray, George R., 179
Madero, Francisco I., 133
Magdaleno, Mauricio, 128–129
Magical realism, 11, 86–87, 97–106
passim, 110, 134, 147, 154–155,

165, 183, 189–191, 214, 216, 224,
226. *See also* Asturias, Carpentier,
García Márquez, Rulfo
Magnarelli, Sharon, 217
Mallea, Eduardo, 95–97, 140
Maples Arce, Manuel, 68
Marechal, Leopoldo, 106–107
Mariani, Roberto, 6, 60, 61, 223
Mariátegui, José Carlos, 49, 111–112,
113
Marinetti, F. T., 67
Martí, José, 13, 14, 17
Martínfierrismo, 67
Martín Fierro (periodical), 66, 67
Marvelous real (*real maravilloso*),
105–106
Matto de Turner, Clorinda, 49
Maupassant, Guy de. *See* De Maupassant, Guy
Maya narrative. See *Popol-Vuh*
Menchú, Rigoberta, 5, 210, 220, 222
Méndez, Evar, 66
Méndez-M., Miguel, 7
Menton, Seymour, 193
Mexican-American narrative, 6–7
Meyrinck, Gustav, 65
Microcuento, 4, 151–152, 156
Mier, Fray Servando Teresa de,
210–211
Minicuento. See *Microcuento*
Mistral, Gabriela. *See* Godoy de Alcayaga, Lucila
Modernism, international (early twentieth century), 7–8, 63–64, 142–144, 198–199. *See also* Eliot, Dos Passos, Faulkner, Joyce, Pound
Modernism, Spanish American (turn of century), 4, 7–8, 9, 10, 13–33,
34, 35–36, 39, 44, 53–54, 62,
63–64, 86, 143, 223, 224, 226
Modernismo. See Modernism
Monegal. *See* Rodríguez Monegal
Montejo, Esteban, 208, 209

Monterroso, Augusto, 4
Mora, Gabriela, 89–90
Mundo, 78

Nación, 75, 95
Nahuatl, 159
Native peoples and languages. *See* Indians as authors, Indian-theme fiction, *Indigenismo*
Nativism. *See Criollismo*
Naturalism, 34–35, 36–44, 52, 60, 61, 145–146
Neobaroque, 191. *See also* Baroque
Neofantastic writing, 167
Neo-indigenismo. See Indigenismo, new
Neo-Platonism, 107
Nervo, Amado, 23, 25–26
New narrative. *See* New novel
New novel, 2, 98, 141–142, 218. *See also* Boom, Magical realism
Nonfiction novel. *See* Documentary literature
Novela testimonio. See Documentary literature
Novo, Salvador, 72
Nueva narrativa. See New novel

Ocampo, Silvina, 91
Ocampo, Victoria, 91–92
Onda, 6, 204–206
Onetti, Juan Carlos, 144–147
Onís, Harriet de, 5, 119, 140, 151
Ortiz [Fernández], Fernando, 208
Orwell, George, 217
Otomí tribe, 128–129
Owen, Gilberto, 72

Pacheco, José Emilio, 206–207
Padilla, Heberto, 6
Palancares, Jesusa, 209
Pareja Diezcanseco, Alfredo, 116
Parra Sanojo, Ana Teresa (pseud. Teresa de la Parra), 57–60, 224

Payró, Roberto J., 36–37
Paz, Octavio, 4–5, 19, 158–159, 194
Peden, Margaret Sayers, 5, 14, 56, 159, 197
Pérez Firmat, Gustavo, 148
Poe, Edgar Allan, 166
Poniatowska, Elena, 209–210, 220
Popol-Vuh, 11, 100, 102
Postboom, as term and concept, 195–200, 219–221; as literary phenomenon, 2–3, 6, 12, 195–221, 225
Postmodernism, international (late twentieth century), 7–8, 143–144, 199–200, 212
Postmodernism, Spanish American (early twentieth century), 7–8, 54, 57, 66
Pound, Ezra, 7, 63
Pozas A., Ricardo, 134–135
Prado, Pedro, 29–33, 53
Puig, Manuel, 6, 200–203, 220

Quechua language, in Spanish American fiction, 114–115, 122, 126–127, 136, 138
Quiché Maya, 210
Quiroga, Horacio, 4, 14, 53–57, 167

Rabassa, Gregory, 5, 190, 191
Rama, Angel, 18
Ramírez Gómez, José Agustín (pseud. José Agustín), 204–205, 206
Realism, 9–11, 34–61, 64, 97, 106, 108–109, 110–139, 141, 145–146, 154–155, 159–160, 176, 177, 196, 198, 223. *See also Criollismo, Indigenismo*, Magical realism, Soviet realism
Realism, magical. *See* Magical realism
Real maravilloso. See Marvelous real
Reeve, Richard M., 164
Revista Azul, 25

Revista Moderna, 25
Revueltas, José, 139, 204
Reyles, Carlos, 14
Rivera, José Eustasio, 80–83, 85
Rivera, Tomás, 7
Roa Bastos, Augusto, 138–139
Robles, Humberto, 117
Rodó, José Enrique, 4, 14–17
Rodríguez Monegal, Emir, 192
Rojas, Manuel, 52–53
Rubín, Ramón, 134
Rulfo, Juan, 2, 152–156

Sábato, Ernesto, 91, 107–108
Sainz, Gustavo, 204, 205, 206
Saldívar, Ramón, 7
Sánchez, Luis Rafael, 214–215
Sarduy, Severo, 191, 193–194
Scrimaglio, Marta, 65
Shakespeare, William, 15
Silva, José Asunción, 14
Silva, Julio, 168
Simms, Ruth L. C., 194
Sinchi Roca, 137
Sinclair, Upton, 138
Socialist realism. *See* Soviet realism
Sommers, Joseph, 128, 133, 155, 160, 162
Soviet realism, 60, 113
Stabb, Martin S., 92
Storni, Alfonsina, 57
Stowe, Harriet Beecher, 49
Sudamericana publishing house, 202
Sur, 91
Surrealism, 67–68, 91, 103, 105, 107, 108, 167, 168, 176, 179

Tel Quel group, 193
Testimonial literature. *See* Documentary literature

Thompson, Augusto Geomine (pseud. Augusto d'Halmar), 38, 52
Torres Bodet, Jaime, 72–73
Torres-Rioseco, Arturo, 31, 48
Totalizing novel, 70, 77, 195
Tzotzil, 134, 135–136

Ultraísmo, 65, 68, 107
Urbina, Luis Gonzaga, 23, 25
Uslar Pietri, Arturo, 86–88, 98

Valenzuela, Luisa, 3, 6, 214, 217–218, 225
Vargas Llosa, Mario, 172–176, 192, 224
Vega, Ana Lydia, 215–217
Vela, Arqueles, 69, 70
Verne, Jules, 166, 168
Viana, Javier de, 36
Vidal, Hernán, 24
Villa, Francisco (Pancho), 44, 45
Villaurrutia, Xavier, 72
Viñas, David, 139
Virgillo, Carmelo, 41

Williams, Raymond Leslie, 82, 143, 199, 218, 219
Woolf, Virginia, 213

Yáñez, Agustín, 130–134
Yunque, Alvaro. *See* Arístides Gandolfi Herrero

Zig Zag publishing house, 130
Zola, Emile, 35, 41, 42
Zona de Carga y Descarga, 213